Garfield
says a
mouthful

BY JIM DAVIS

Ballantine Books • **New York**

2010 Ballantine Books Trade Paperback Edition

Published in the United States by Ballantine Books, an imprint of The Random House Publishing Group, a division of Random House, Inc., New York.

BALLANTINE and colophon are registered trademarks of Random House, Inc.

Originally published in slightly different form in the United States by Ballantine Books, an imprint of The Random House Publishing Group, a division of Random House, Inc., in 1991.

ISBN 978-0-345-49179-4

Printed in China

www.ballantinebooks.com

9 8 7 6 5 4 3 2

First Colorized Edition

Top Ten Signs That Your Cat Is a "Garfield"

10. Your food bill surpasses the national debt

9. He gets a court order requiring you to pamper him

8. He takes over everything in the house except the mortgage payment

7. Dogs in the neighborhood get anonymous hate mail

6. He has never strayed farther than three feet from the house

5. He treats you with no more respect than the drapes

4. Your plants die mysterious deaths

3. He's sometimes mistaken for Rhode Island

2. He tries to have **you** declawed

1. Can't tell if he's sleeping or dead

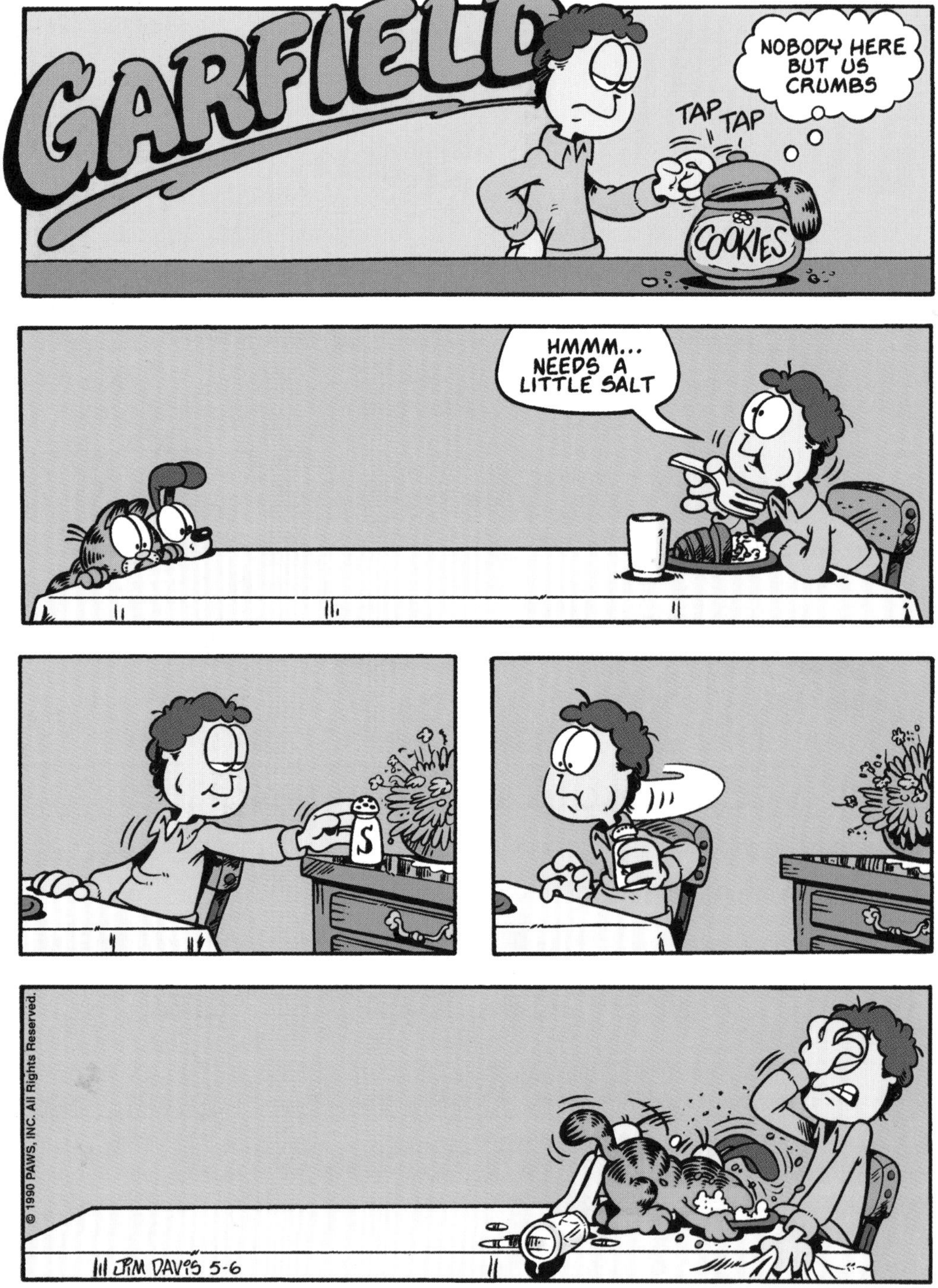
GARFIELD
NOBODY HERE BUT US CRUMBS
TAP TAP
COOKIES
HMMM... NEEDS A LITTLE SALT
S
JIM DAVIS 5-6

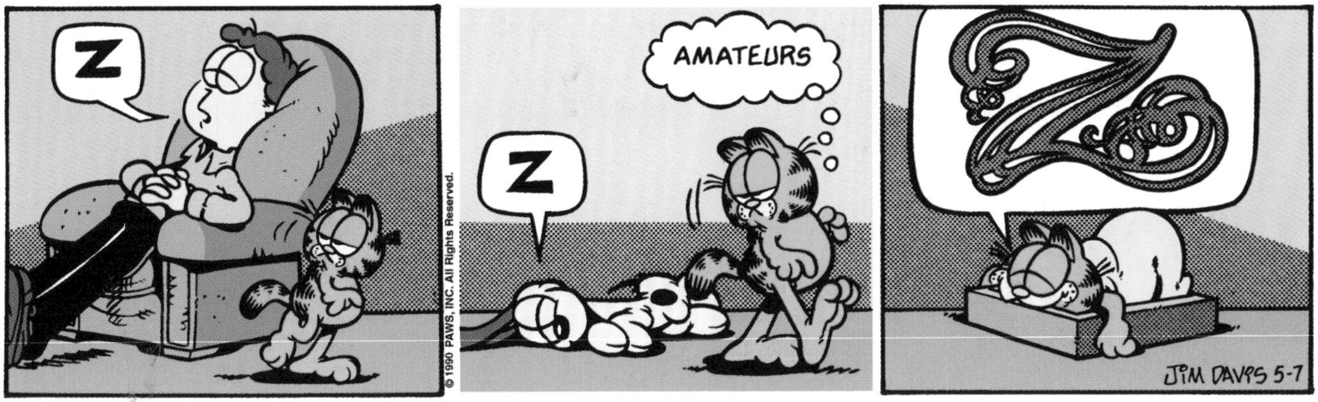
Z
Z
AMATEURS
JIM DAVIS 5-7

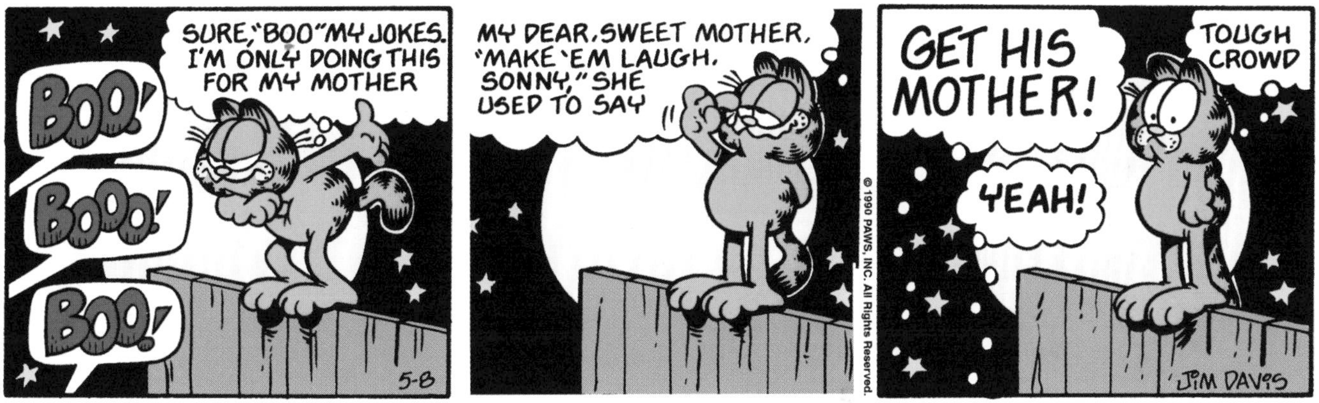
BOO!
BOOO!
BOO!
SURE, "BOO" MY JOKES. I'M ONLY DOING THIS FOR MY MOTHER
5-8
MY DEAR, SWEET MOTHER. "MAKE 'EM LAUGH, SONNY," SHE USED TO SAY
GET HIS MOTHER!
YEAH!
TOUGH CROWD
JIM DAVIS

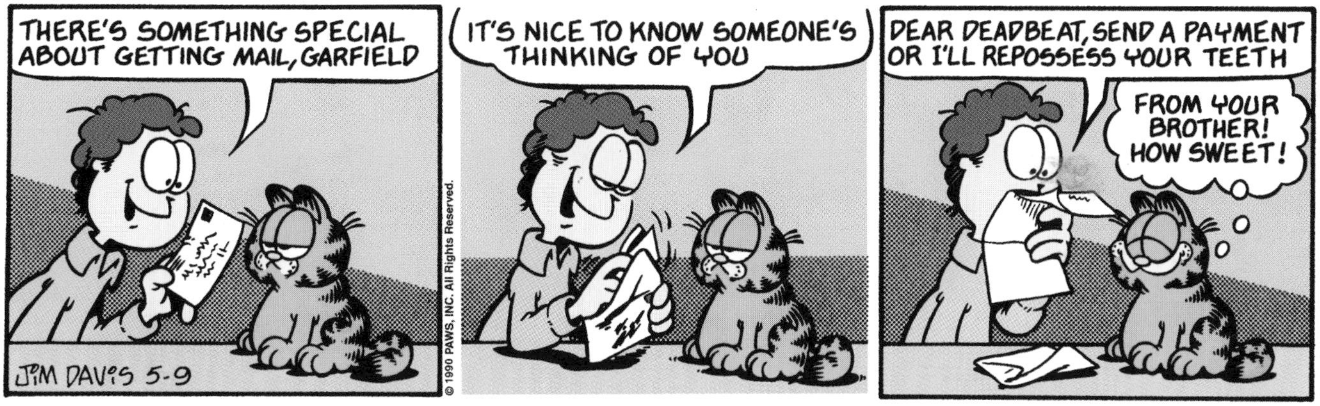
THERE'S SOMETHING SPECIAL ABOUT GETTING MAIL, GARFIELD
JIM DAVIS 5-9
IT'S NICE TO KNOW SOMEONE'S THINKING OF YOU
DEAR DEADBEAT, SEND A PAYMENT OR I'LL REPOSSESS YOUR TEETH
FROM YOUR BROTHER! HOW SWEET!

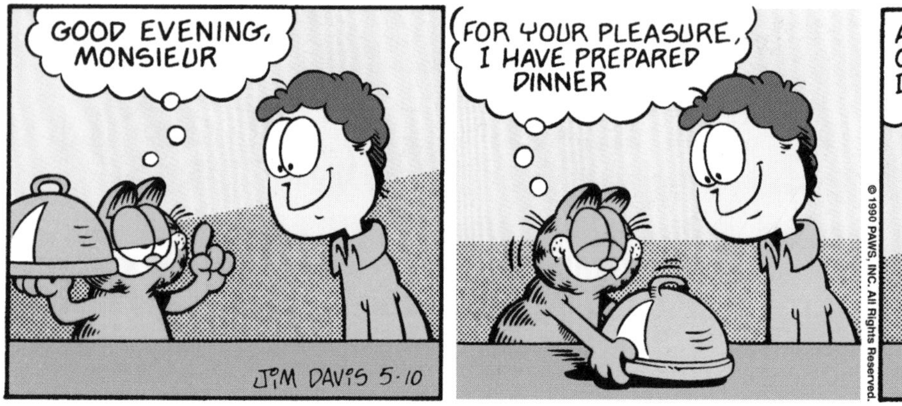
GOOD EVENING, MONSIEUR
JIM DAVIS 5-10
FOR YOUR PLEASURE, I HAVE PREPARED DINNER
© 1990 PAWS, INC. All Rights Reserved.
AND, FOR YOUR CONVENIENCE, I HAVE EATEN IT

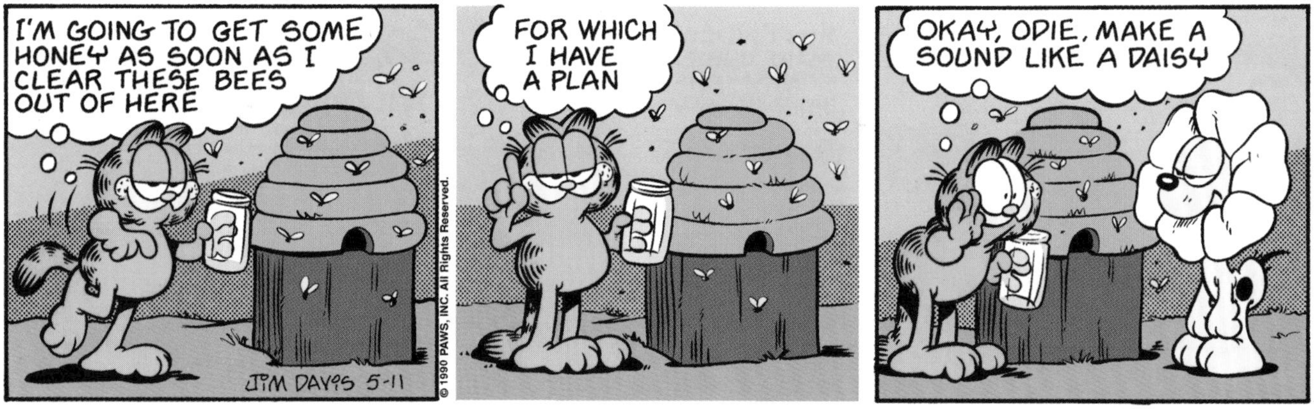
I'M GOING TO GET SOME HONEY AS SOON AS I CLEAR THESE BEES OUT OF HERE
JIM DAVIS 5-11
© 1990 PAWS, INC. All Rights Reserved.
FOR WHICH I HAVE A PLAN
OKAY, ODIE, MAKE A SOUND LIKE A DAISY

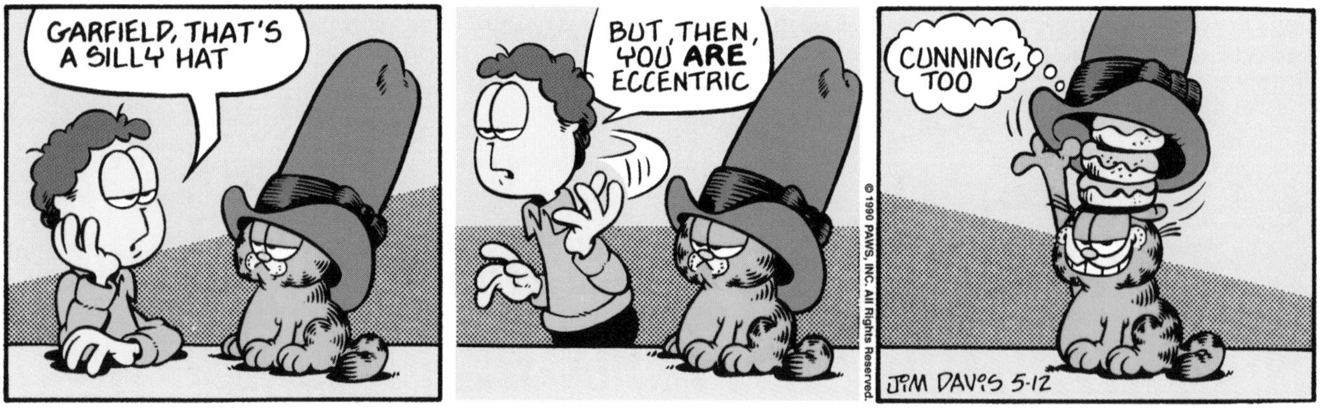
GARFIELD, THAT'S A SILLY HAT
BUT, THEN, YOU **ARE** ECCENTRIC
© 1990 PAWS, INC. All Rights Reserved.
CUNNING, TOO
JIM DAVIS 5-12

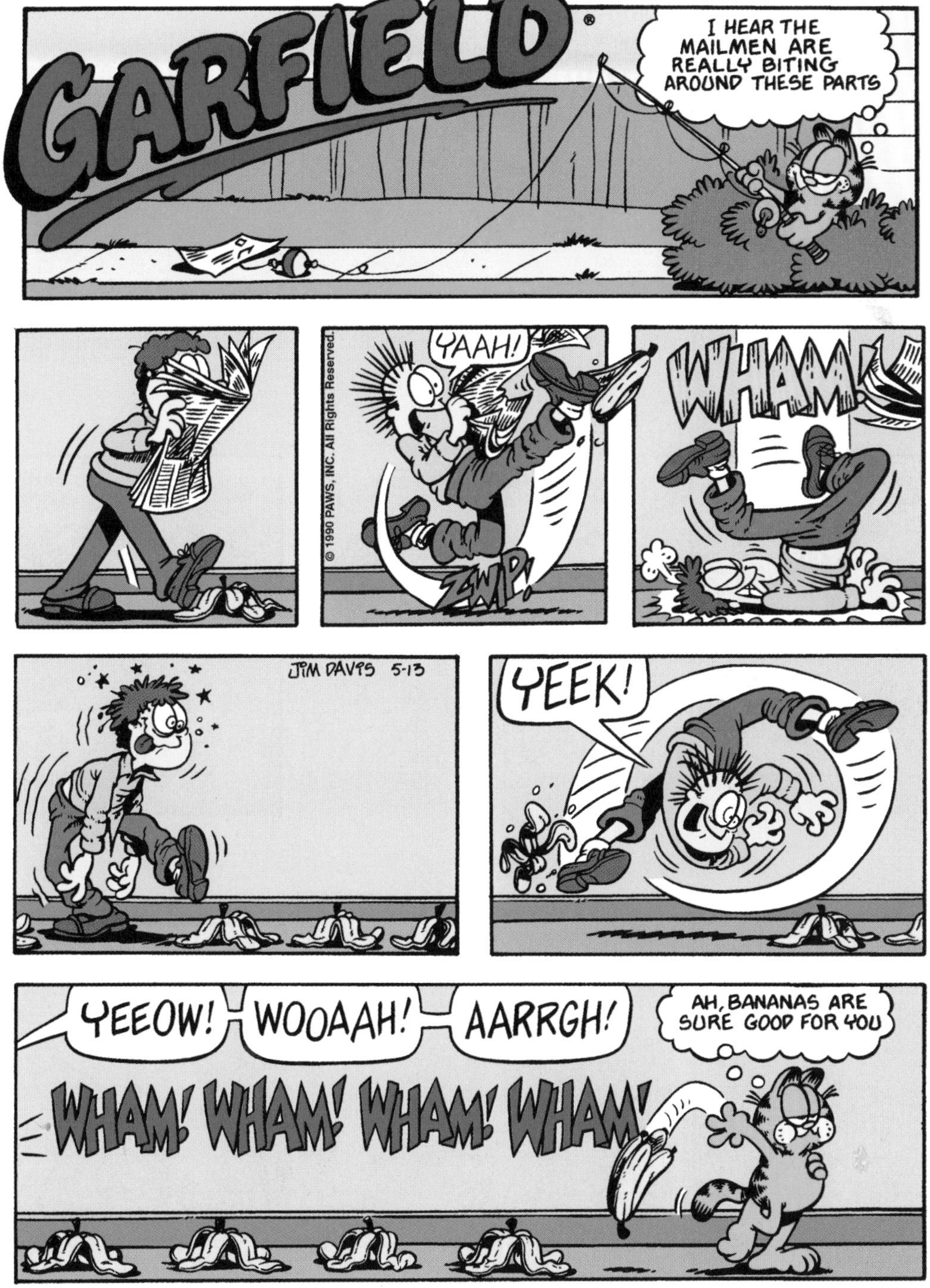
GARFIELD
I HEAR THE MAILMEN ARE REALLY BITING AROUND THESE PARTS
© 1990 PAWS, INC. All Rights Reserved.
YAAH!
ZWIP!
WHAM!
JIM DAVIS 5-13
YEEK!
YEEOW!
WOOAAH!
AARRGH!
AH, BANANAS ARE SURE GOOD FOR YOU
WHAM! WHAM! WHAM! WHAM!

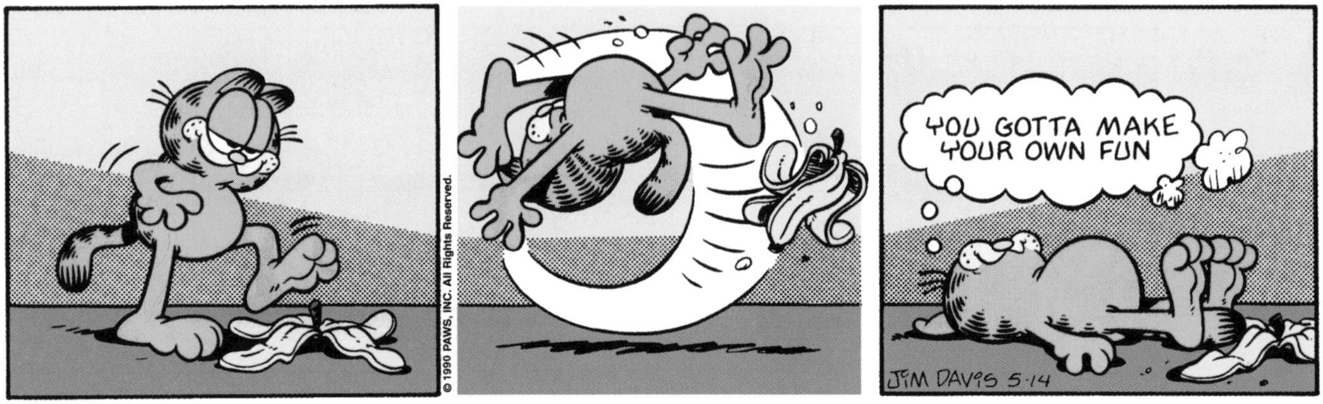
© 1990 PAWS, INC. All Rights Reserved.
YOU GOTTA MAKE YOUR OWN FUN
JIM DAVIS 5-14

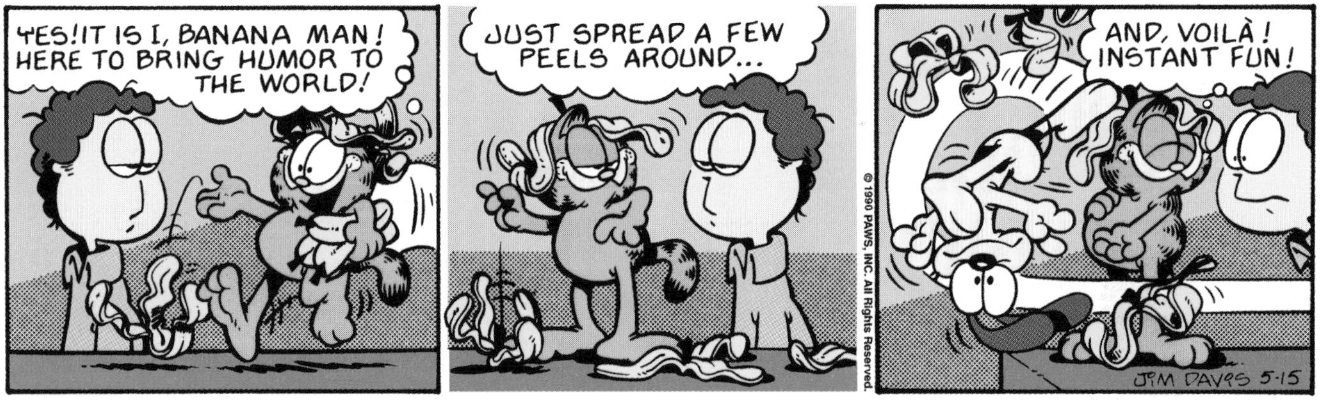
YES! IT IS I, BANANA MAN! HERE TO BRING HUMOR TO THE WORLD!
JUST SPREAD A FEW PEELS AROUND...
© 1990 PAWS, INC. All Rights Reserved.
AND, VOILÀ! INSTANT FUN!
JIM DAVIS 5-15

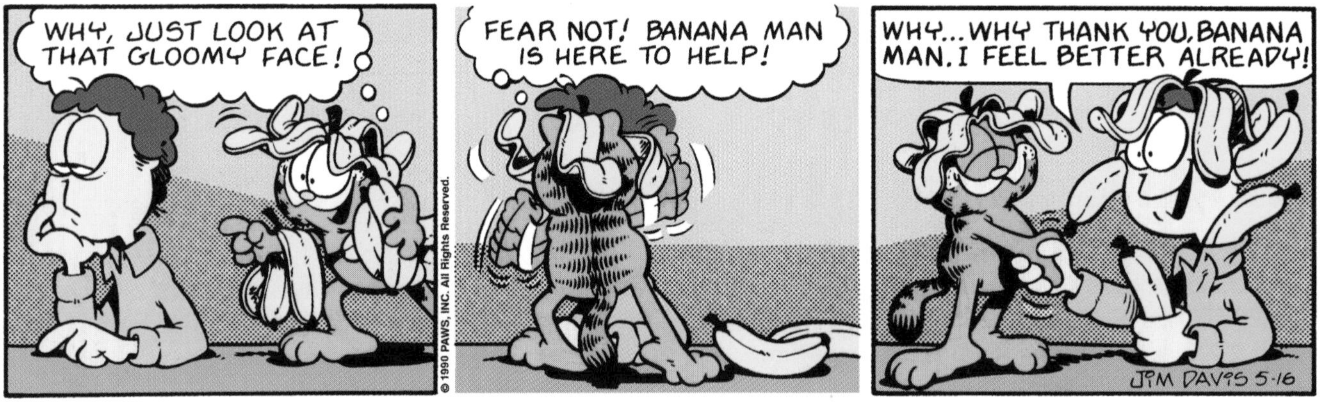
WHY, JUST LOOK AT THAT GLOOMY FACE!
© 1990 PAWS, INC. All Rights Reserved.
FEAR NOT! BANANA MAN IS HERE TO HELP!
WHY... WHY THANK YOU, BANANA MAN. I FEEL BETTER ALREADY!
JIM DAVIS 5-16

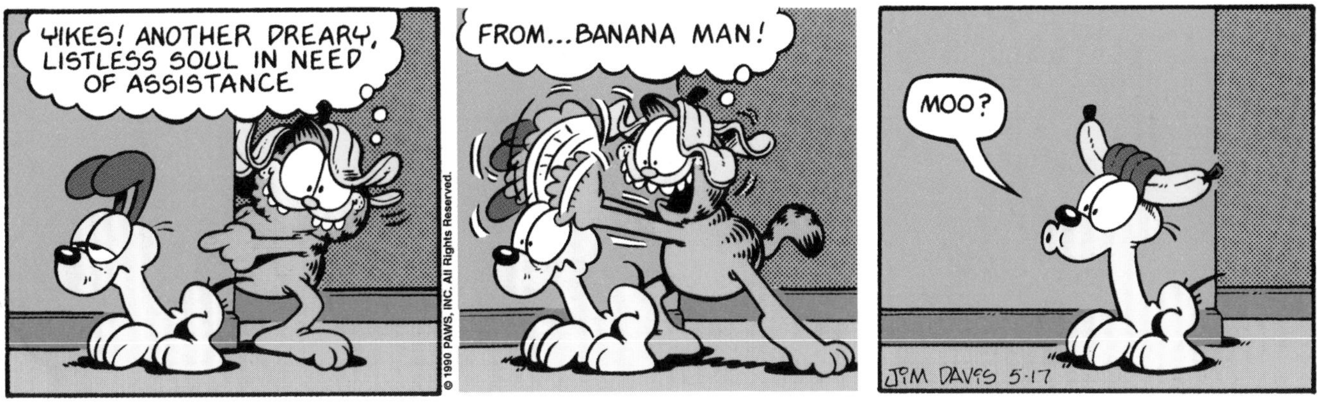
YIKES! ANOTHER DREARY, LISTLESS SOUL IN NEED OF ASSISTANCE
© 1990 PAWS, INC. All Rights Reserved.
FROM...BANANA MAN!
MOO?
JIM DAVIS 5·17

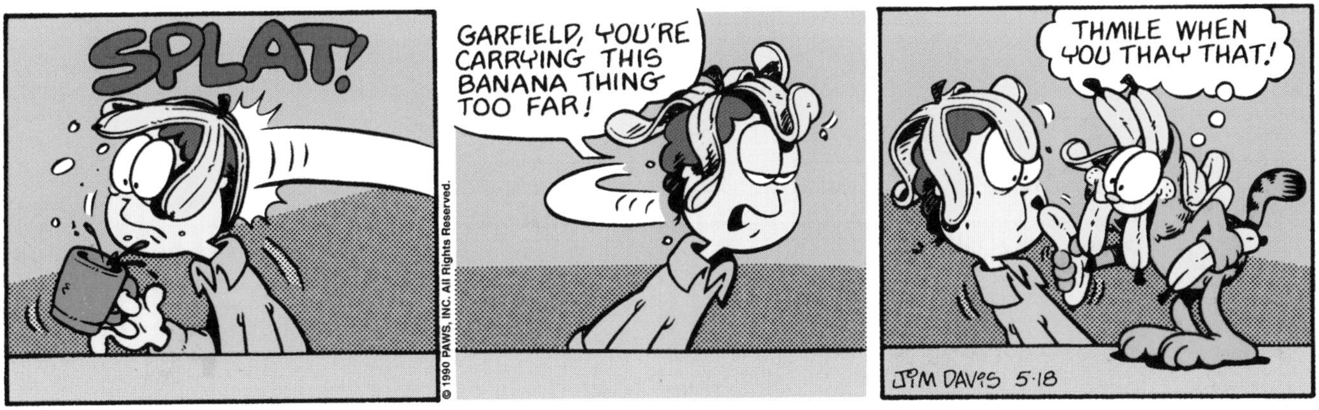
SPLAT!
© 1990 PAWS, INC. All Rights Reserved.
GARFIELD, YOU'RE CARRYING THIS BANANA THING TOO FAR!
THMILE WHEN YOU THAY THAT!
JIM DAVIS 5·18

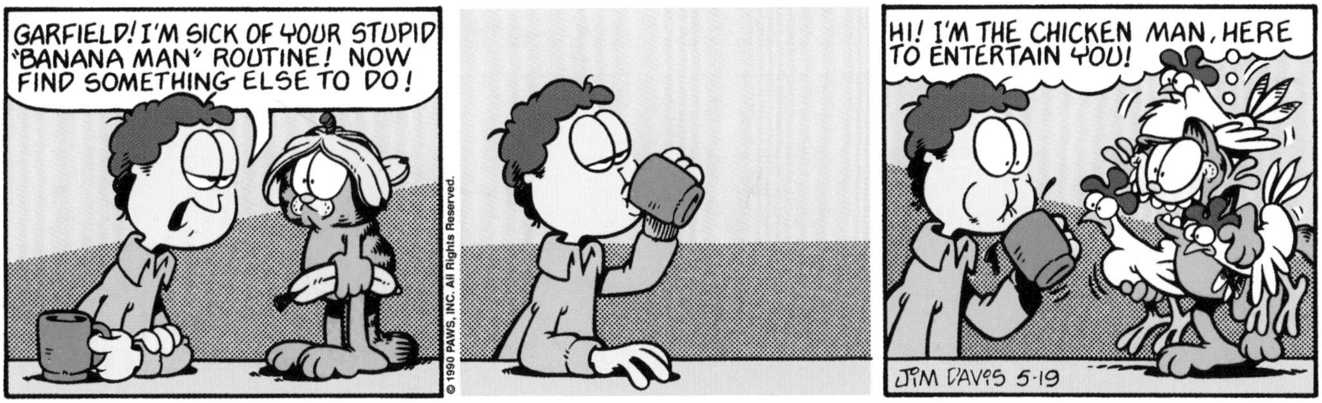
GARFIELD! I'M SICK OF YOUR STUPID "BANANA MAN" ROUTINE! NOW FIND SOMETHING ELSE TO DO!
© 1990 PAWS, INC. All Rights Reserved.
HI! I'M THE CHICKEN MAN, HERE TO ENTERTAIN YOU!
JIM DAVIS 5·19

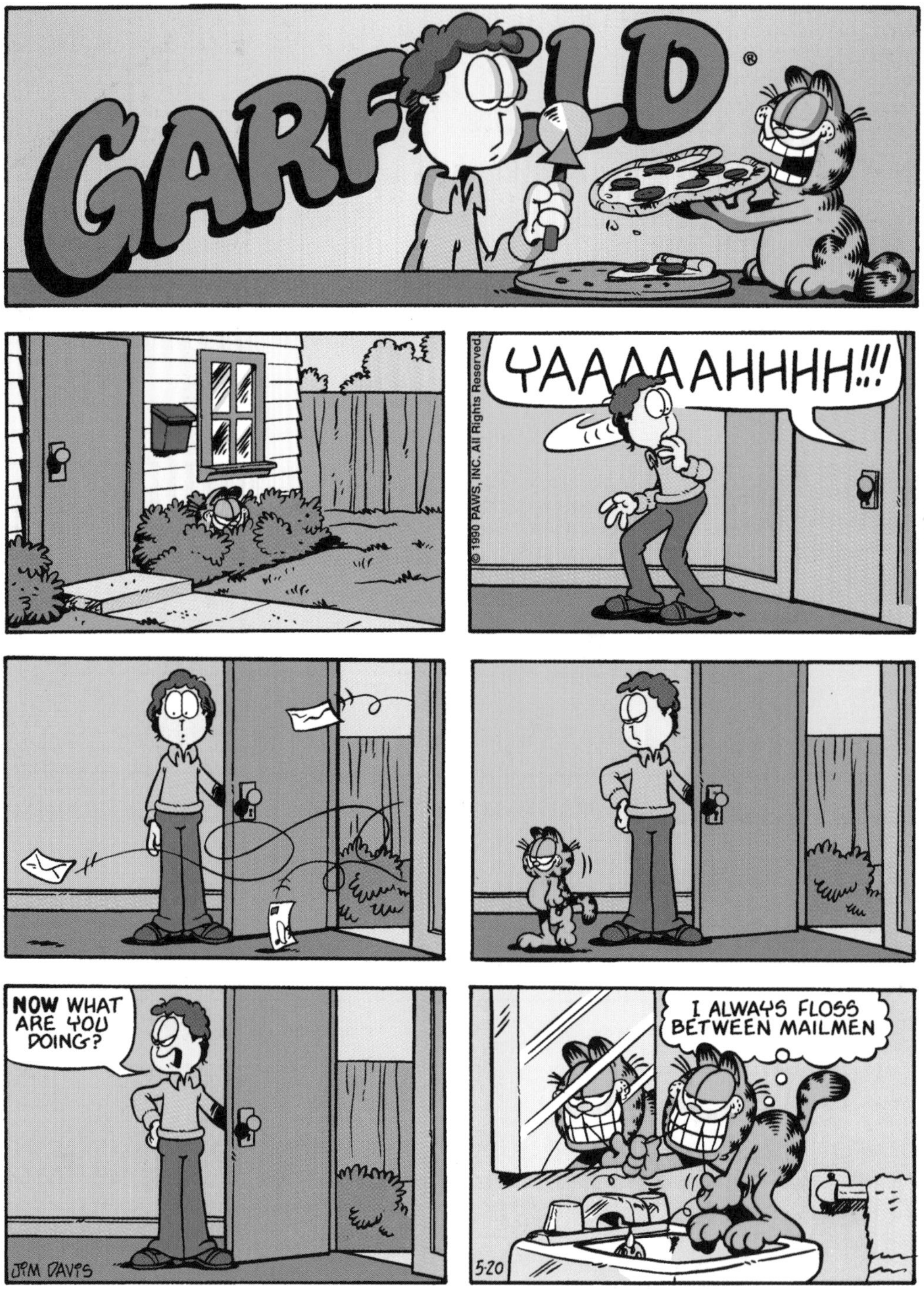
GARFIELD®
© 1990 PAWS, INC. All Rights Reserved.
YAAAAAHHHH!!!
NOW WHAT ARE YOU DOING?
I ALWAYS FLOSS BETWEEN MAILMEN
JIM DAVIS
5-20

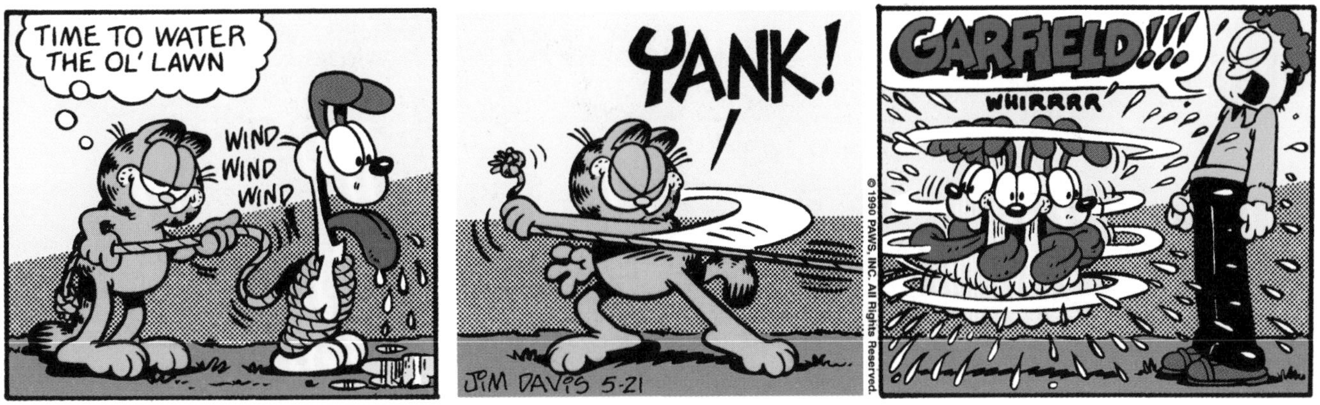
TIME TO WATER THE OL' LAWN
WIND WIND WIND
YANK!
JIM DAVIS 5-21
© 1990 PAWS, INC. All Rights Reserved.
GARFIELD!!!
WHIRRRR

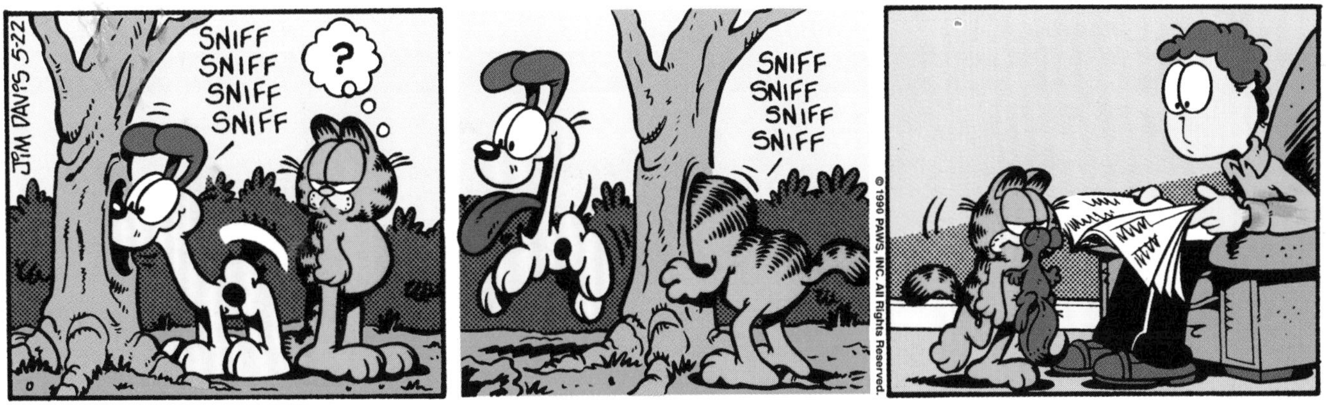
JIM DAVIS 5-22
SNIFF SNIFF SNIFF SNIFF
?
SNIFF SNIFF SNIFF SNIFF
© 1990 PAWS, INC. All Rights Reserved.

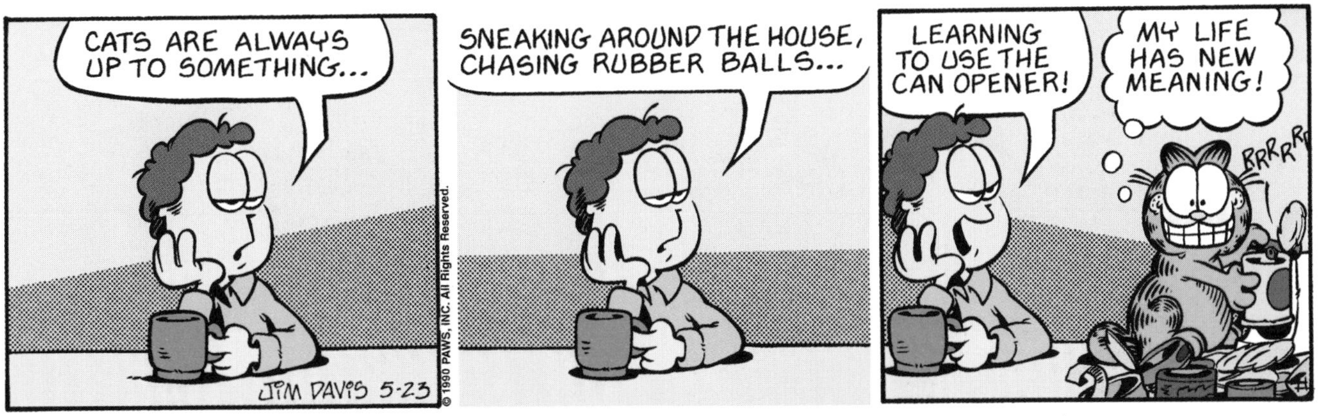
CATS ARE ALWAYS UP TO SOMETHING...
JIM DAVIS 5-23
© 1990 PAWS, INC. All Rights Reserved.
SNEAKING AROUND THE HOUSE, CHASING RUBBER BALLS...
LEARNING TO USE THE CAN OPENER!
MY LIFE HAS NEW MEANING!
RRRRR

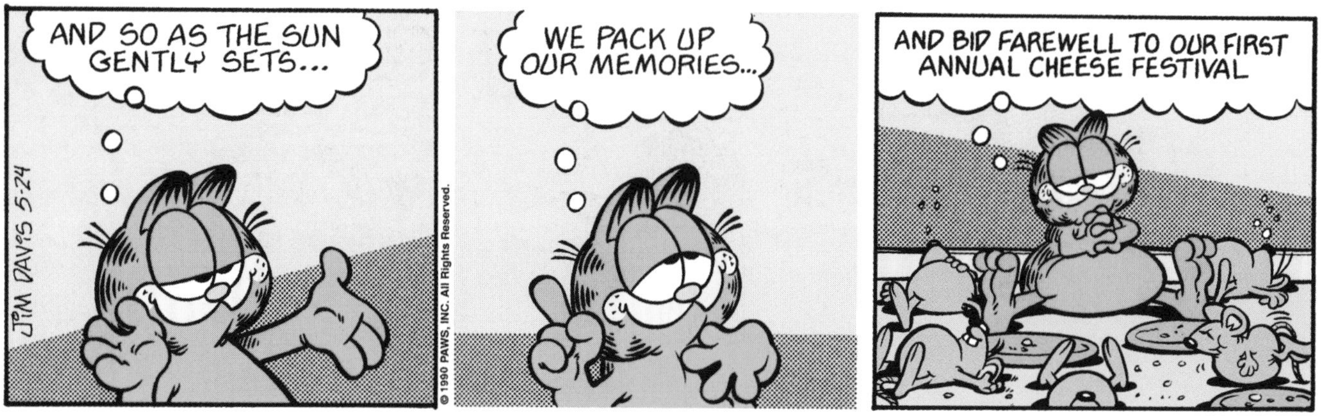
JIM DAVIS 5-24
AND SO AS THE SUN GENTLY SETS...
© 1990 PAWS, INC. All Rights Reserved.
WE PACK UP OUR MEMORIES...
AND BID FAREWELL TO OUR FIRST ANNUAL CHEESE FESTIVAL

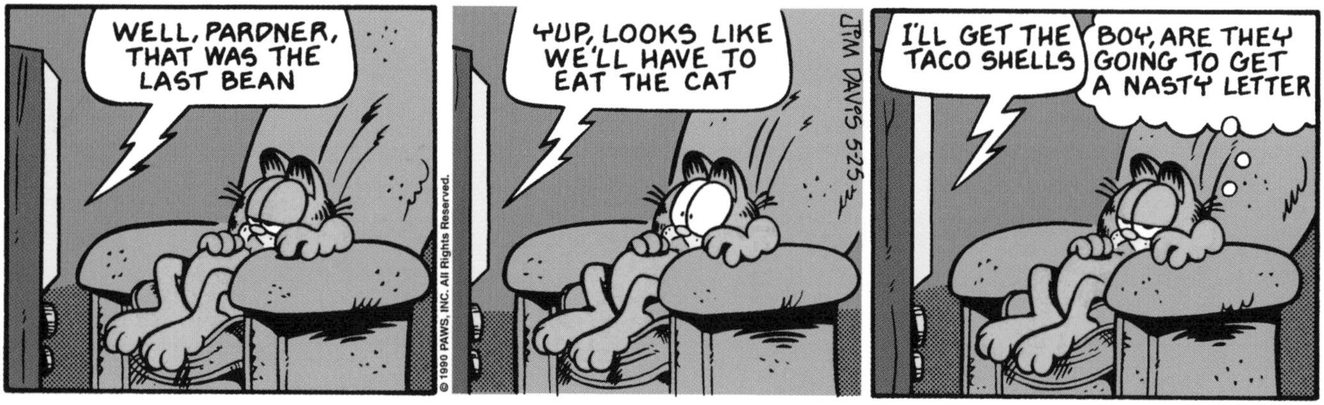
WELL, PARDNER, THAT WAS THE LAST BEAN
© 1990 PAWS, INC. All Rights Reserved.
YUP, LOOKS LIKE WE'LL HAVE TO EAT THE CAT
JIM DAVIS 5-25
I'LL GET THE TACO SHELLS
BOY, ARE THEY GOING TO GET A NASTY LETTER

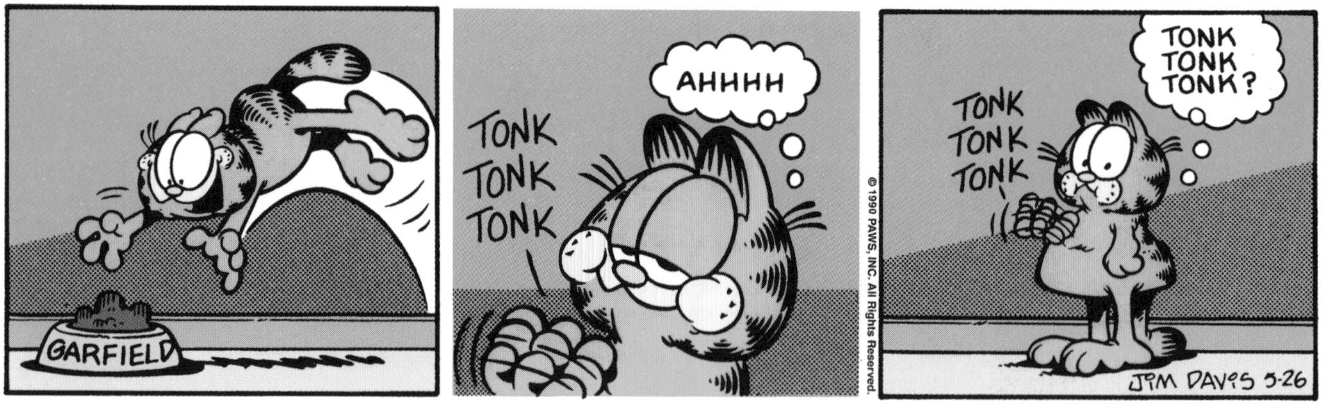
GARFIELD
TONK TONK TONK
AHHHH
© 1990 PAWS, INC. All Rights Reserved.
TONK TONK TONK
TONK TONK TONK?
JIM DAVIS 5-26

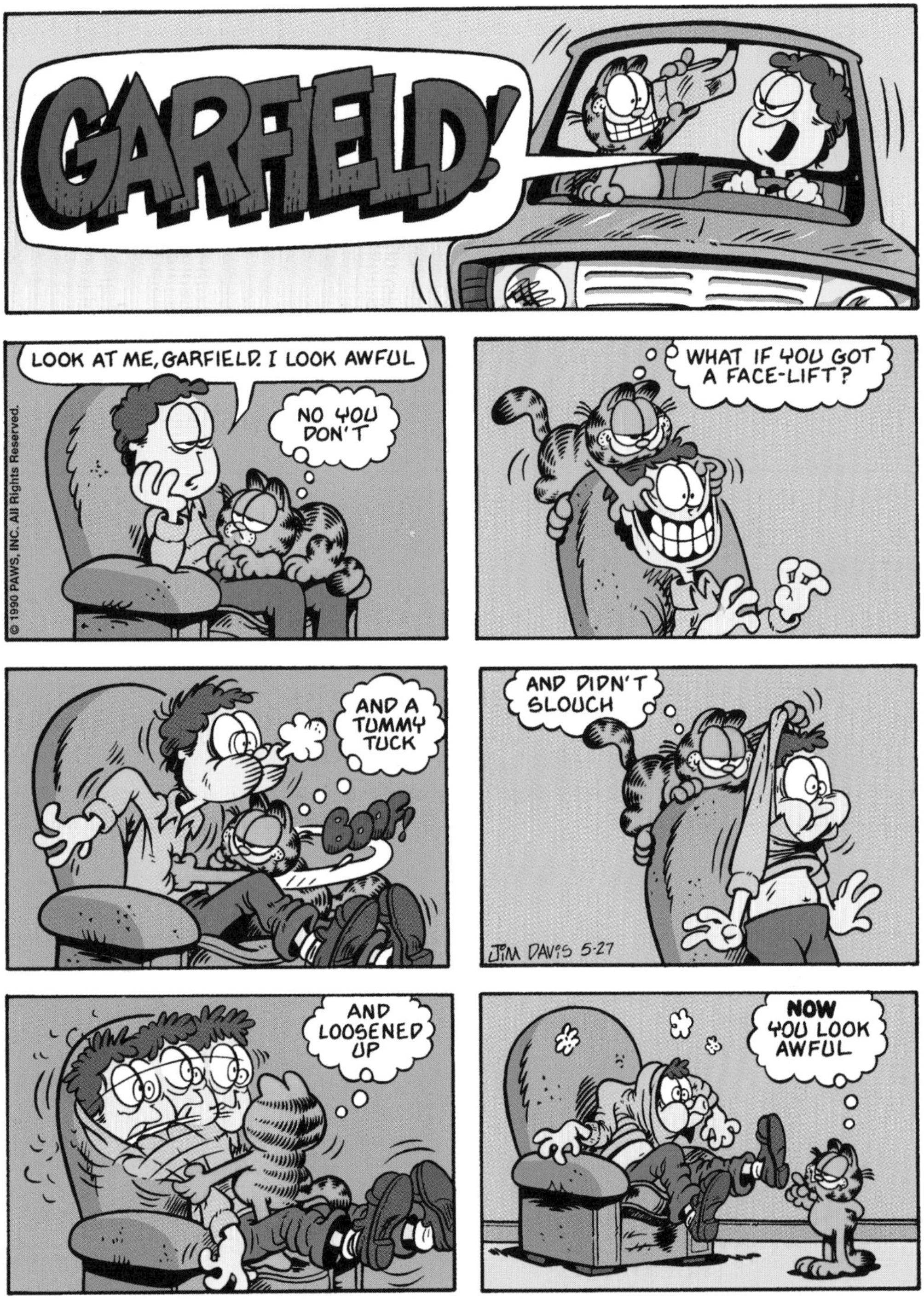
GARFIELD!
LOOK AT ME, GARFIELD. I LOOK AWFUL
NO YOU DON'T
WHAT IF YOU GOT A FACE-LIFT?
AND A TUMMY TUCK
BOOF!
AND DIDN'T SLOUCH
JIM DAVIS 5-27
AND LOOSENED UP
NOW YOU LOOK AWFUL

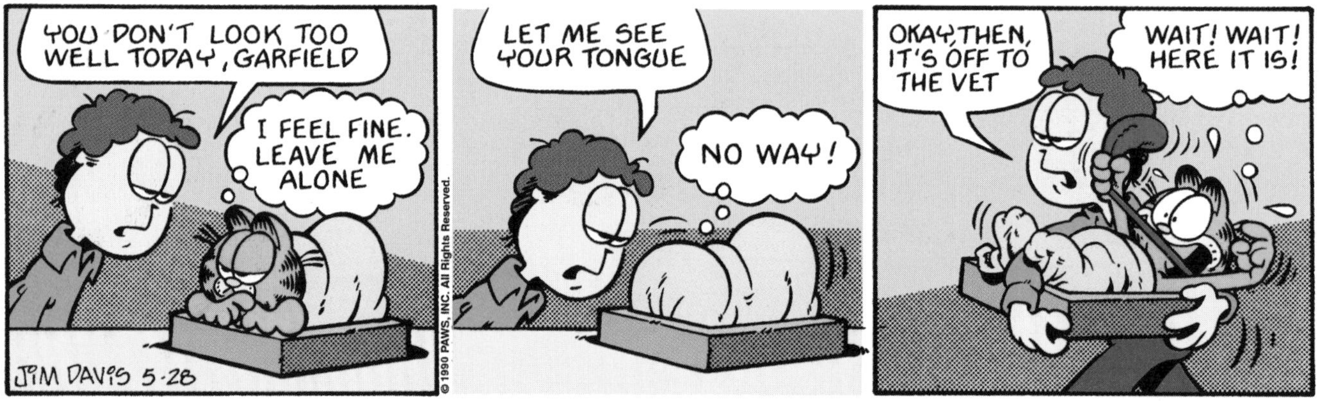
YOU DON'T LOOK TOO WELL TODAY, GARFIELD
I FEEL FINE. LEAVE ME ALONE
JIM DAVIS 5-28
© 1990 PAWS, INC. All Rights Reserved.
LET ME SEE YOUR TONGUE
NO WAY!
OKAY, THEN, IT'S OFF TO THE VET
WAIT! WAIT! HERE IT IS!

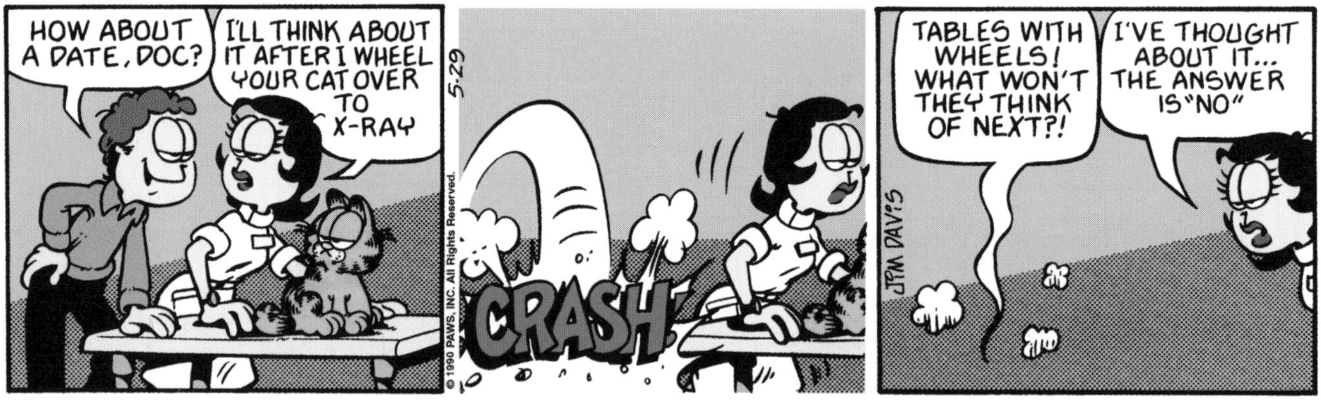
HOW ABOUT A DATE, DOC?
I'LL THINK ABOUT IT AFTER I WHEEL YOUR CAT OVER TO X-RAY
5-29
© 1990 PAWS, INC. All Rights Reserved.
CRASH
JIM DAVIS
TABLES WITH WHEELS! WHAT WON'T THEY THINK OF NEXT?!
I'VE THOUGHT ABOUT IT... THE ANSWER IS "NO"

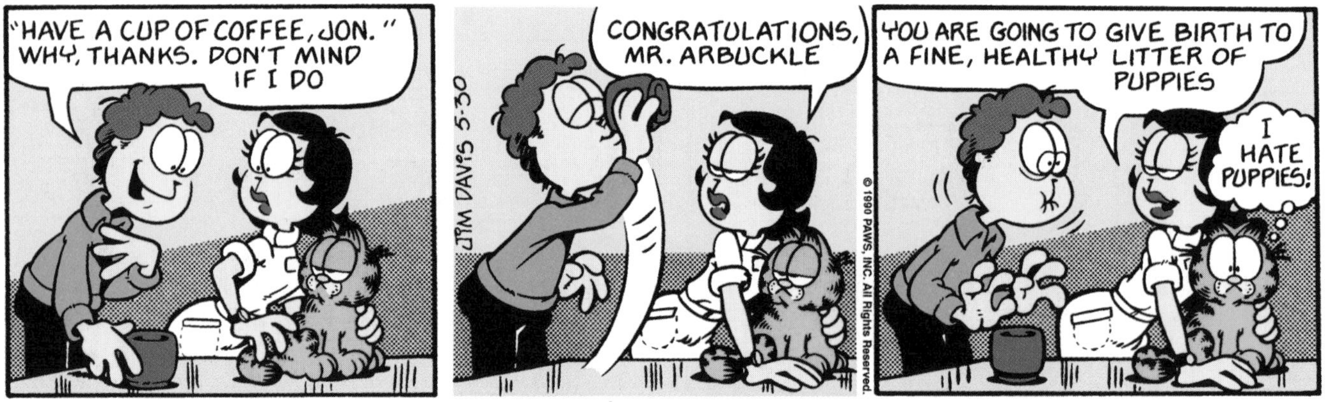
"HAVE A CUP OF COFFEE, JON." WHY, THANKS. DON'T MIND IF I DO
JIM DAVIS 5-30
CONGRATULATIONS, MR. ARBUCKLE
© 1990 PAWS, INC. All Rights Reserved.
YOU ARE GOING TO GIVE BIRTH TO A FINE, HEALTHY LITTER OF PUPPIES
I HATE PUPPIES!

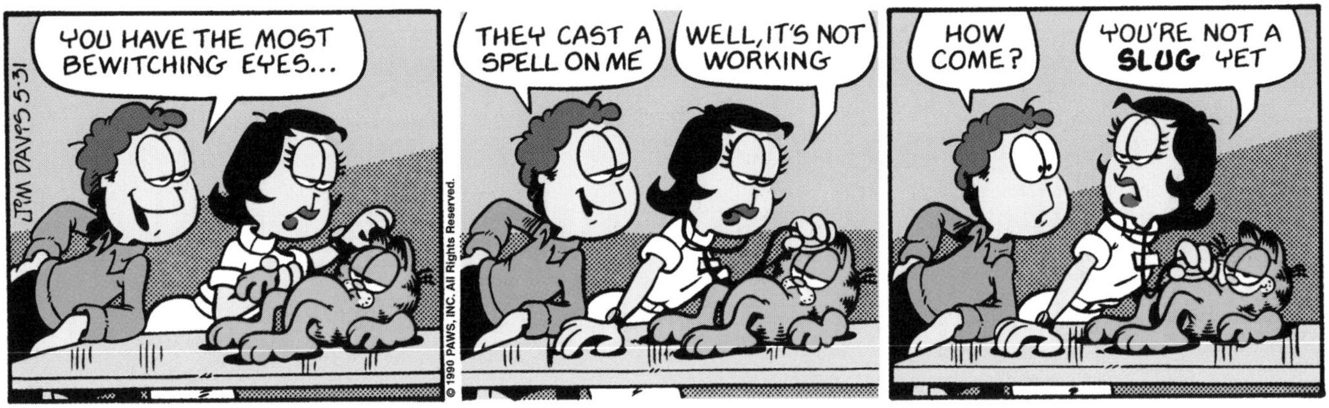
YOU HAVE THE MOST BEWITCHING EYES...
JIM DAVIS 5-31
THEY CAST A SPELL ON ME
WELL, IT'S NOT WORKING
© 1990 PAWS, INC. All Rights Reserved.
HOW COME?
YOU'RE NOT A **SLUG** YET

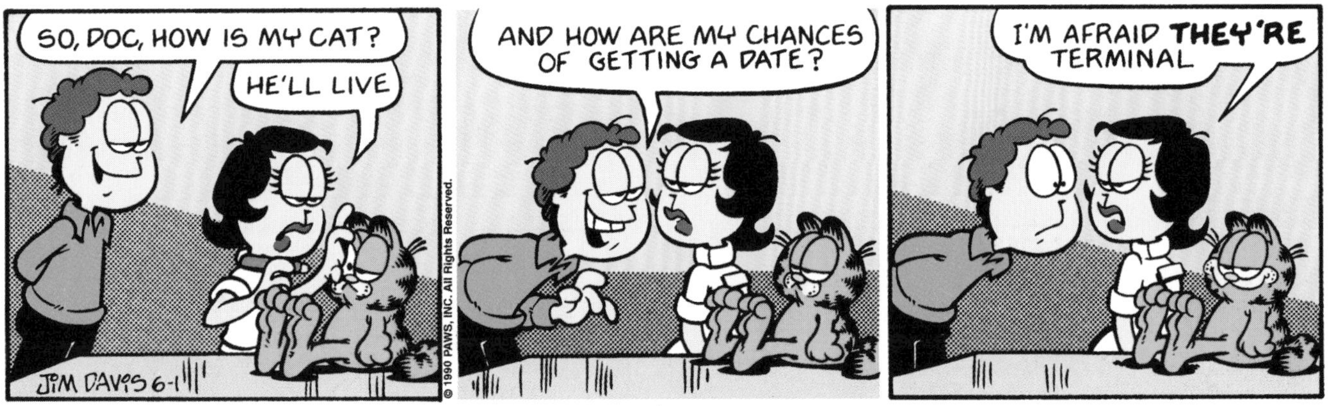
SO, DOC, HOW IS MY CAT?
HE'LL LIVE
JIM DAVIS 6-1
© 1990 PAWS, INC. All Rights Reserved.
AND HOW ARE MY CHANCES OF GETTING A DATE?
I'M AFRAID **THEY'RE** TERMINAL

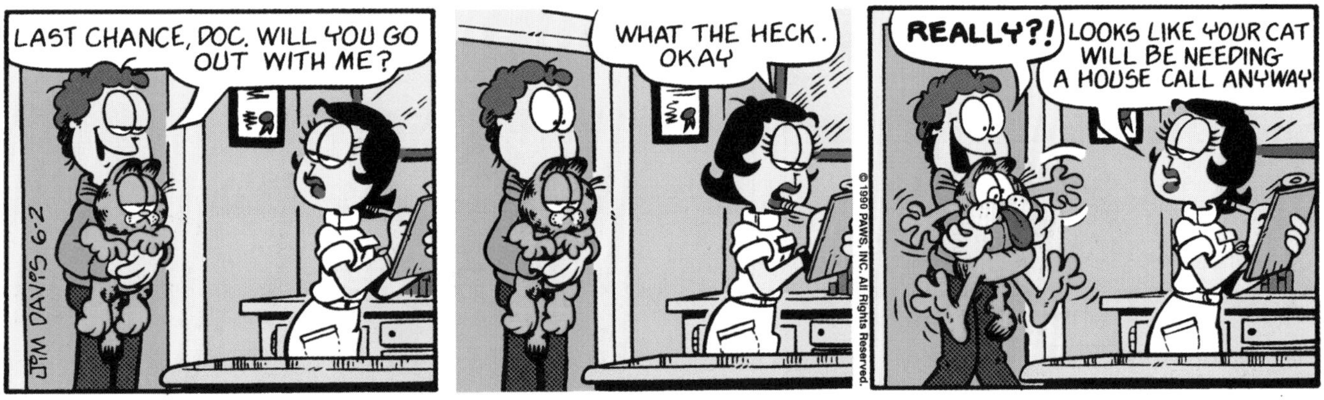
LAST CHANCE, DOC. WILL YOU GO OUT WITH ME?
JIM DAVIS 6-2
WHAT THE HECK. OKAY
© 1990 PAWS, INC. All Rights Reserved.
REALLY?!
LOOKS LIKE YOUR CAT WILL BE NEEDING A HOUSE CALL ANYWAY

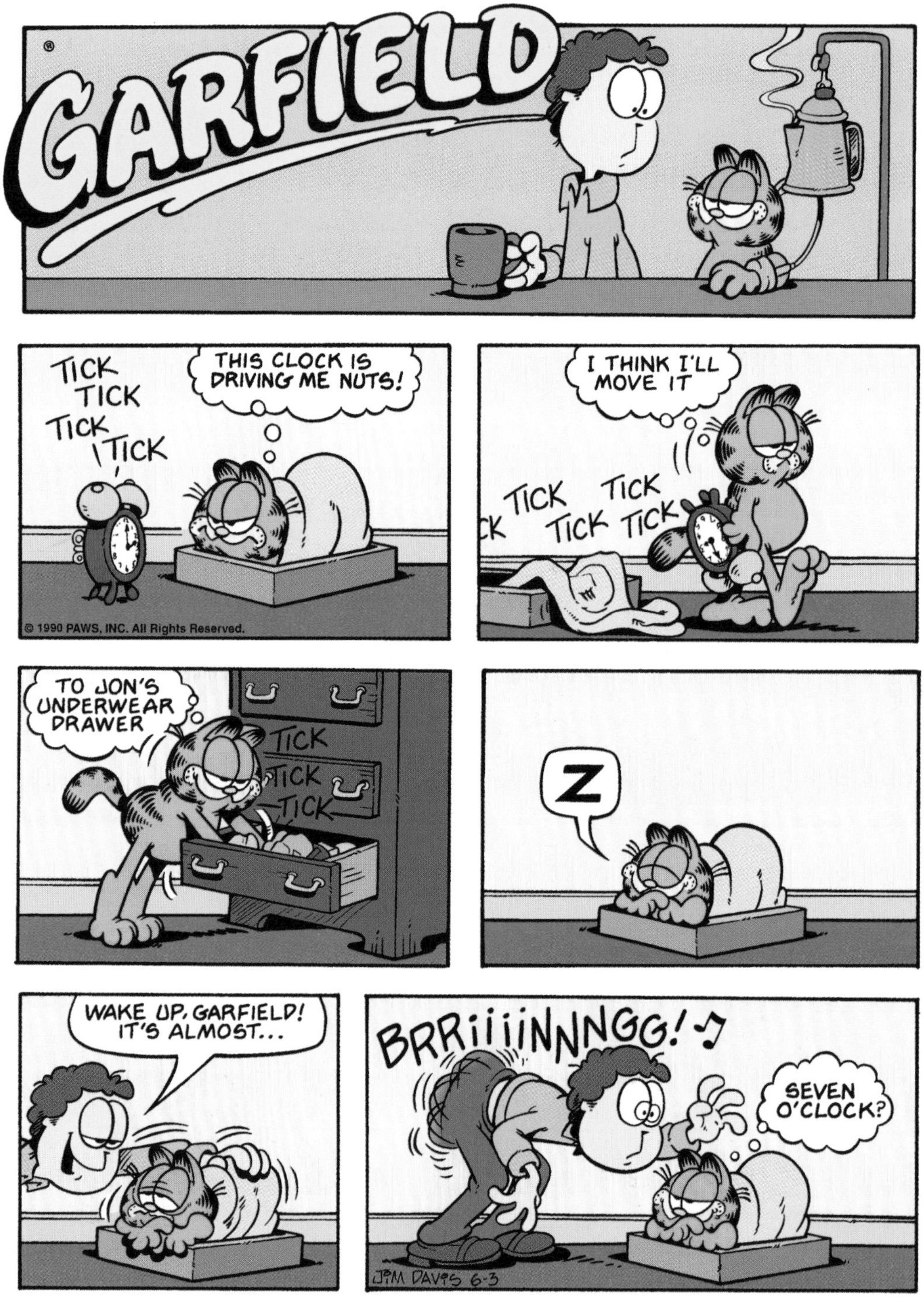
GARFIELD
TICK TICK TICK TICK
THIS CLOCK IS DRIVING ME NUTS!
I THINK I'LL MOVE IT
TICK TICK TICK TICK
TO JON'S UNDERWEAR DRAWER
TICK TICK TICK
Z
WAKE UP, GARFIELD! IT'S ALMOST...
BRRiiiiNNNGG!
SEVEN O'CLOCK?
JIM DAVIS 6-3

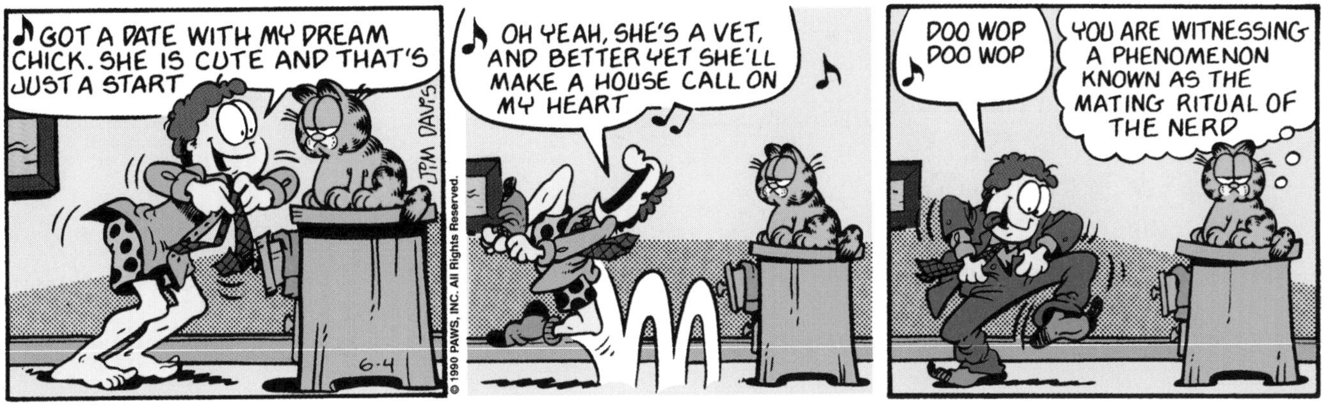
GOT A DATE WITH MY DREAM CHICK. SHE IS CUTE AND THAT'S JUST A START
JIM DAVIS
6-4
© 1990 PAWS, INC. All Rights Reserved.
OH YEAH, SHE'S A VET, AND BETTER YET SHE'LL MAKE A HOUSE CALL ON MY HEART
DOO WOP DOO WOP
YOU ARE WITNESSING A PHENOMENON KNOWN AS THE MATING RITUAL OF THE NERD

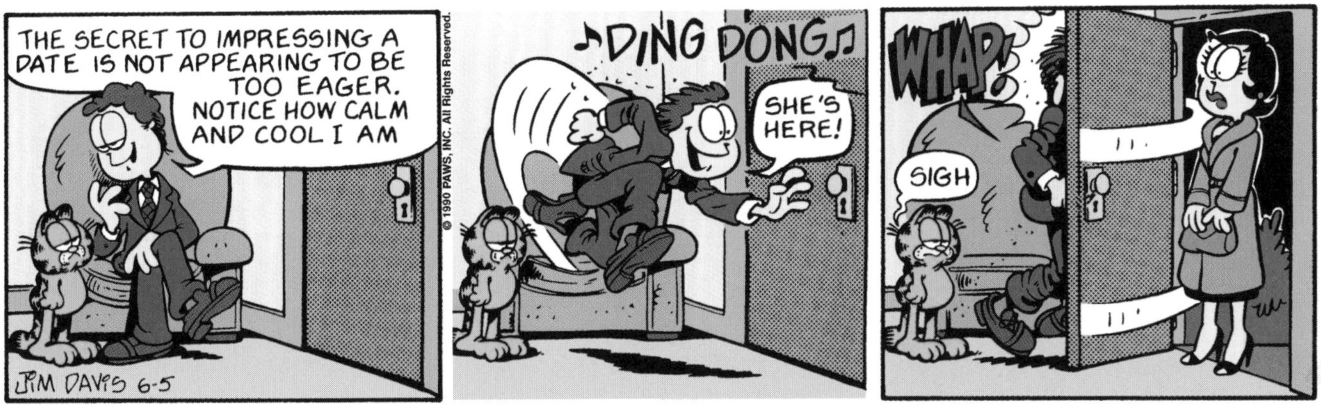
THE SECRET TO IMPRESSING A DATE IS NOT APPEARING TO BE TOO EAGER. NOTICE HOW CALM AND COOL I AM
JIM DAVIS 6-5
© 1990 PAWS, INC. All Rights Reserved.
DING DONG
SHE'S HERE!
WHAP!
SIGH

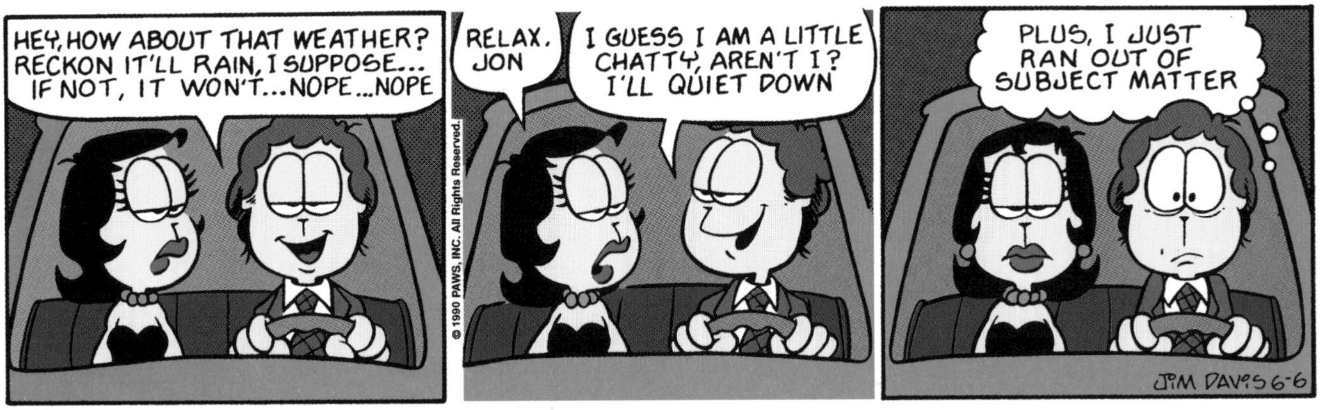
HEY, HOW ABOUT THAT WEATHER? RECKON IT'LL RAIN, I SUPPOSE... IF NOT, IT WON'T...NOPE...NOPE
© 1990 PAWS, INC. All Rights Reserved.
RELAX, JON
I GUESS I AM A LITTLE CHATTY, AREN'T I? I'LL QUIET DOWN
PLUS, I JUST RAN OUT OF SUBJECT MATTER
JIM DAVIS 6-6

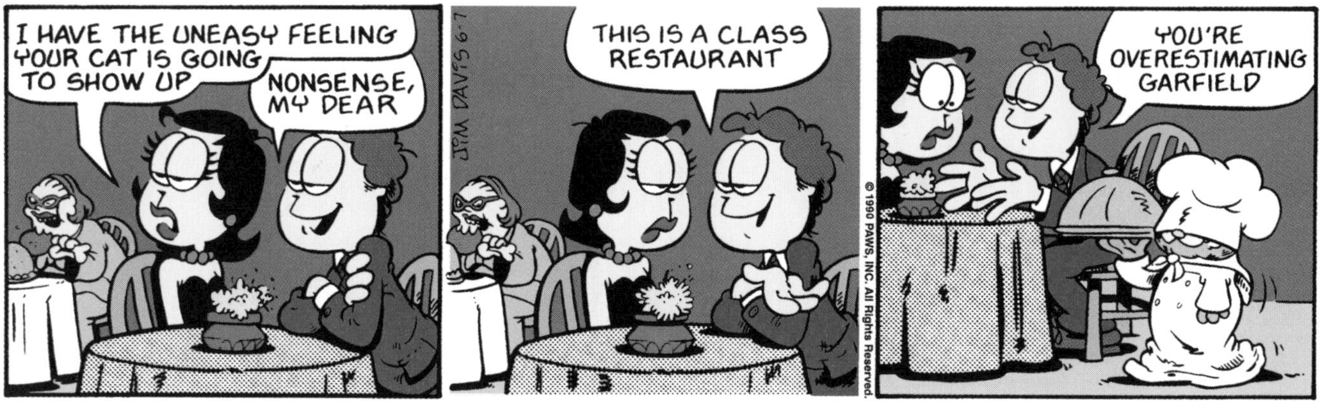
I HAVE THE UNEASY FEELING YOUR CAT IS GOING TO SHOW UP
NONSENSE, MY DEAR
JIM DAVIS 6-7
THIS IS A CLASS RESTAURANT
© 1990 PAWS, INC. All Rights Reserved.
YOU'RE OVERESTIMATING GARFIELD

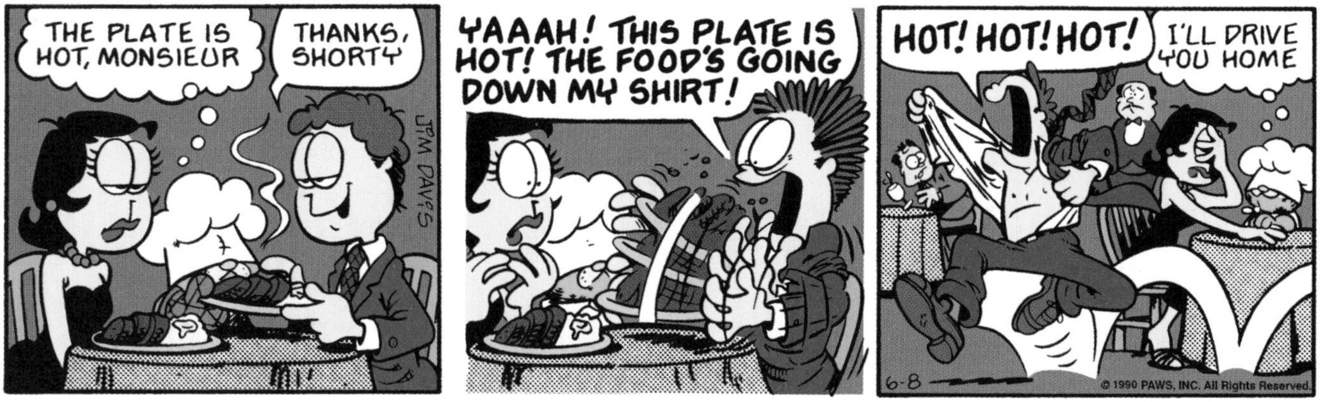
THE PLATE IS HOT, MONSIEUR
THANKS, SHORTY
JIM DAVIS
YAAAH! THIS PLATE IS HOT! THE FOOD'S GOING DOWN MY SHIRT!
HOT! HOT! HOT!
I'LL DRIVE YOU HOME
6-8
© 1990 PAWS, INC. All Rights Reserved.

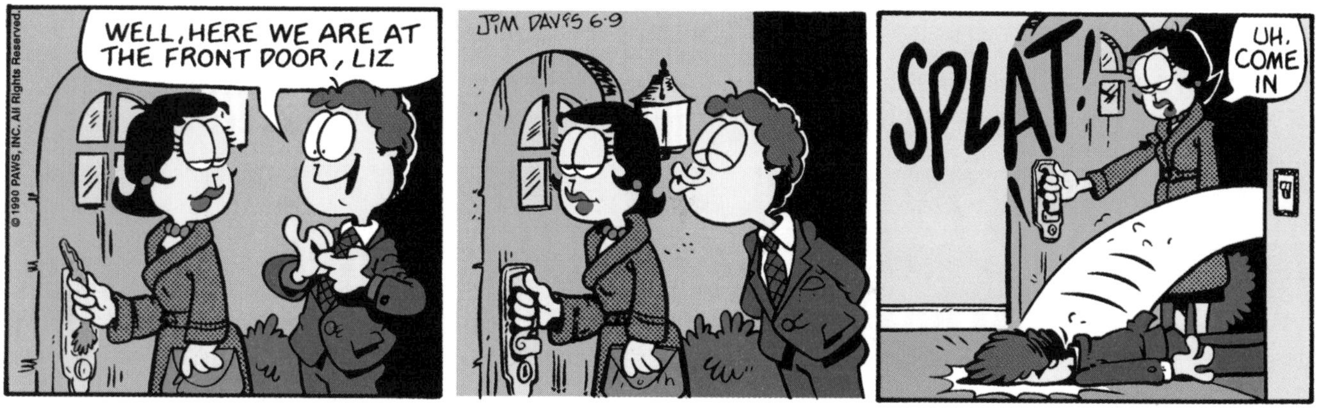
© 1990 PAWS, INC. All Rights Reserved.
WELL, HERE WE ARE AT THE FRONT DOOR, LIZ
JIM DAVIS 6-9
SPLAT!
UH, COME IN

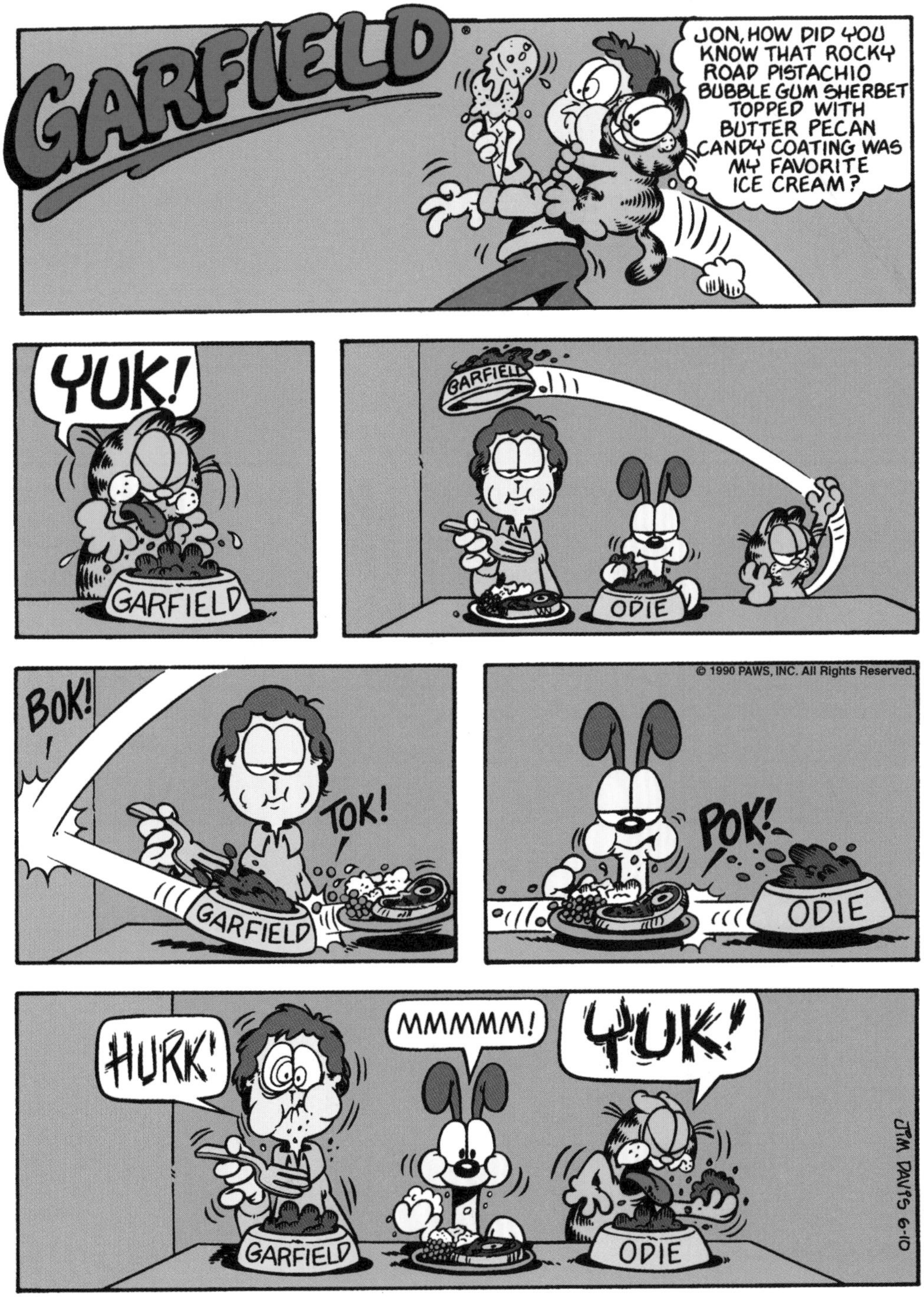
GARFIELD
JON, HOW DID YOU KNOW THAT ROCKY ROAD PISTACHIO BUBBLE GUM SHERBET TOPPED WITH BUTTER PECAN CANDY COATING WAS MY FAVORITE ICE CREAM?
YUK!
GARFIELD
GARFIELD
ODIE
BOK!
TOK!
GARFIELD
POK!
ODIE
HURK!
MMMMM!
YUK!
GARFIELD
ODIE
JIM DAVIS 6-10

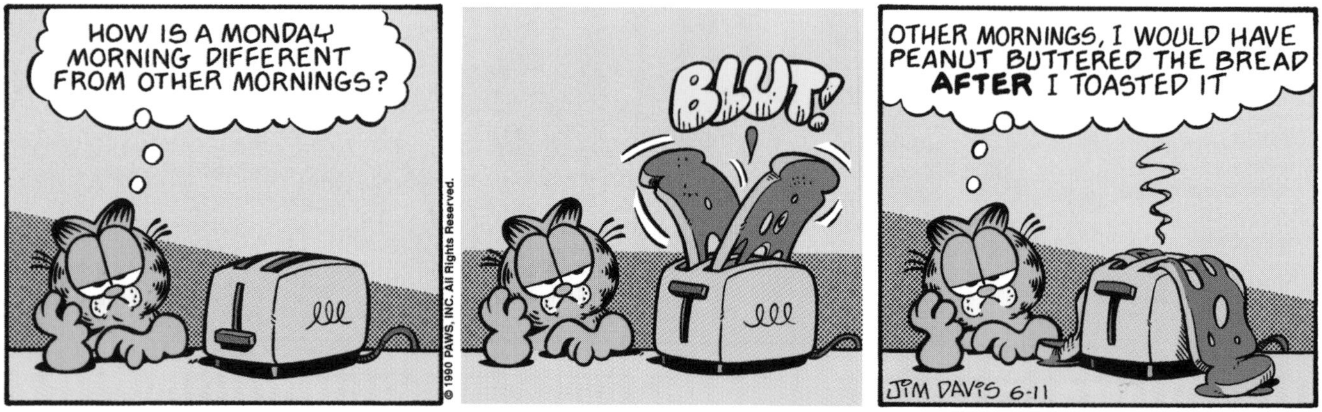
HOW IS A MONDAY MORNING DIFFERENT FROM OTHER MORNINGS?
© 1990 PAWS, INC. All Rights Reserved.
BLUT!
OTHER MORNINGS, I WOULD HAVE PEANUT BUTTERED THE BREAD **AFTER** I TOASTED IT
JIM DAVIS 6-11

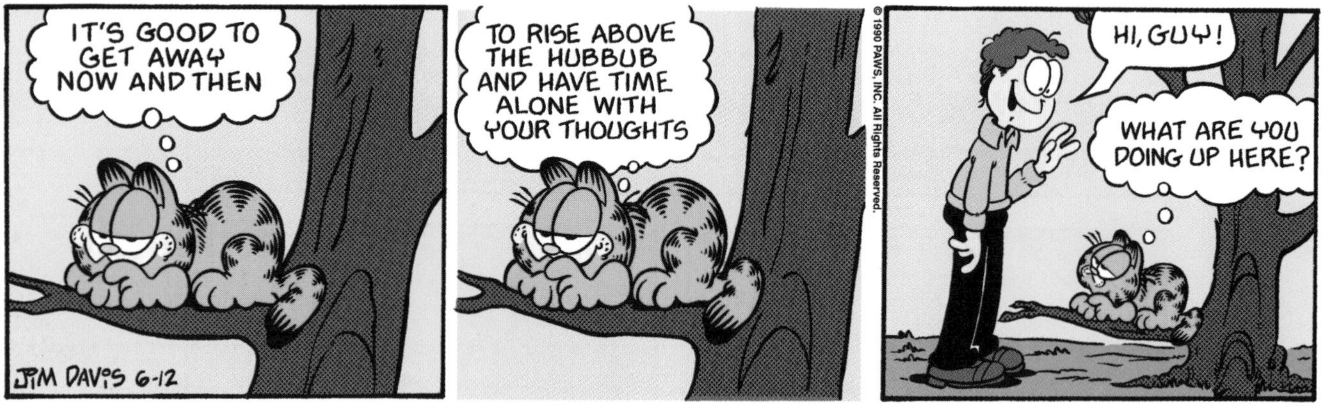
IT'S GOOD TO GET AWAY NOW AND THEN
JIM DAVIS 6-12
TO RISE ABOVE THE HUBBUB AND HAVE TIME ALONE WITH YOUR THOUGHTS
© 1990 PAWS, INC. All Rights Reserved.
HI, GUY!
WHAT ARE YOU DOING UP HERE?

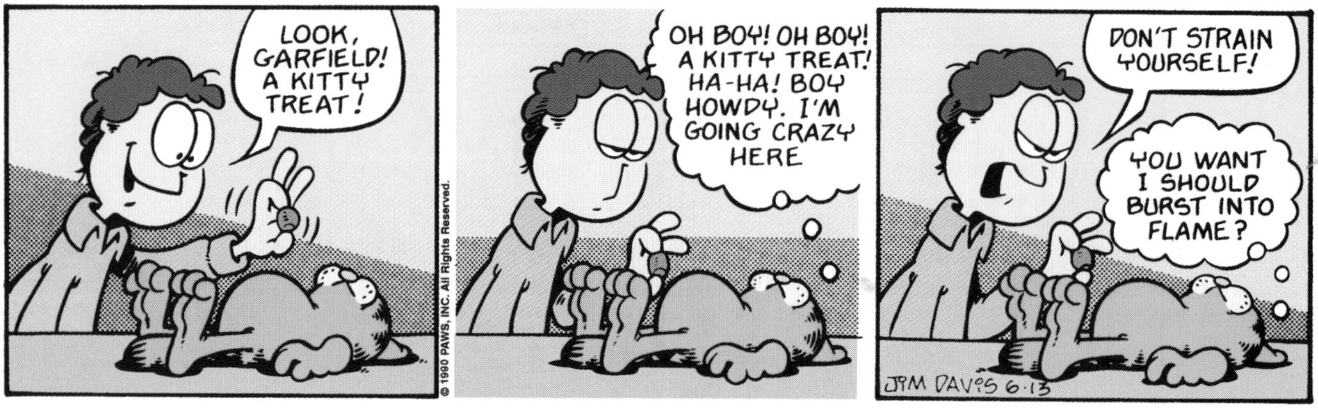
LOOK, GARFIELD! A KITTY TREAT!
© 1990 PAWS, INC. All Rights Reserved.
OH BOY! OH BOY! A KITTY TREAT! HA-HA! BOY HOWDY. I'M GOING CRAZY HERE
DON'T STRAIN YOURSELF!
YOU WANT I SHOULD BURST INTO FLAME?
JIM DAVIS 6-13

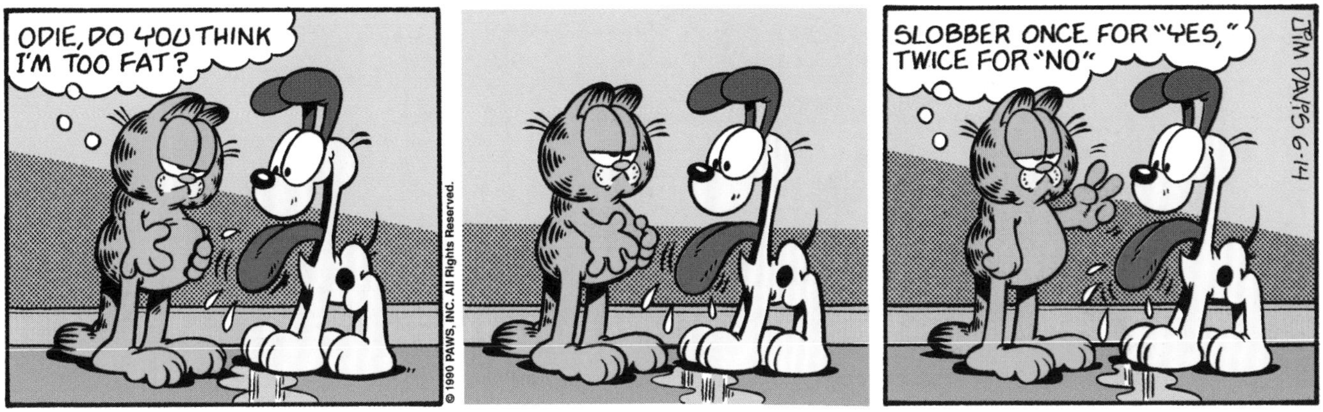
ODIE, DO YOU THINK I'M TOO FAT?
© 1990 PAWS, INC. All Rights Reserved.
SLOBBER ONCE FOR "YES," TWICE FOR "NO"
JIM DAVIS 6-14

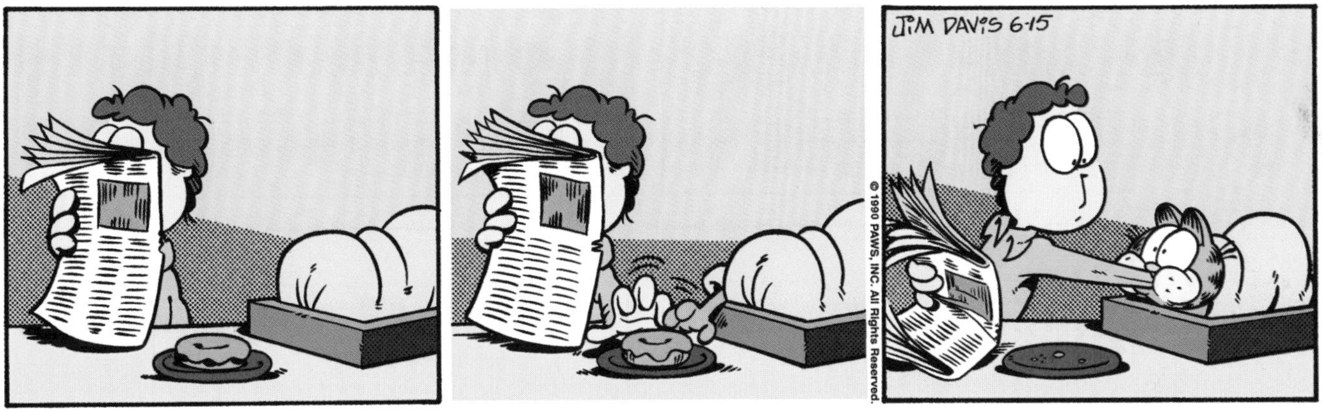
© 1990 PAWS, INC. All Rights Reserved.
JIM DAVIS 6-15

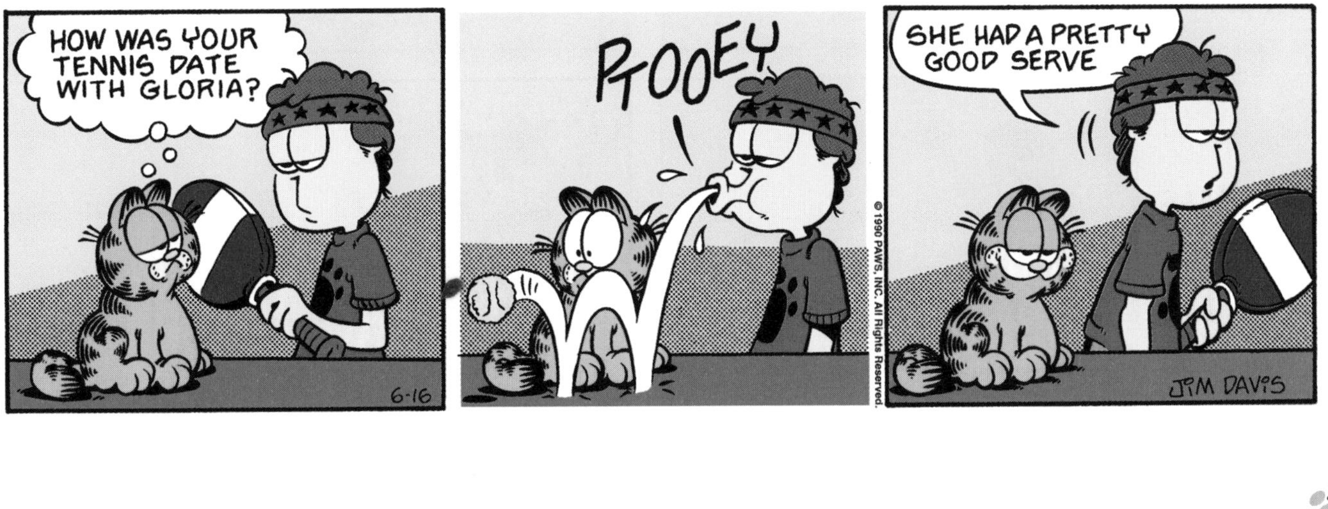
HOW WAS YOUR TENNIS DATE WITH GLORIA?
6-16
PTOOEY
© 1990 PAWS, INC. All Rights Reserved.
SHE HAD A PRETTY GOOD SERVE
JIM DAVIS

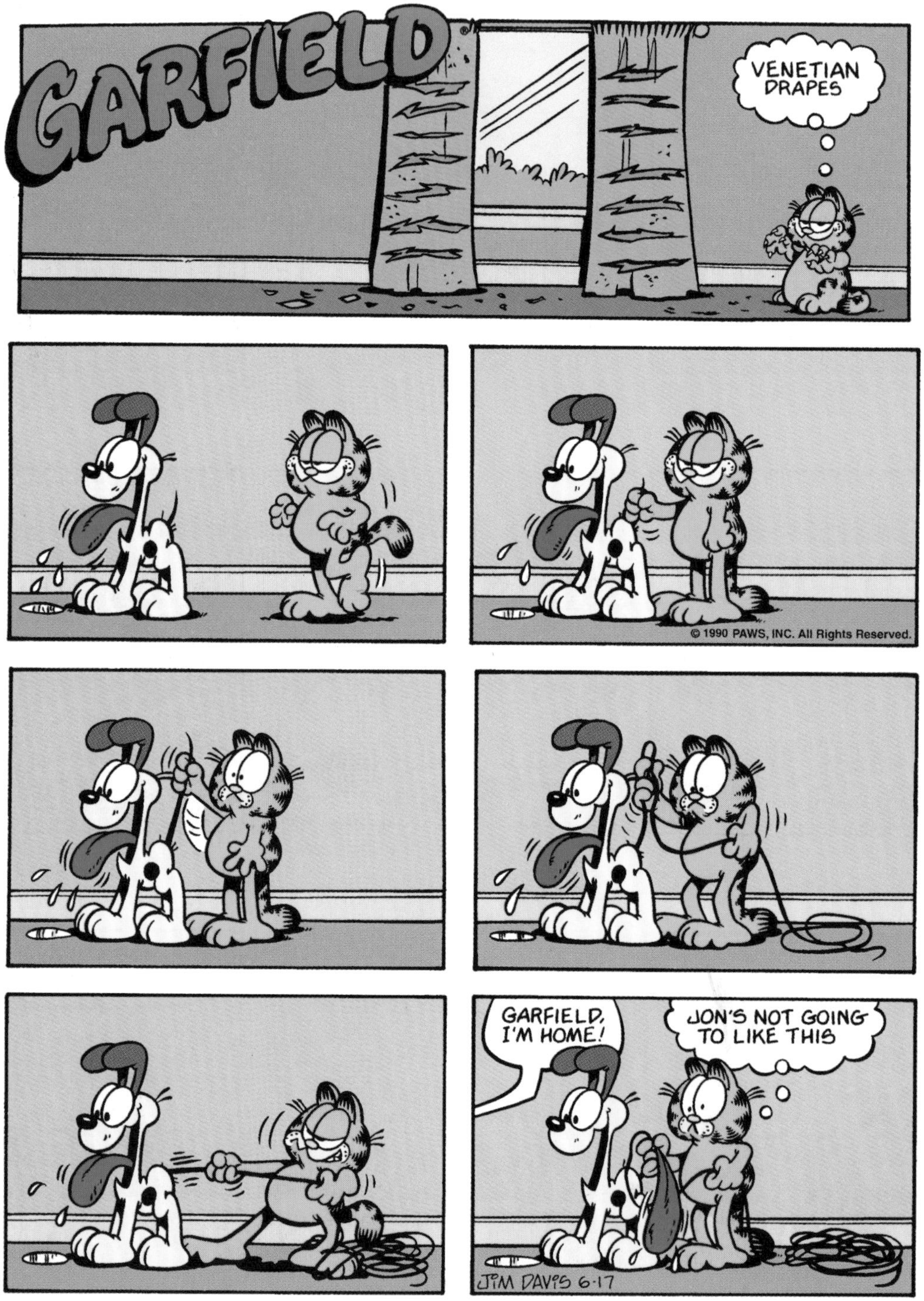
GARFIELD
VENETIAN DRAPES
© 1990 PAWS, INC. All Rights Reserved.
GARFIELD, I'M HOME!
JON'S NOT GOING TO LIKE THIS
JIM DAVIS 6-17

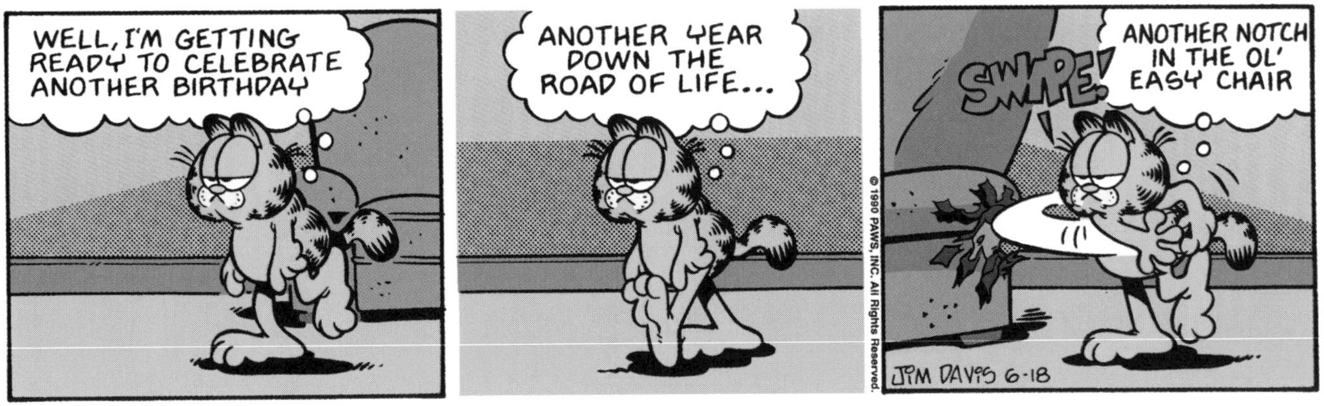
WELL, I'M GETTING READY TO CELEBRATE ANOTHER BIRTHDAY
ANOTHER YEAR DOWN THE ROAD OF LIFE...
© 1990 PAWS, INC. All Rights Reserved.
SWIPE!
ANOTHER NOTCH IN THE OL' EASY CHAIR
JIM DAVIS 6-18

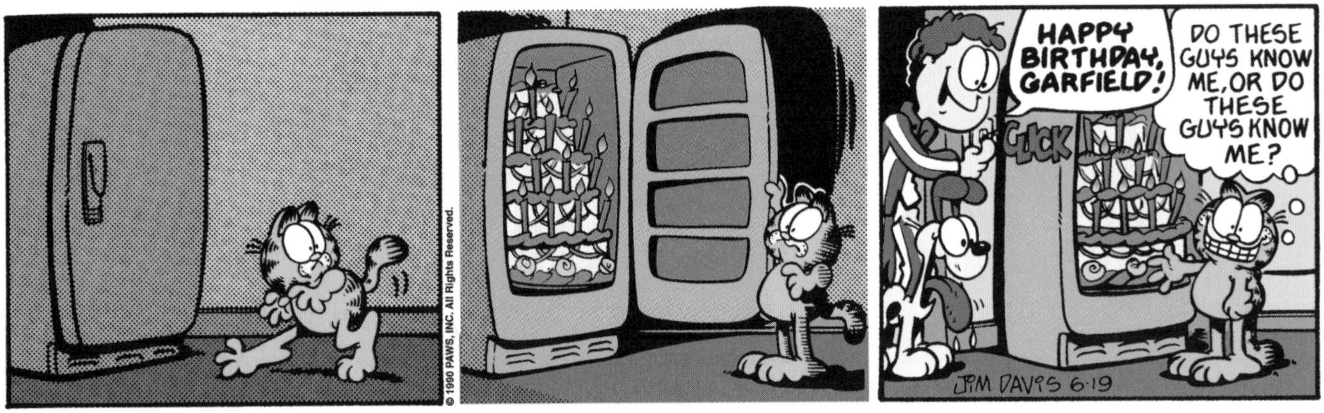
© 1990 PAWS, INC. All Rights Reserved.
CLICK
HAPPY BIRTHDAY, GARFIELD!
DO THESE GUYS KNOW ME, OR DO THESE GUYS KNOW ME?
JIM DAVIS 6-19

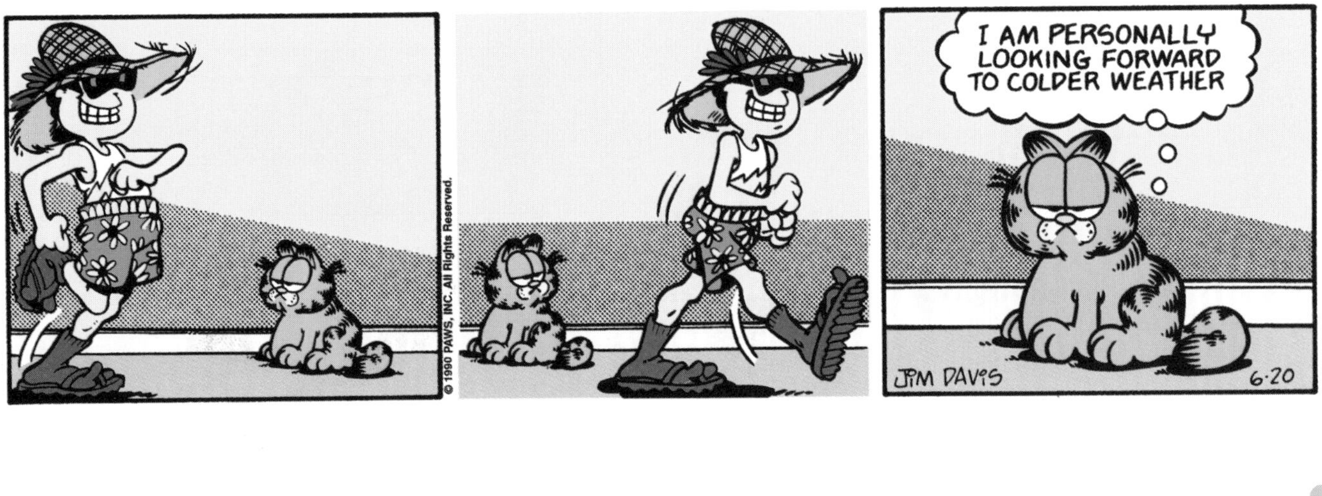
© 1990 PAWS, INC. All Rights Reserved.
I AM PERSONALLY LOOKING FORWARD TO COLDER WEATHER
JIM DAVIS
6-20

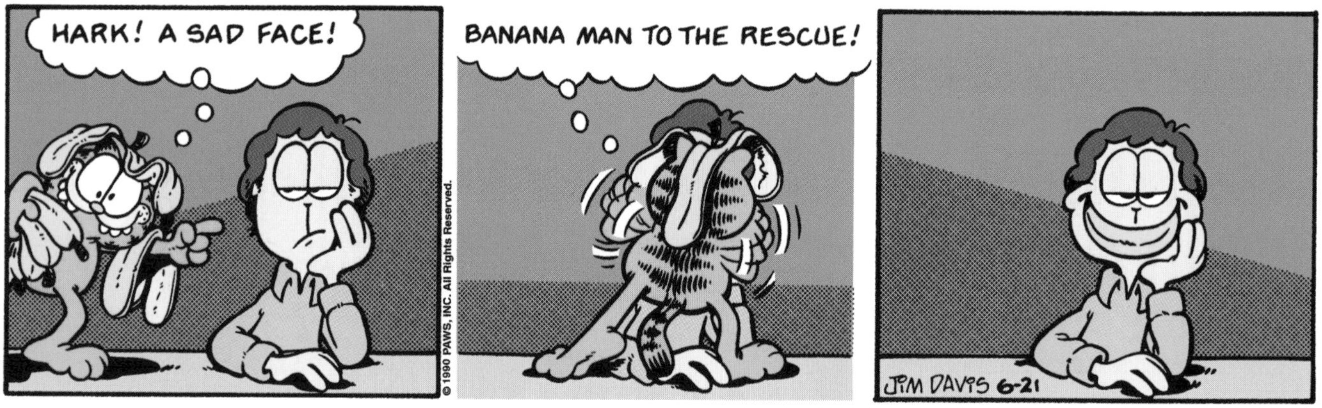
HARK! A SAD FACE!
© 1990 PAWS, INC. All Rights Reserved.
BANANA MAN TO THE RESCUE!
JIM DAVIS 6-21

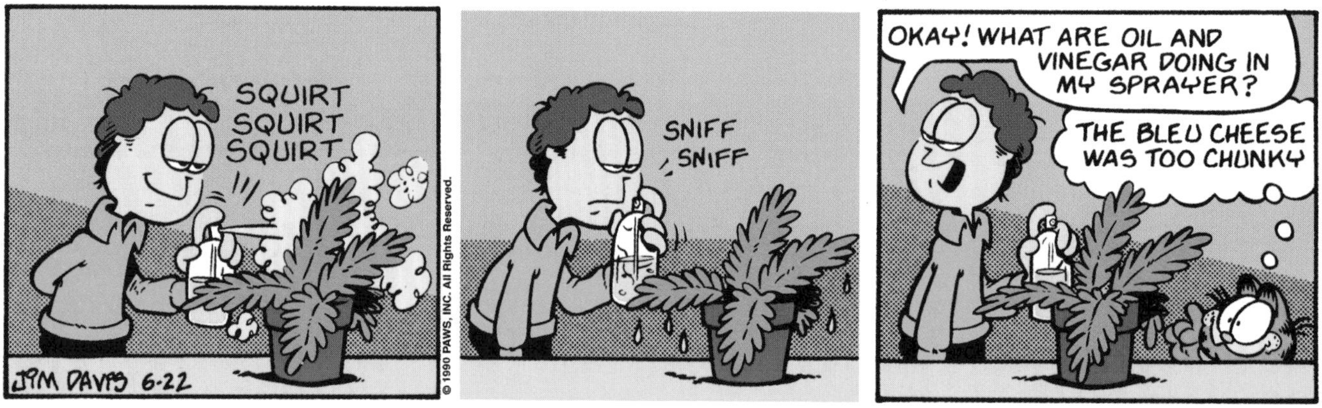
SQUIRT SQUIRT SQUIRT
JIM DAVIS 6-22
© 1990 PAWS, INC. All Rights Reserved.
SNIFF SNIFF
OKAY! WHAT ARE OIL AND VINEGAR DOING IN MY SPRAYER?
THE BLEU CHEESE WAS TOO CHUNKY

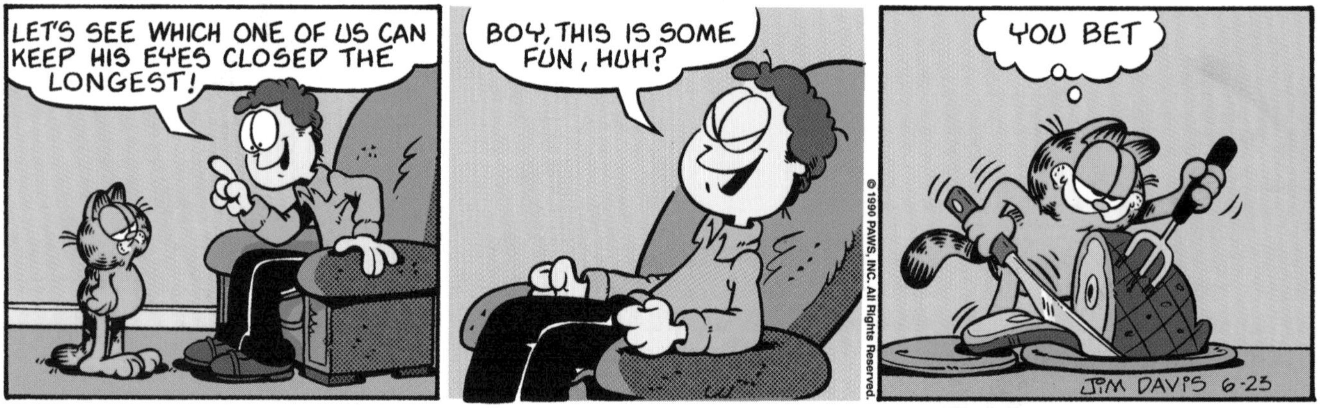
LET'S SEE WHICH ONE OF US CAN KEEP HIS EYES CLOSED THE LONGEST!
BOY, THIS IS SOME FUN, HUH?
© 1990 PAWS, INC. All Rights Reserved.
YOU BET
JIM DAVIS 6-23

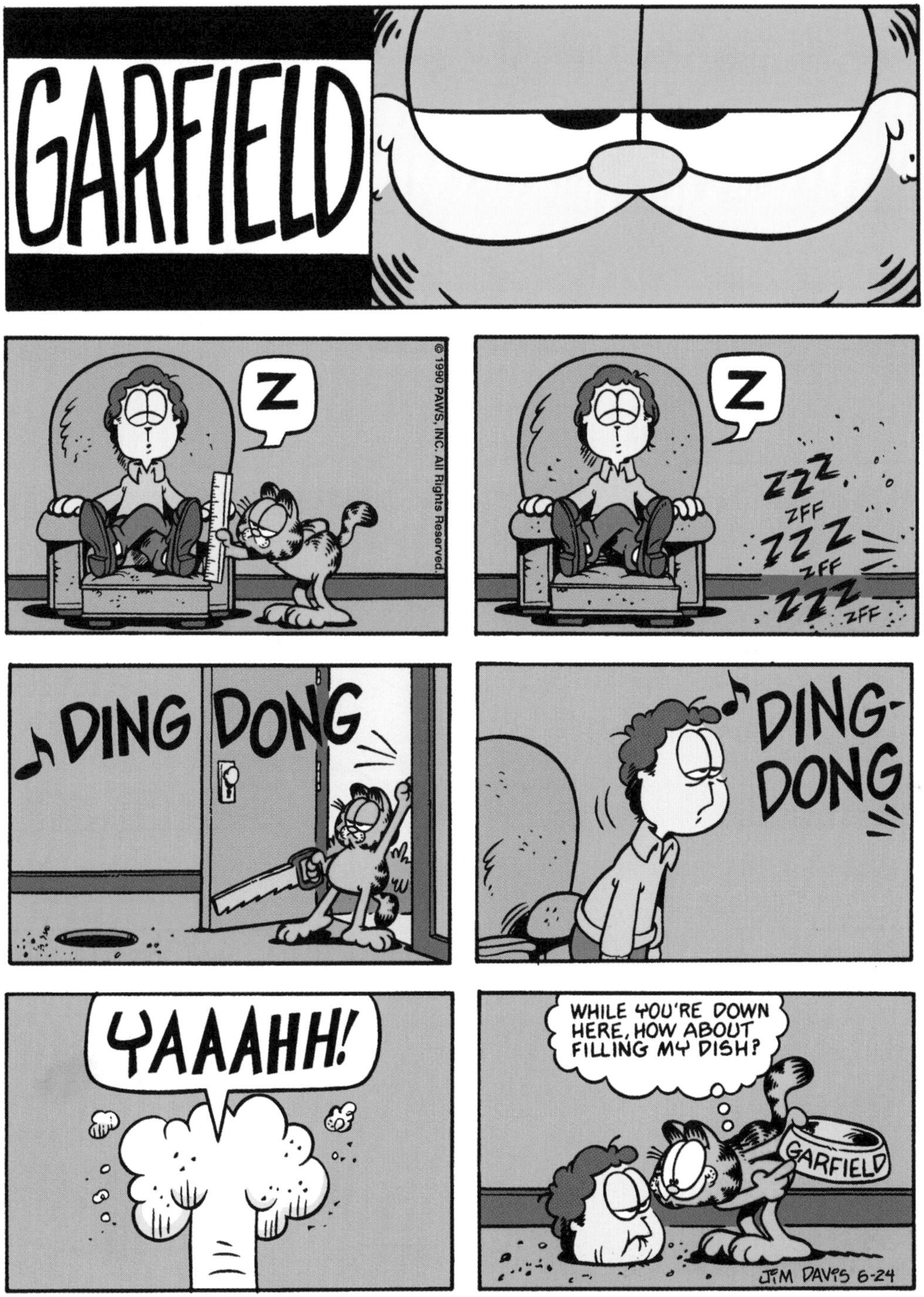
GARFIELD
© 1990 PAWS, INC. All Rights Reserved.
Z
Z
ZZZ ZFF ZZZ ZFF ZZZ ZFF
DING DONG
DING-DONG
YAAAHH!
WHILE YOU'RE DOWN HERE, HOW ABOUT FILLING MY DISH?
GARFIELD
JIM DAVIS 6-24

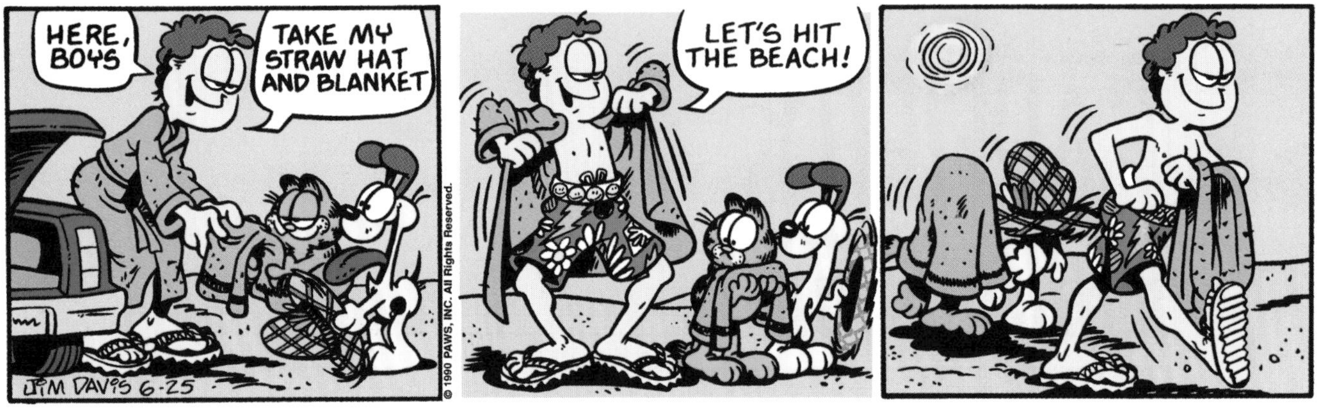
HERE, BOYS
TAKE MY STRAW HAT AND BLANKET
JIM DAVIS 6-25
LET'S HIT THE BEACH!

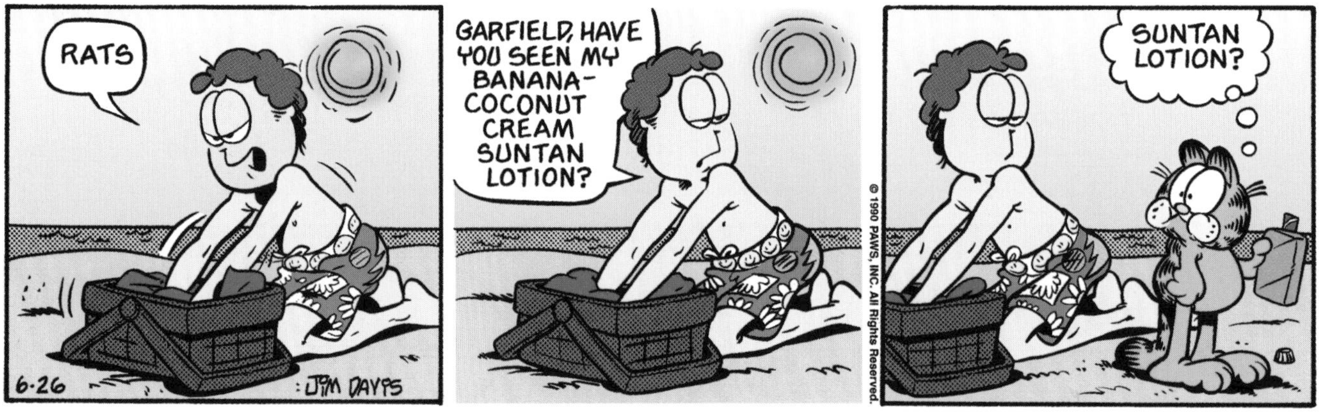
RATS
6-26
JIM DAVIS
GARFIELD, HAVE YOU SEEN MY BANANA-COCONUT CREAM SUNTAN LOTION?
SUNTAN LOTION?

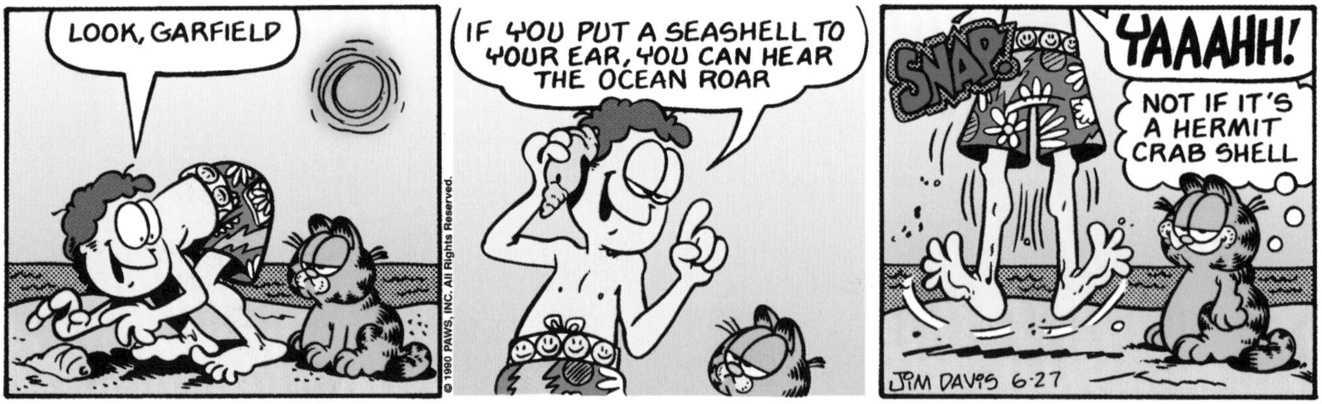
LOOK, GARFIELD
IF YOU PUT A SEASHELL TO YOUR EAR, YOU CAN HEAR THE OCEAN ROAR
SNAP!
YAAAHH!
NOT IF IT'S A HERMIT CRAB SHELL
JIM DAVIS 6-27

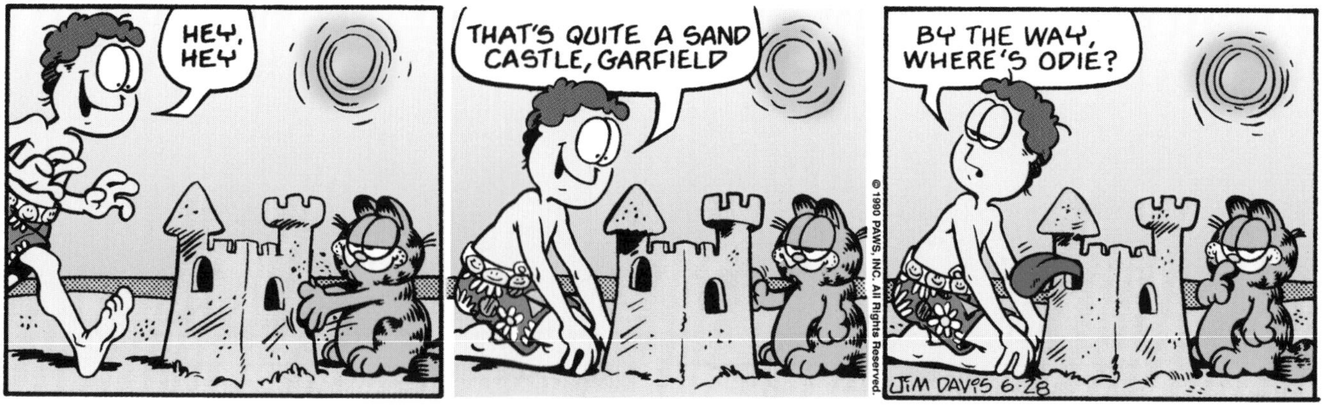
HEY, HEY
THAT'S QUITE A SAND CASTLE, GARFIELD
BY THE WAY, WHERE'S ODIE?
JIM DAVIS 6-28

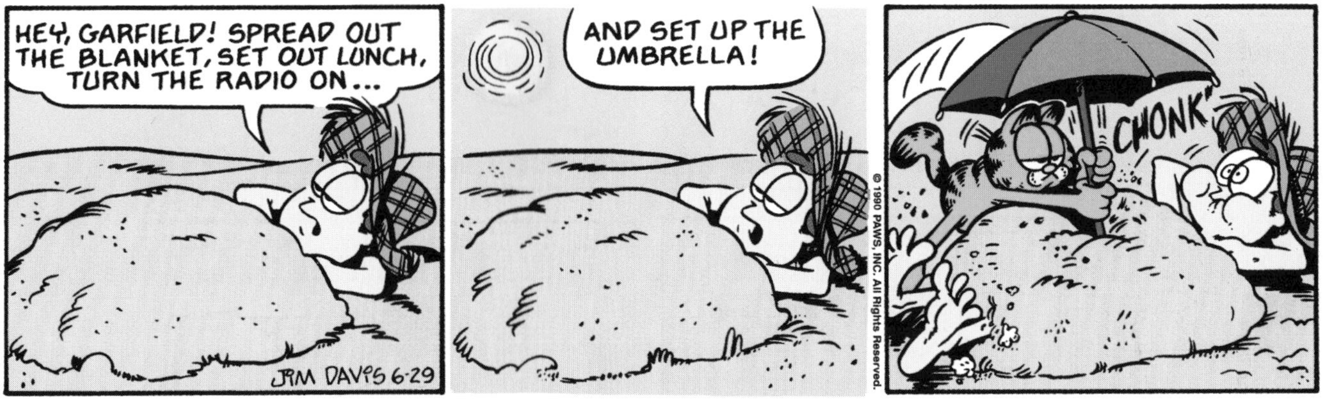
HEY, GARFIELD! SPREAD OUT THE BLANKET, SET OUT LUNCH, TURN THE RADIO ON...
AND SET UP THE UMBRELLA!
CHONK
JIM DAVIS 6-29

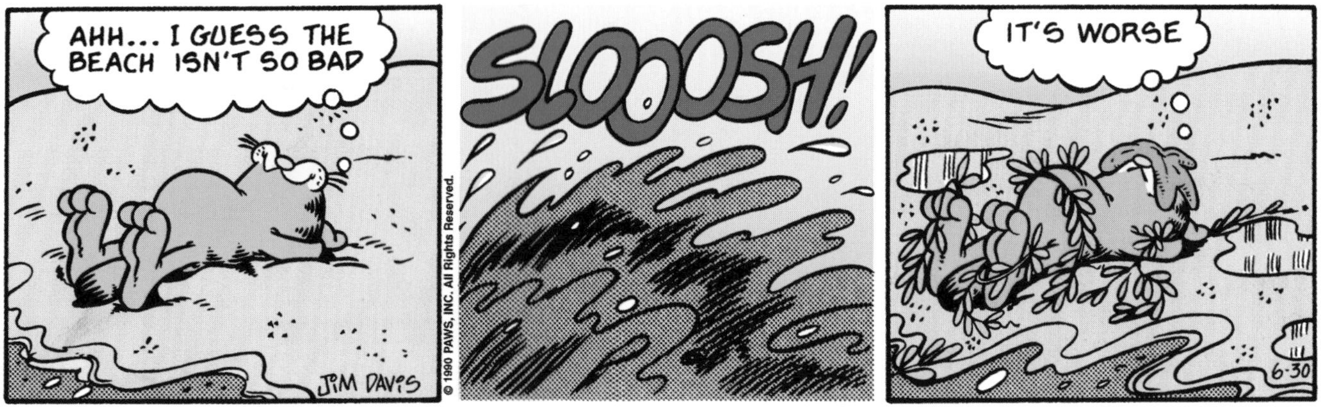
AHH... I GUESS THE BEACH ISN'T SO BAD
SLOOOSH!
IT'S WORSE
JIM DAVIS
6-30

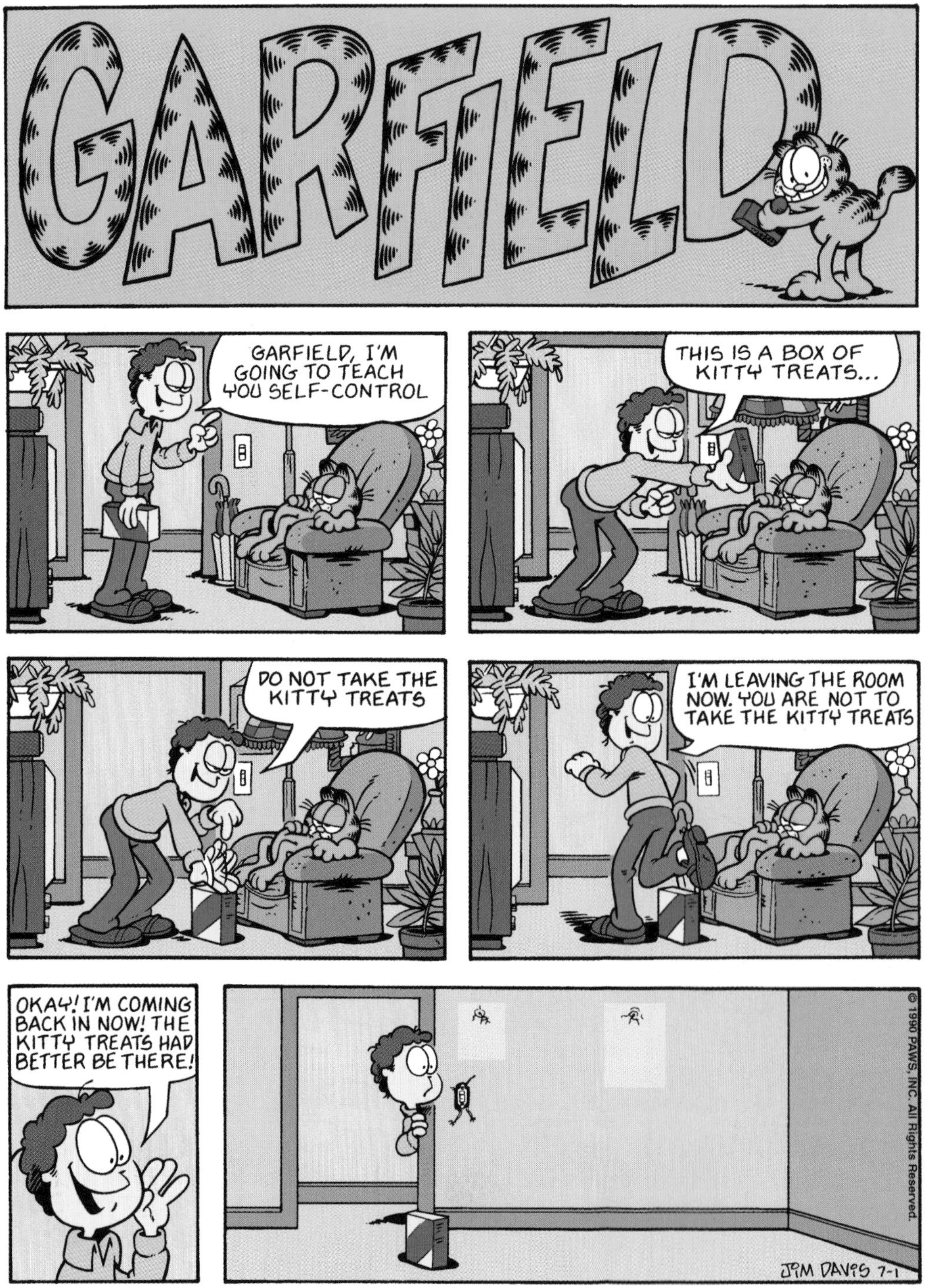
GARFIELD
GARFIELD, I'M GOING TO TEACH YOU SELF-CONTROL
THIS IS A BOX OF KITTY TREATS...
DO NOT TAKE THE KITTY TREATS
I'M LEAVING THE ROOM NOW. YOU ARE NOT TO TAKE THE KITTY TREATS
OKAY! I'M COMING BACK IN NOW! THE KITTY TREATS HAD BETTER BE THERE!
© 1990 PAWS, INC. All Rights Reserved.
JIM DAVIS 7-1

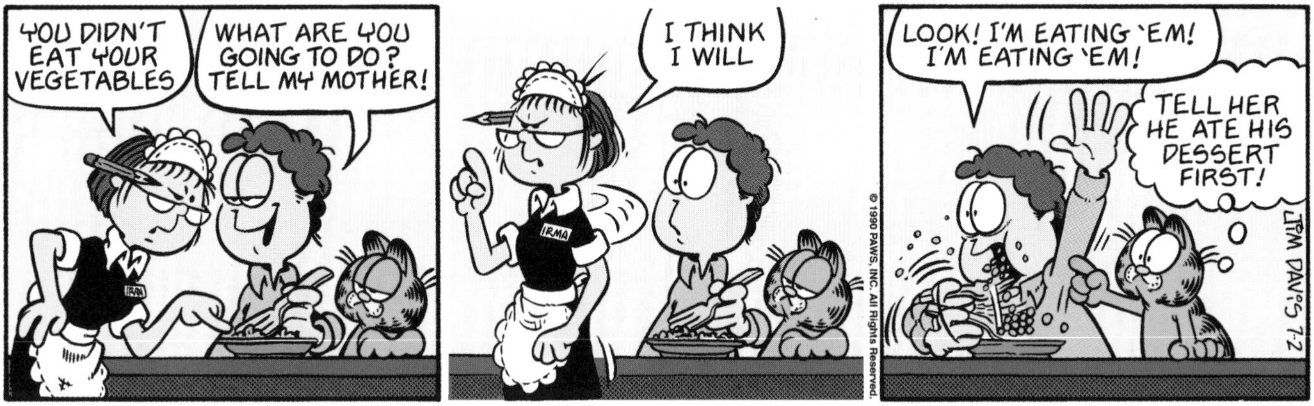
YOU DIDN'T EAT YOUR VEGETABLES
WHAT ARE YOU GOING TO DO? TELL MY MOTHER!
I THINK I WILL
LOOK! I'M EATING 'EM! I'M EATING 'EM!
TELL HER HE ATE HIS DESSERT FIRST!
JIM DAVIS 7-2

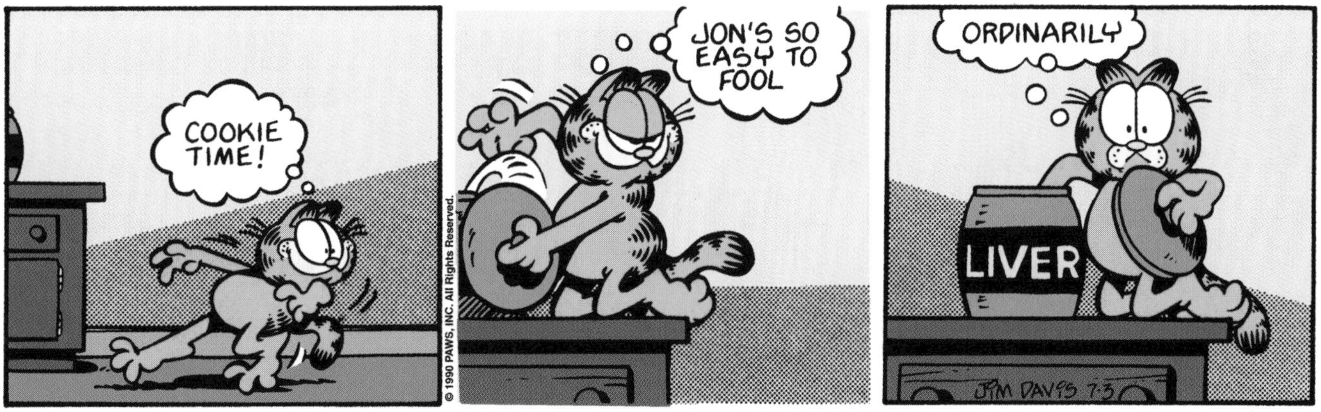
COOKIE TIME!
JON'S SO EASY TO FOOL
ORDINARILY
LIVER
JIM DAVIS 7-3

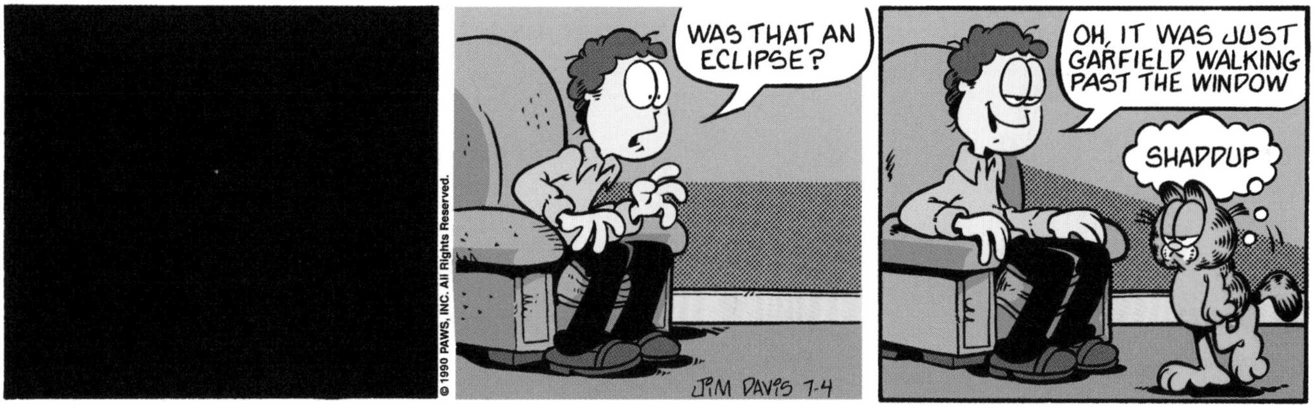
WAS THAT AN ECLIPSE?
JIM DAVIS 7-4
OH, IT WAS JUST GARFIELD WALKING PAST THE WINDOW
SHADDUP

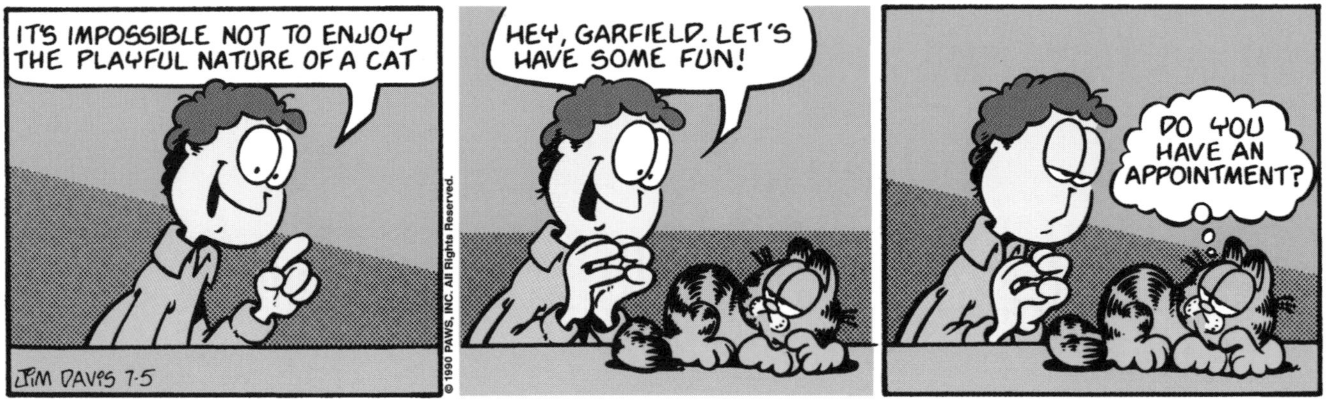
IT'S IMPOSSIBLE NOT TO ENJOY THE PLAYFUL NATURE OF A CAT
HEY, GARFIELD. LET'S HAVE SOME FUN!
DO YOU HAVE AN APPOINTMENT?
JIM DAVIS 7-5
© 1990 PAWS, INC. All Rights Reserved.

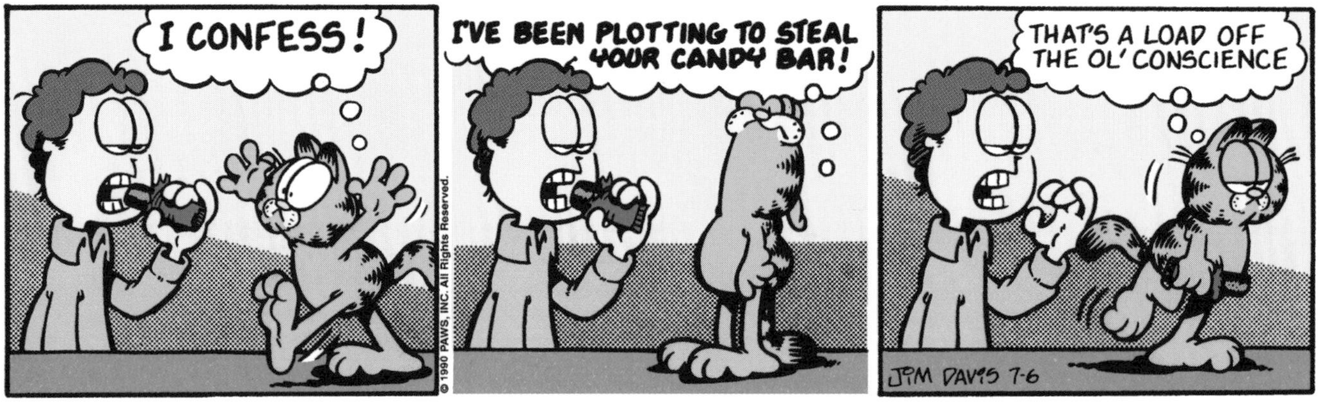
I CONFESS!
I'VE BEEN PLOTTING TO STEAL YOUR CANDY BAR!
THAT'S A LOAD OFF THE OL' CONSCIENCE
JIM DAVIS 7-6
© 1990 PAWS, INC. All Rights Reserved.

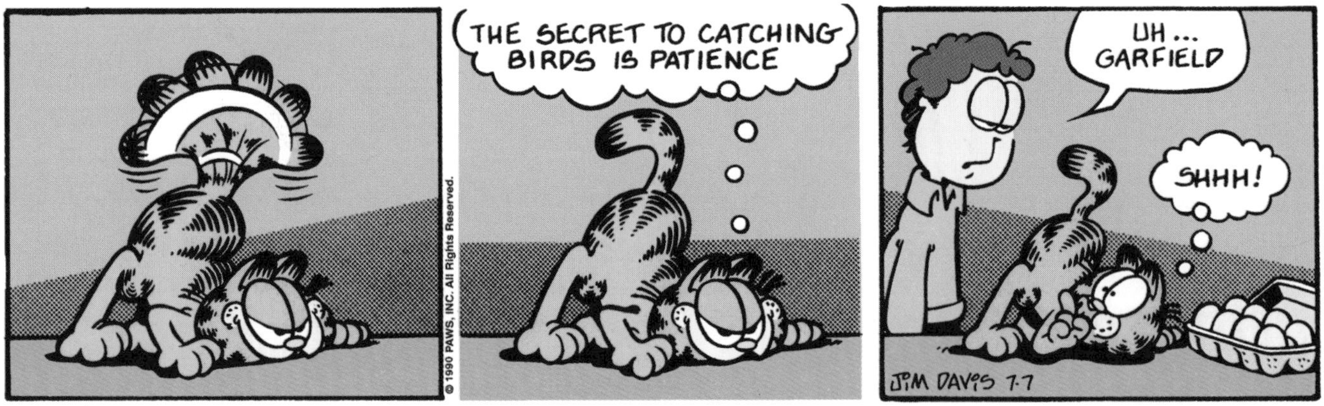
THE SECRET TO CATCHING BIRDS IS PATIENCE
UH... GARFIELD
SHHH!
JIM DAVIS 7-7
© 1990 PAWS, INC. All Rights Reserved.

GARFIELD

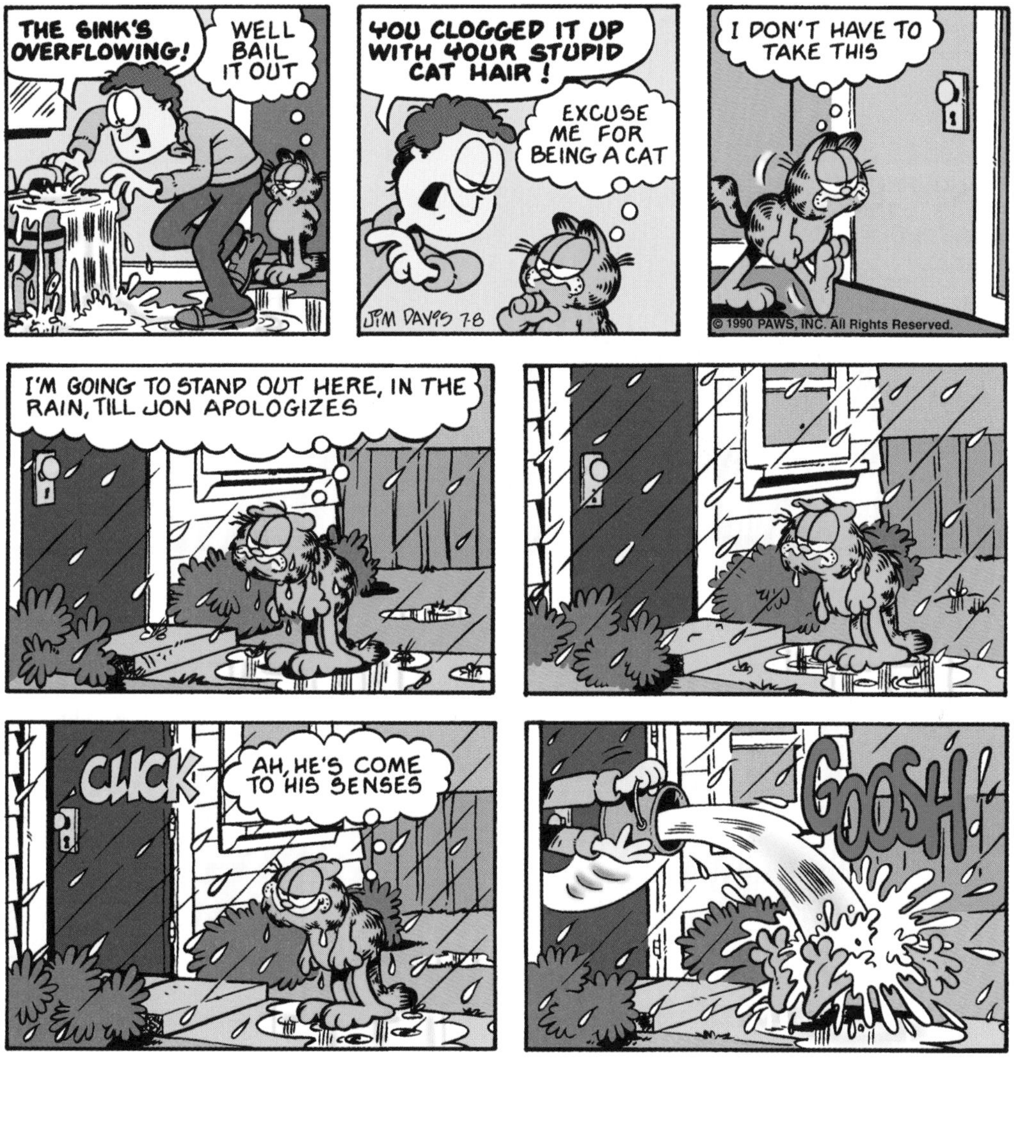

THE SINK'S OVERFLOWING!
WELL BAIL IT OUT
YOU CLOGGED IT UP WITH YOUR STUPID CAT HAIR!
EXCUSE ME FOR BEING A CAT
JIM DAVIS 7-8
I DON'T HAVE TO TAKE THIS
© 1990 PAWS, INC. All Rights Reserved.
I'M GOING TO STAND OUT HERE, IN THE RAIN, TILL JON APOLOGIZES
CLICK
AH, HE'S COME TO HIS SENSES
GOOSH!

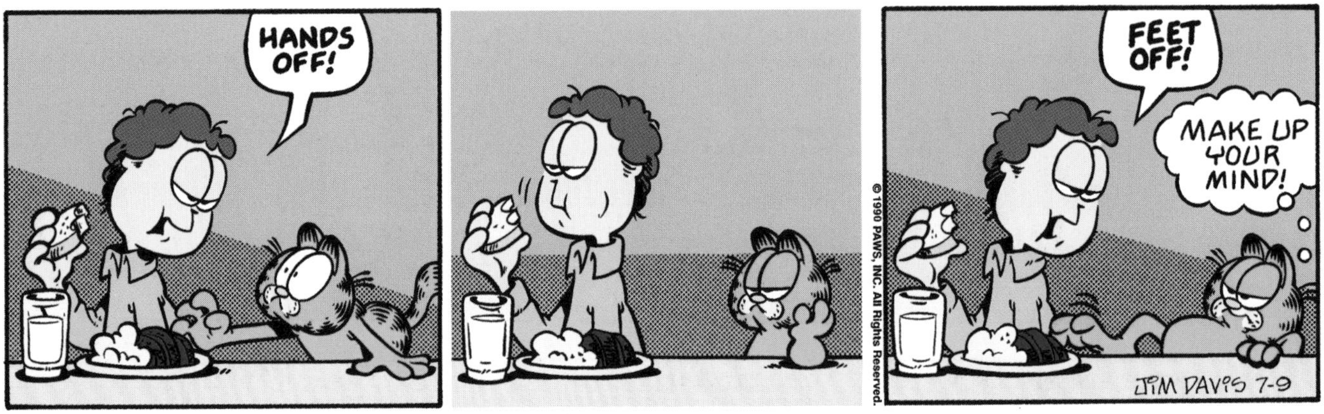
HANDS OFF!
FEET OFF!
MAKE UP YOUR MIND!
© 1990 PAWS, INC. All Rights Reserved.
JIM DAVIS 7-9

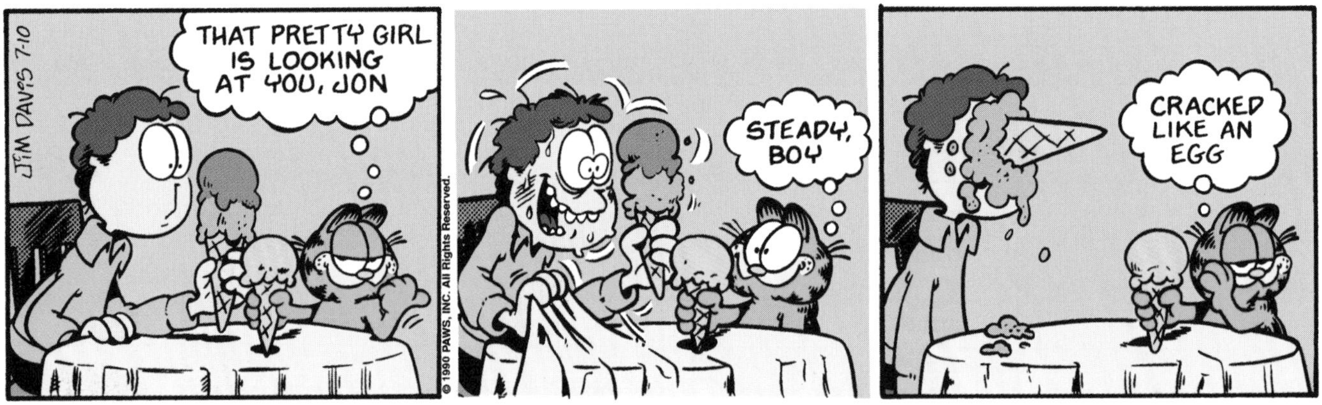
JIM DAVIS 7-10
THAT PRETTY GIRL IS LOOKING AT YOU, JON
© 1990 PAWS, INC. All Rights Reserved.
STEADY, BOY
CRACKED LIKE AN EGG

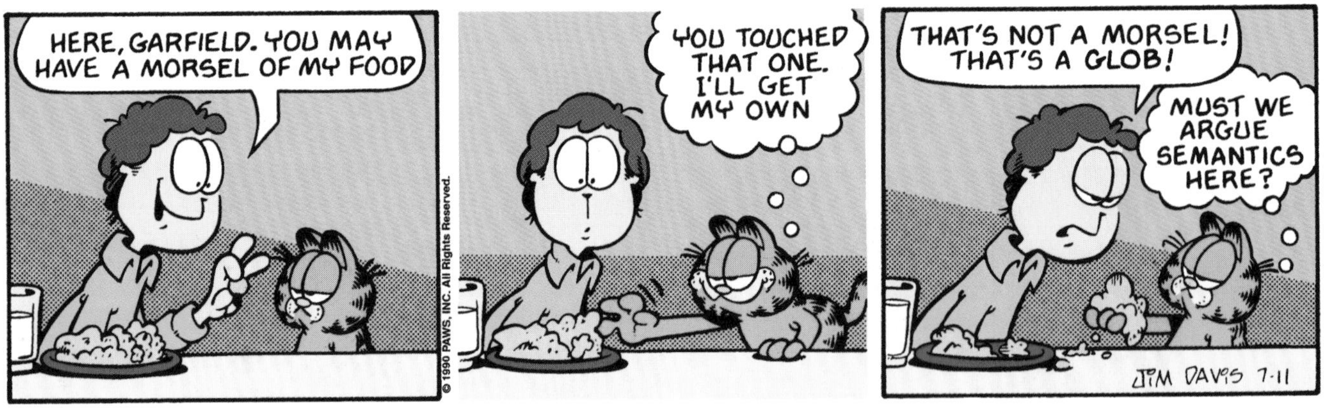
HERE, GARFIELD. YOU MAY HAVE A MORSEL OF MY FOOD
© 1990 PAWS, INC. All Rights Reserved.
YOU TOUCHED THAT ONE. I'LL GET MY OWN
THAT'S NOT A MORSEL! THAT'S A GLOB!
MUST WE ARGUE SEMANTICS HERE?
JIM DAVIS 7-11

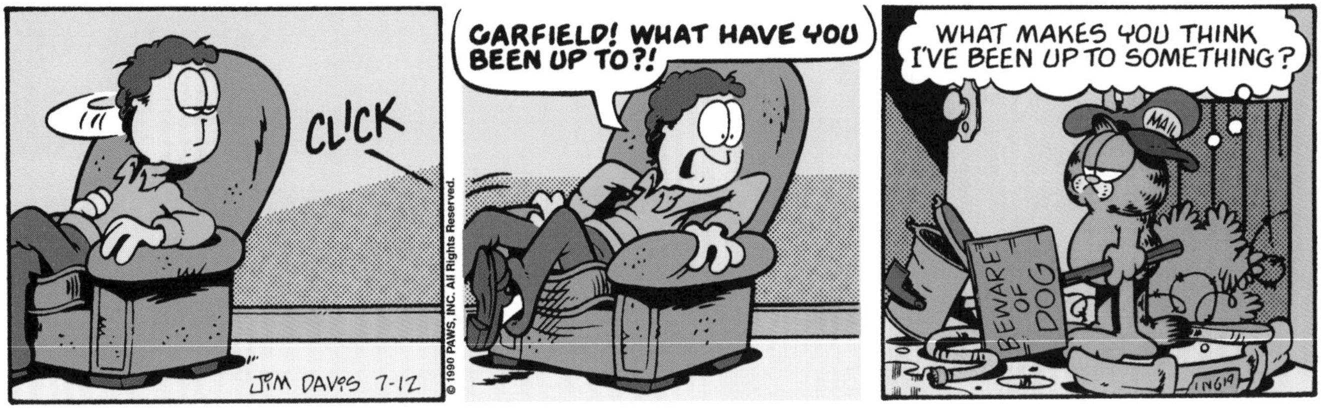
CLICK
JIM DAVIS 7-12
© 1990 PAWS, INC. All Rights Reserved.
GARFIELD! WHAT HAVE YOU BEEN UP TO?!
WHAT MAKES YOU THINK I'VE BEEN UP TO SOMETHING?
MAIL
BEWARE OF DOG

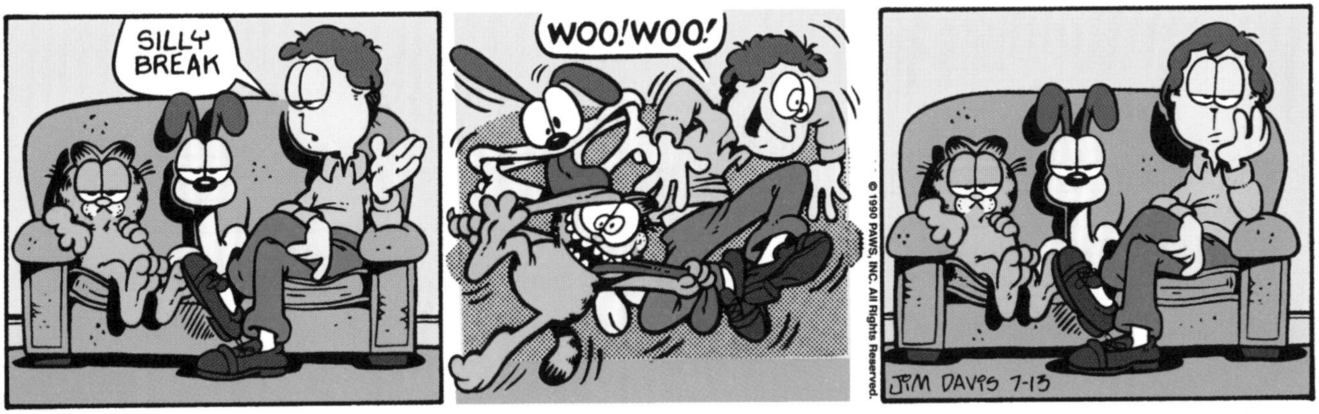
SILLY BREAK
WOO! WOO!
© 1990 PAWS, INC. All Rights Reserved.
JIM DAVIS 7-13

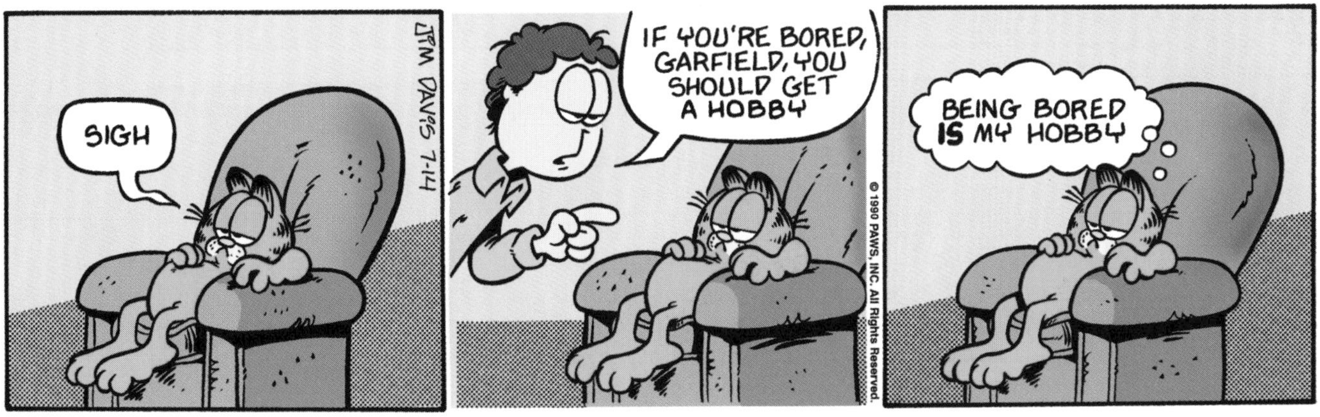
SIGH
JIM DAVIS 7-14
IF YOU'RE BORED, GARFIELD, YOU SHOULD GET A HOBBY
© 1990 PAWS, INC. All Rights Reserved.
BEING BORED **IS** MY HOBBY

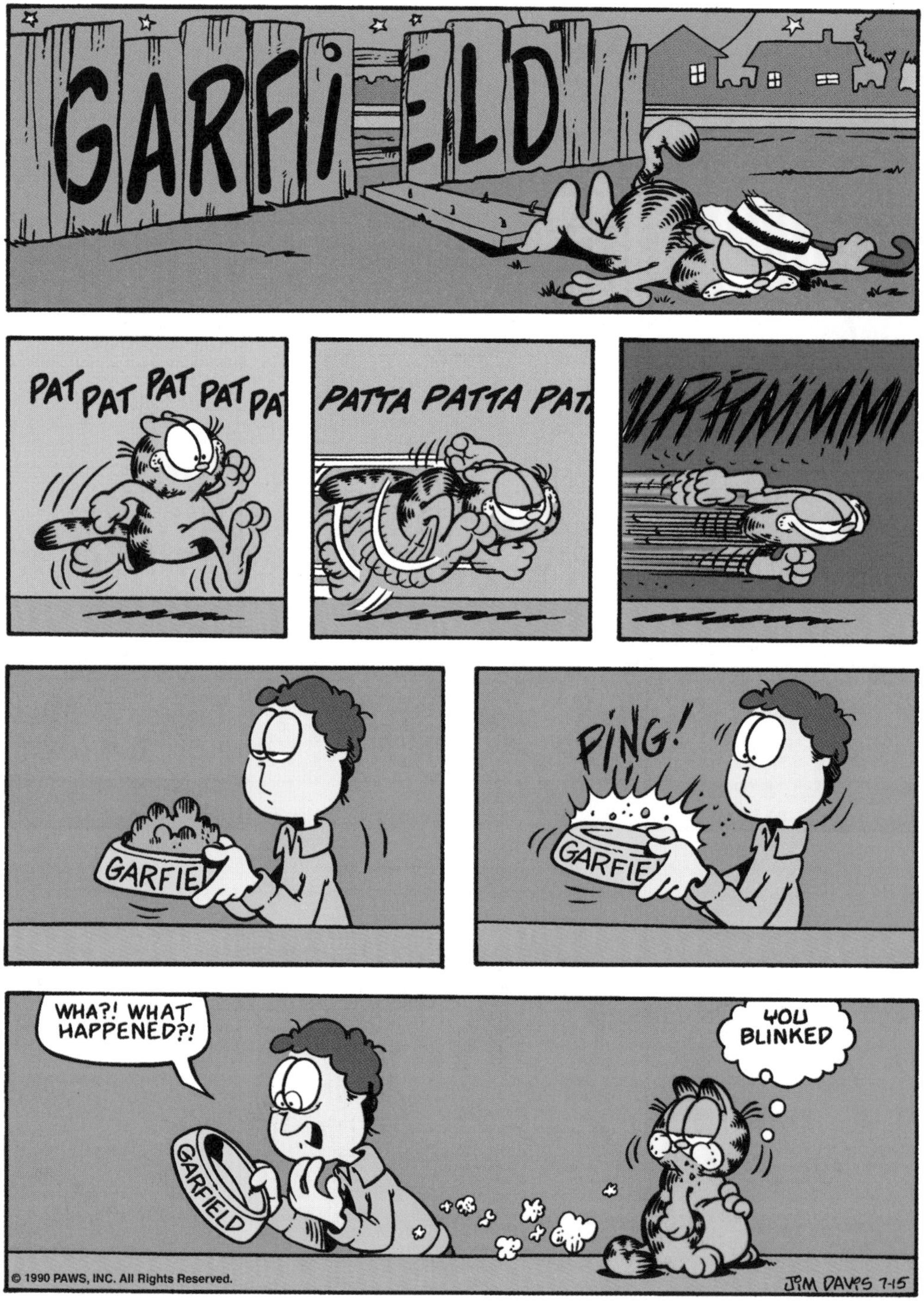
GARFIELD
PAT PAT PAT PAT PA
PATTA PATTA PAT
PING!
GARFIE
WHA?! WHAT HAPPENED?!
YOU BLINKED
GARFIELD
© 1990 PAWS, INC. All Rights Reserved.
JIM DAVIS 7-15

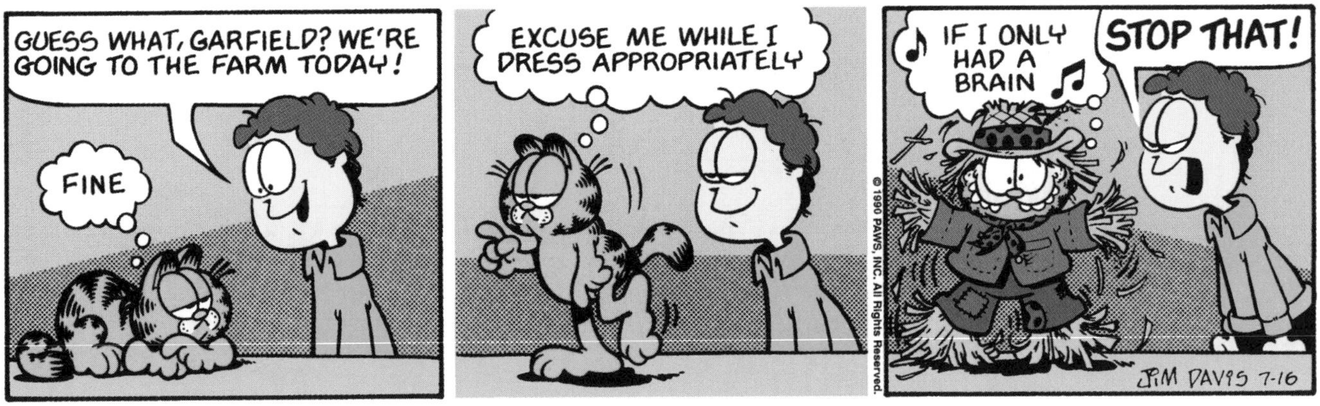
GUESS WHAT, GARFIELD? WE'RE GOING TO THE FARM TODAY!
FINE
EXCUSE ME WHILE I DRESS APPROPRIATELY
IF I ONLY HAD A BRAIN
STOP THAT!
© 1990 PAWS, INC. All Rights Reserved.
JIM DAVIS 7-16

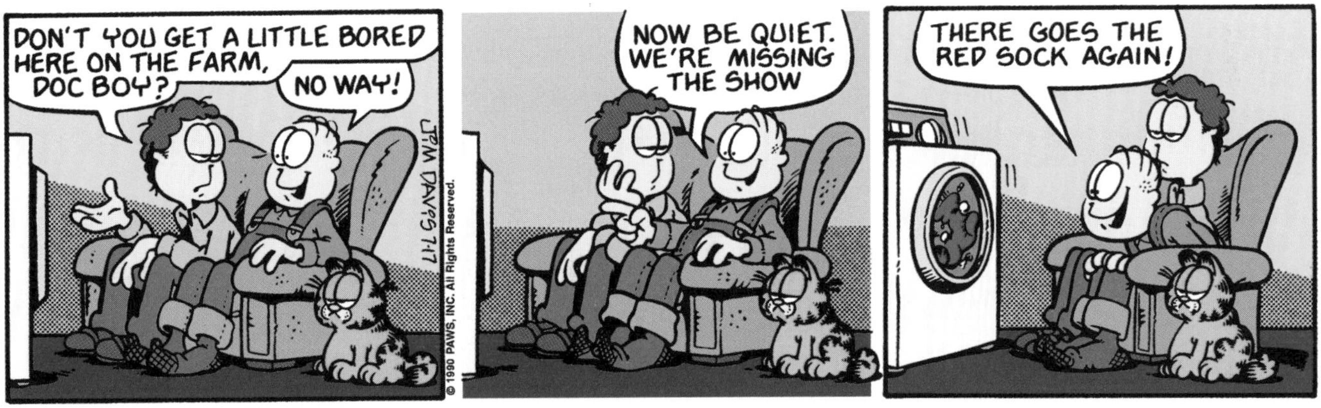
DON'T YOU GET A LITTLE BORED HERE ON THE FARM, DOC BOY?
NO WAY!
JIM DAVIS 7-17
© 1990 PAWS, INC. All Rights Reserved.
NOW BE QUIET. WE'RE MISSING THE SHOW
THERE GOES THE RED SOCK AGAIN!

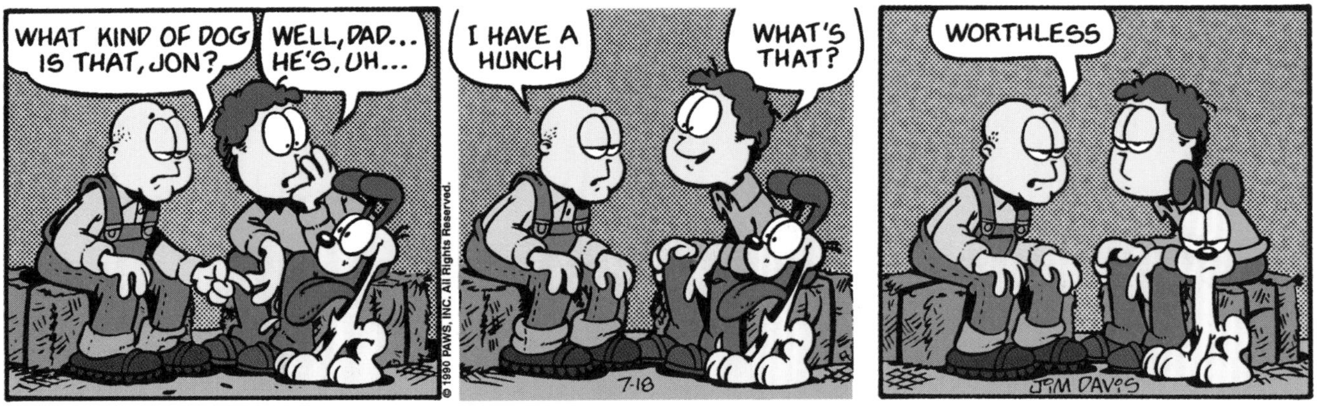
WHAT KIND OF DOG IS THAT, JON?
WELL, DAD... HE'S, UH...
© 1990 PAWS, INC. All Rights Reserved.
I HAVE A HUNCH
WHAT'S THAT?
7-18
WORTHLESS
JIM DAVIS

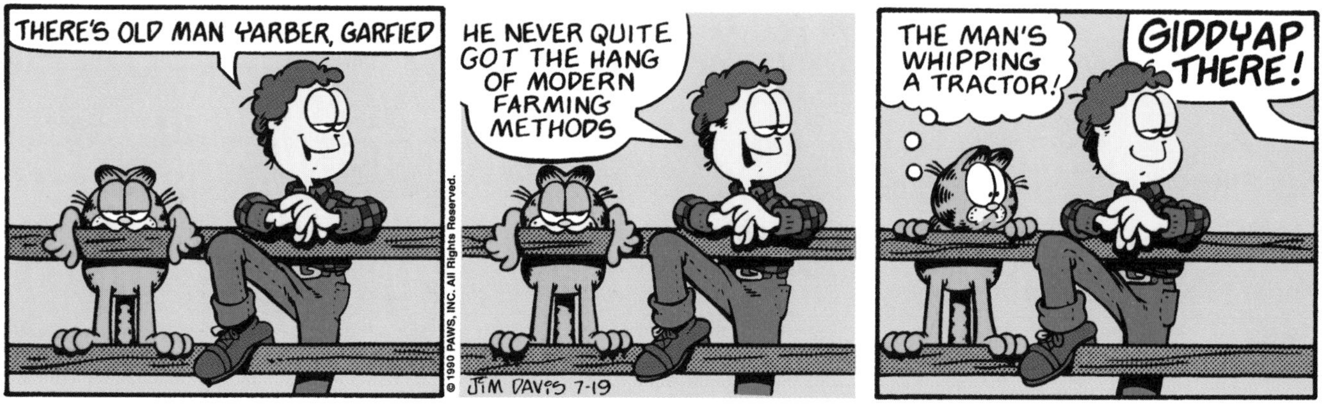
THERE'S OLD MAN YARBER, GARFIED
HE NEVER QUITE GOT THE HANG OF MODERN FARMING METHODS
THE MAN'S WHIPPING A TRACTOR!
GIDDYAP THERE!
© 1990 PAWS, INC. All Rights Reserved.
JIM DAVIS 7-19

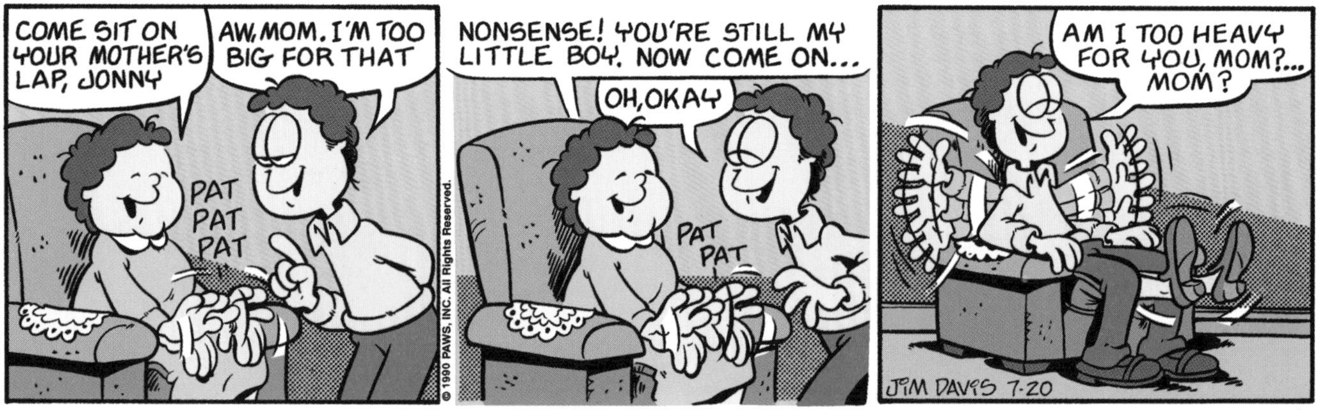
COME SIT ON YOUR MOTHER'S LAP, JONNY
AW, MOM. I'M TOO BIG FOR THAT
PAT PAT PAT
NONSENSE! YOU'RE STILL MY LITTLE BOY. NOW COME ON...
OH, OKAY
PAT PAT
AM I TOO HEAVY FOR YOU, MOM?... MOM?
© 1990 PAWS, INC. All Rights Reserved.
JIM DAVIS 7-20

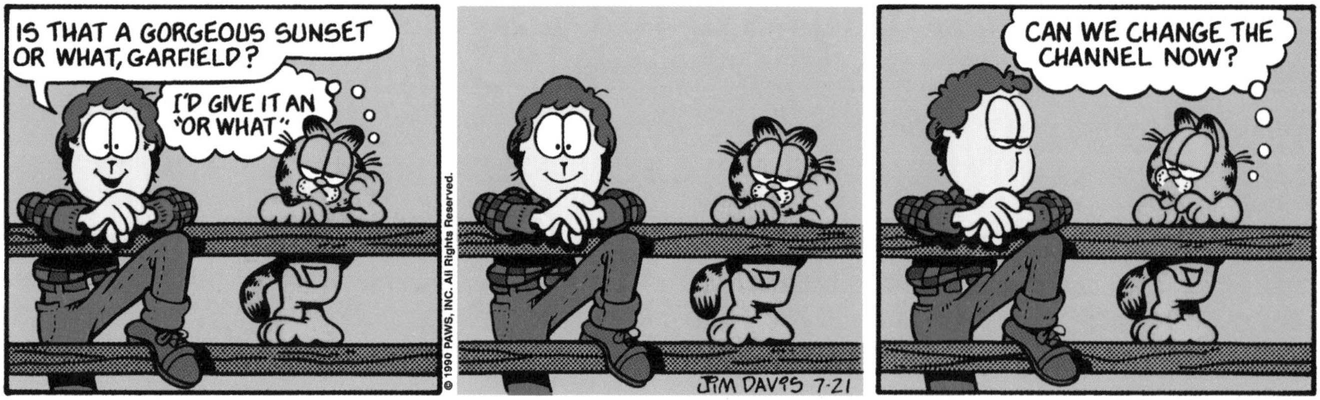
IS THAT A GORGEOUS SUNSET OR WHAT, GARFIELD?
I'D GIVE IT AN "OR WHAT"
CAN WE CHANGE THE CHANNEL NOW?
© 1990 PAWS, INC. All Rights Reserved.
JIM DAVIS 7-21

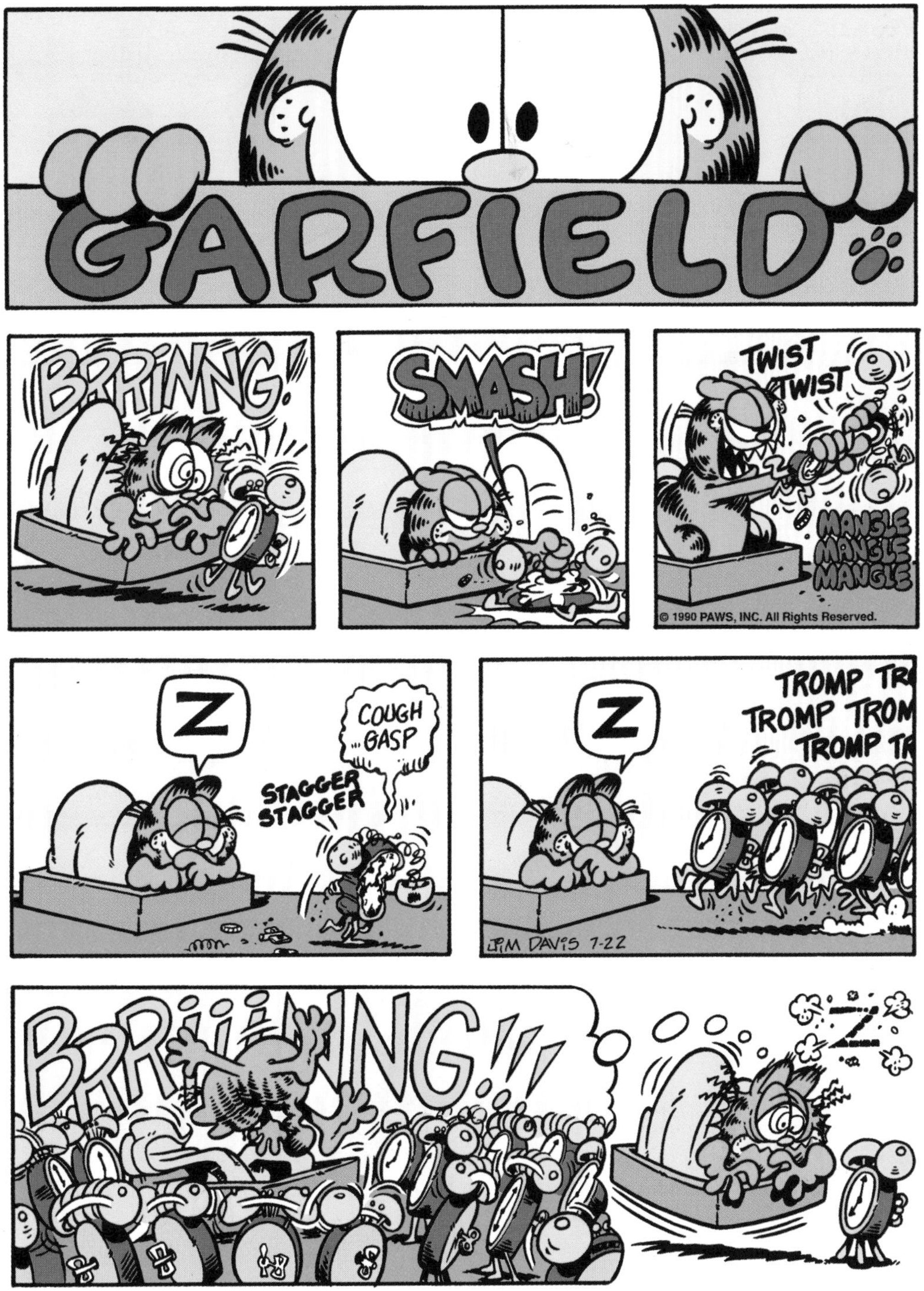
GARFIELD
BRRINNG!
SMASH!
TWIST TWIST
MANGLE MANGLE MANGLE
© 1990 PAWS, INC. All Rights Reserved.
Z
STAGGER STAGGER
COUGH ...GASP
Z
TROMP TROMP TROMP
JIM DAVIS 7-22
BRRiiiiNNG!!!

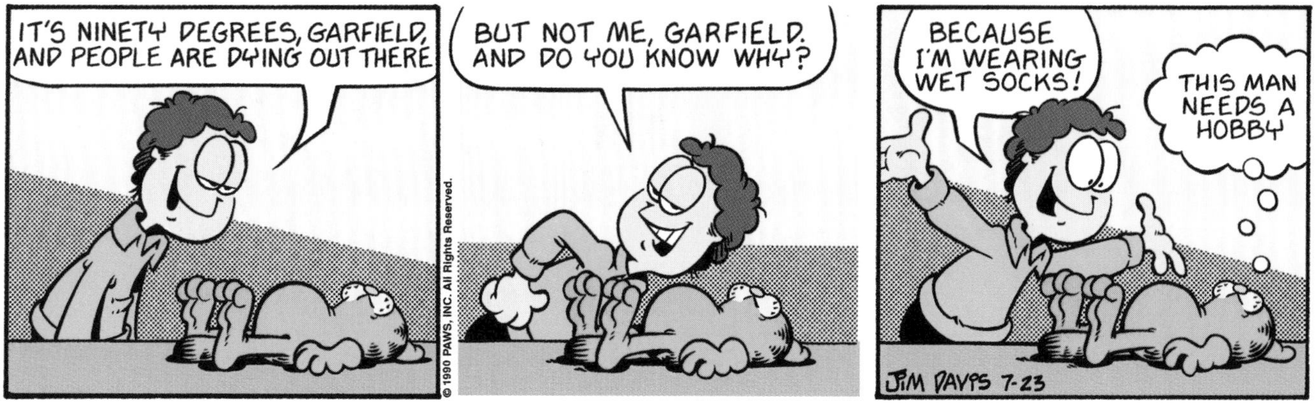
IT'S NINETY DEGREES, GARFIELD, AND PEOPLE ARE DYING OUT THERE
BUT NOT ME, GARFIELD. AND DO YOU KNOW WHY?
BECAUSE I'M WEARING WET SOCKS!
THIS MAN NEEDS A HOBBY
JIM DAVIS 7-23
© 1990 PAWS, INC. All Rights Reserved.

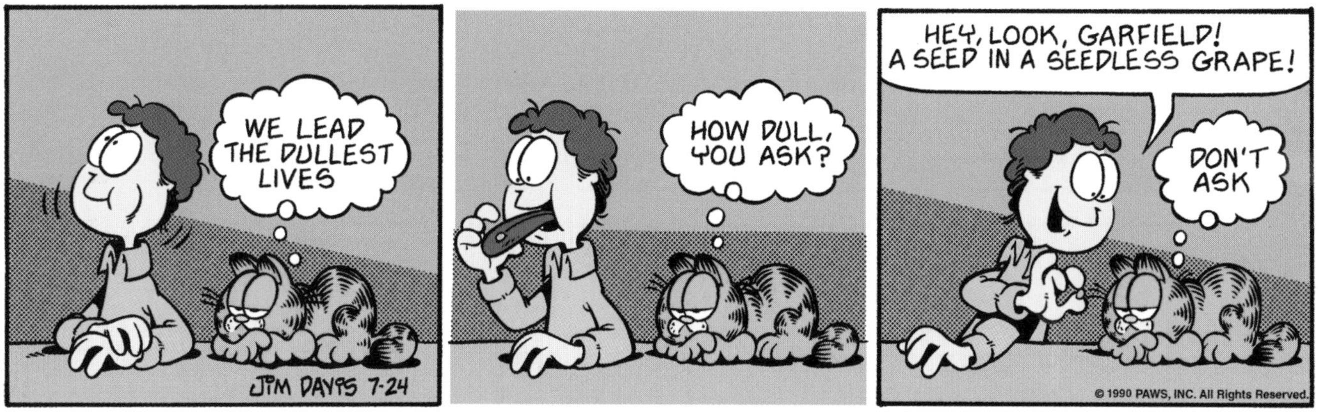
WE LEAD THE DULLEST LIVES
JIM DAVIS 7-24
HOW DULL, YOU ASK?
HEY, LOOK, GARFIELD! A SEED IN A SEEDLESS GRAPE!
DON'T ASK
© 1990 PAWS, INC. All Rights Reserved.

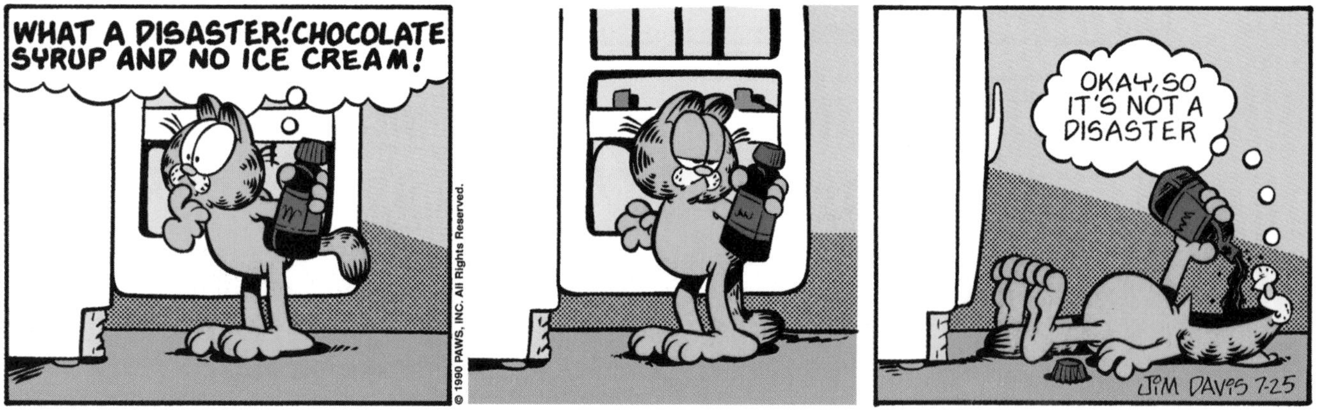
WHAT A DISASTER! CHOCOLATE SYRUP AND NO ICE CREAM!
© 1990 PAWS, INC. All Rights Reserved.
OKAY, SO IT'S NOT A DISASTER
JIM DAVIS 7-25

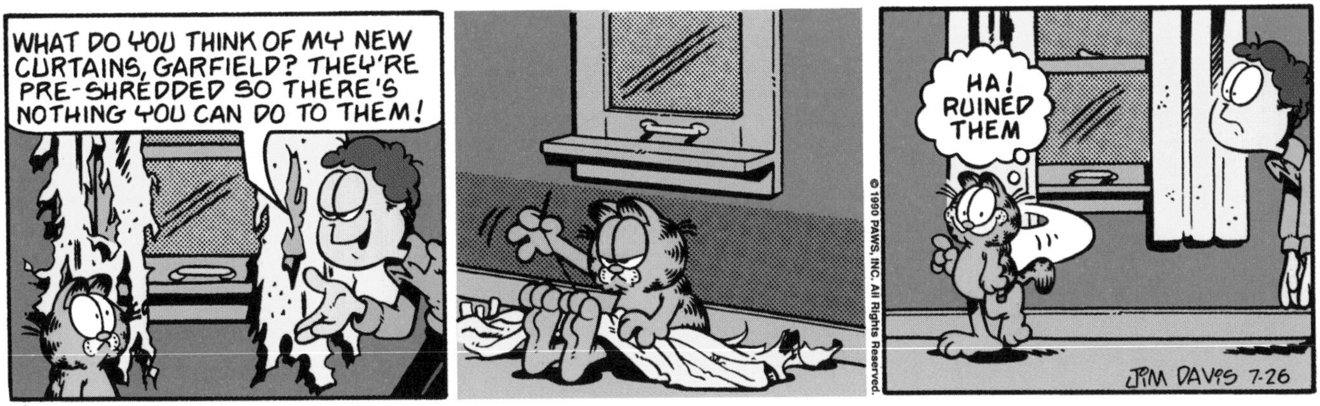
WHAT DO YOU THINK OF MY NEW CURTAINS, GARFIELD? THEY'RE PRE-SHREDDED SO THERE'S NOTHING YOU CAN DO TO THEM!
HA! RUINED THEM
© 1990 PAWS, INC. All Rights Reserved.
JIM DAVIS 7-26

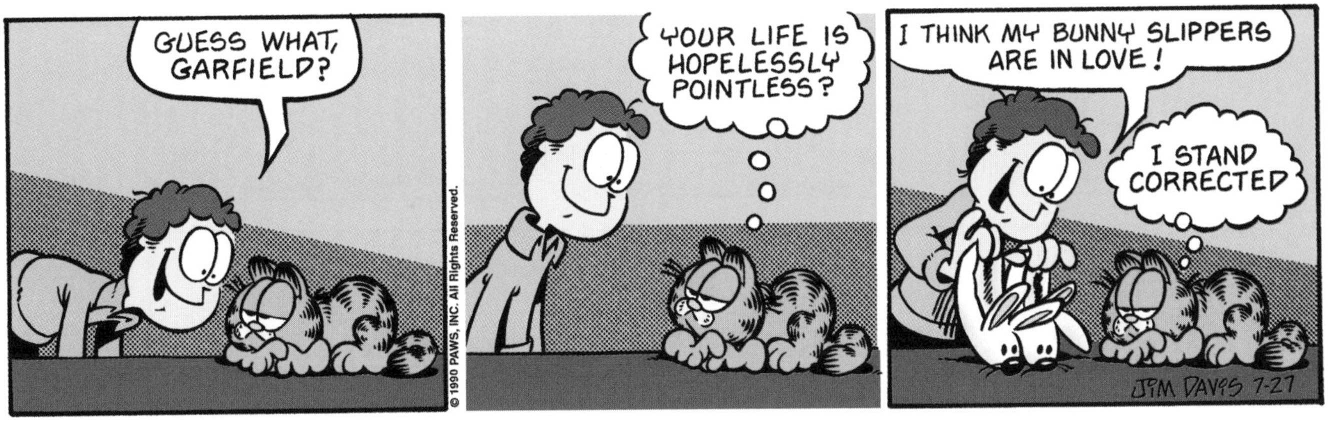
GUESS WHAT, GARFIELD?
YOUR LIFE IS HOPELESSLY POINTLESS?
I THINK MY BUNNY SLIPPERS ARE IN LOVE!
I STAND CORRECTED
© 1990 PAWS, INC. All Rights Reserved.
JIM DAVIS 7-27

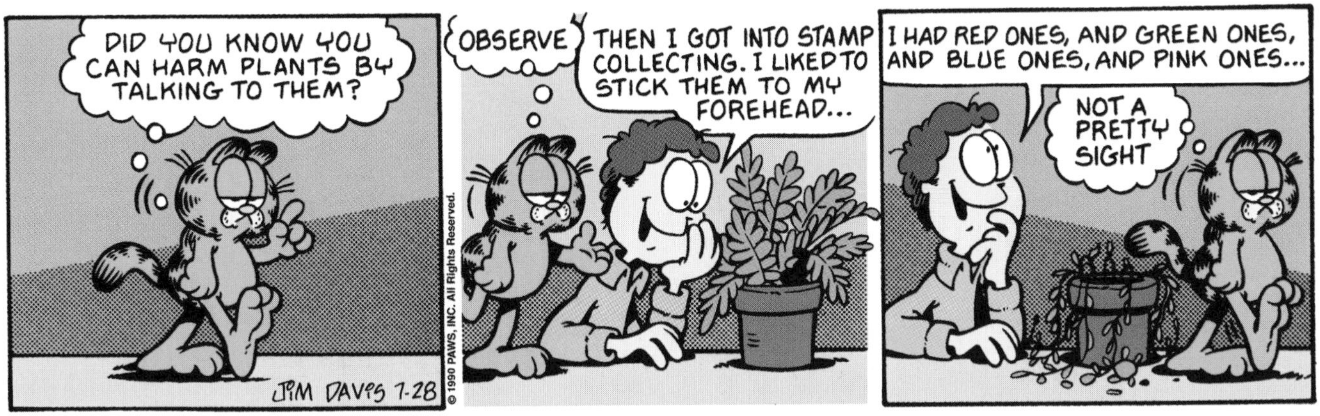
DID YOU KNOW YOU CAN HARM PLANTS BY TALKING TO THEM?
JIM DAVIS 7-28
OBSERVE
THEN I GOT INTO STAMP COLLECTING. I LIKED TO STICK THEM TO MY FOREHEAD...
I HAD RED ONES, AND GREEN ONES, AND BLUE ONES, AND PINK ONES...
NOT A PRETTY SIGHT
© 1990 PAWS, INC. All Rights Reserved.

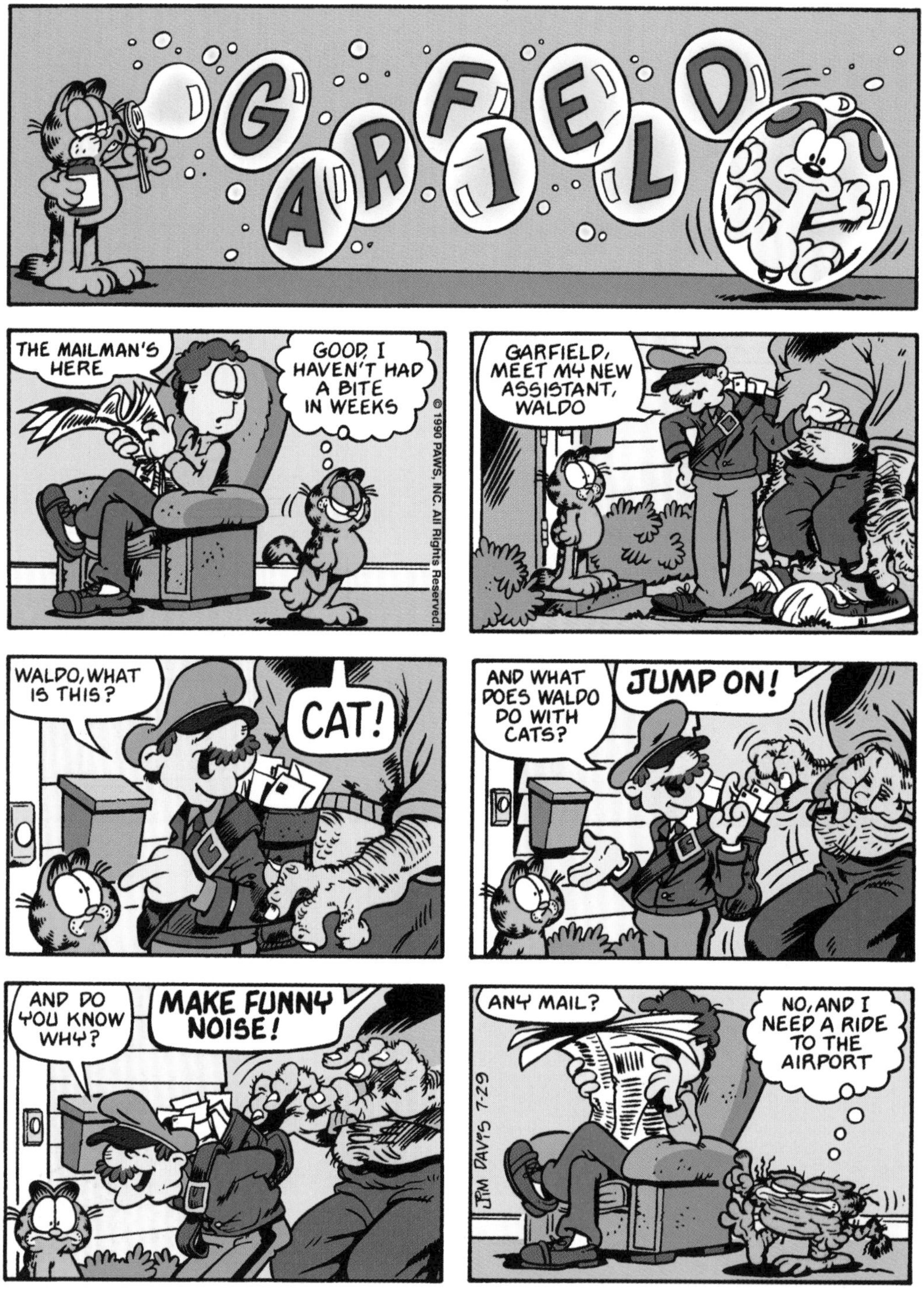
GARFIELD
THE MAILMAN'S HERE
GOOD, I HAVEN'T HAD A BITE IN WEEKS
© 1990 PAWS, INC. All Rights Reserved.
GARFIELD, MEET MY NEW ASSISTANT, WALDO
WALDO, WHAT IS THIS?
CAT!
AND WHAT DOES WALDO DO WITH CATS?
JUMP ON!
AND DO YOU KNOW WHY?
MAKE FUNNY NOISE!
JIM DAVIS 7-29
ANY MAIL?
NO, AND I NEED A RIDE TO THE AIRPORT

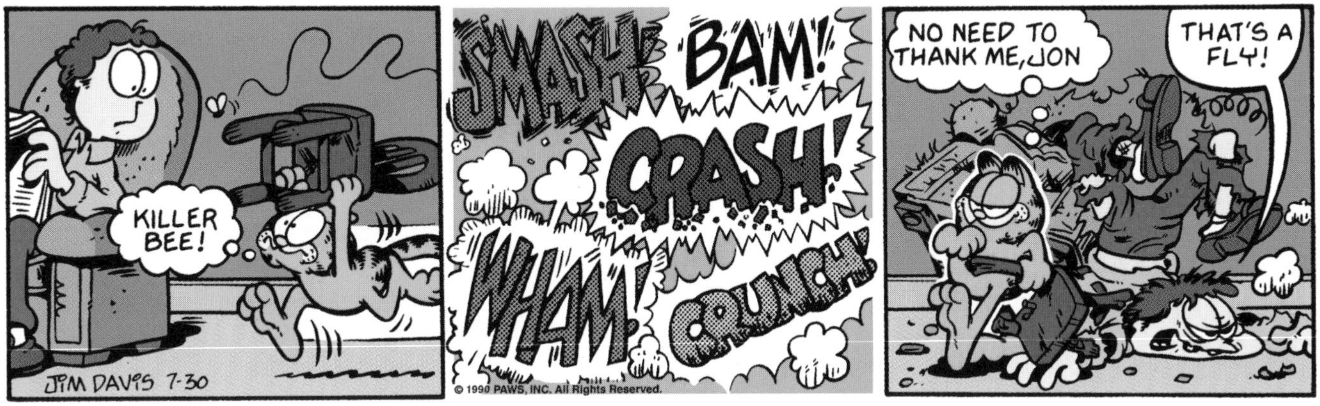
KILLER BEE!
JIM DAVIS 7-30
SMASH! BAM!
CRASH!
WHAM! CRUNCH!
© 1990 PAWS, INC. All Rights Reserved.
NO NEED TO THANK ME, JON
THAT'S A FLY!

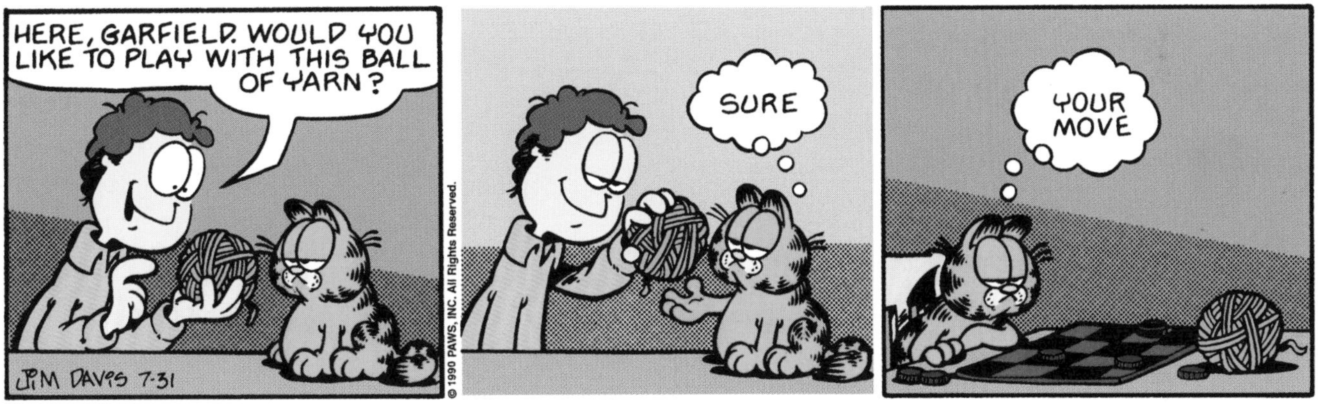
HERE, GARFIELD. WOULD YOU LIKE TO PLAY WITH THIS BALL OF YARN?
JIM DAVIS 7-31
© 1990 PAWS, INC. All Rights Reserved.
SURE
YOUR MOVE

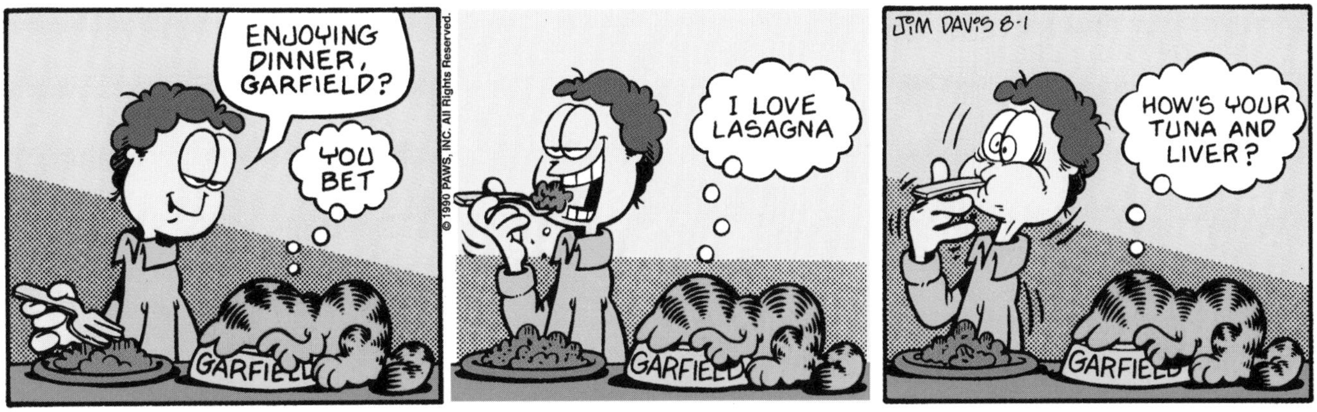
ENJOYING DINNER, GARFIELD?
YOU BET
GARFIELD
© 1990 PAWS, INC. All Rights Reserved.
I LOVE LASAGNA
GARFIELD
JIM DAVIS 8-1
HOW'S YOUR TUNA AND LIVER?
GARFIELD

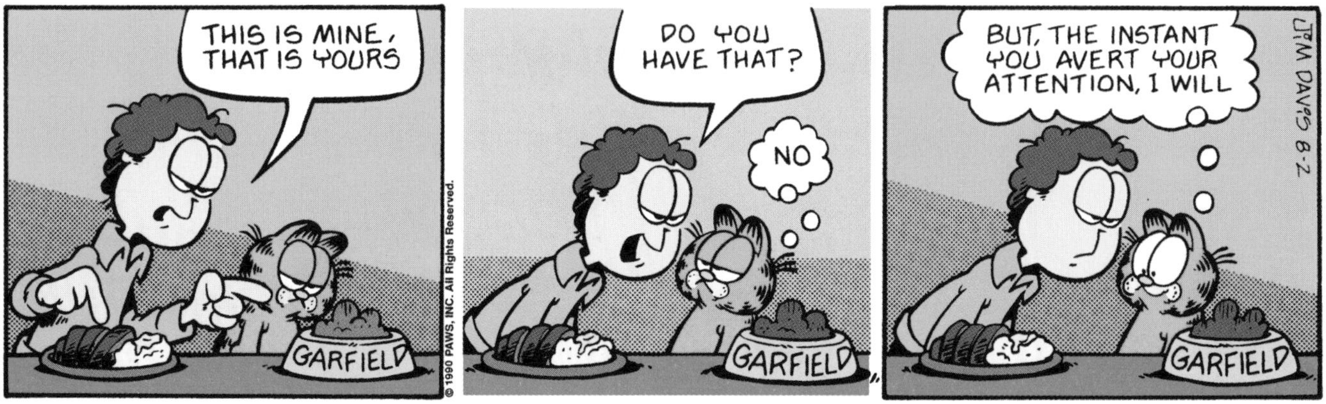
THIS IS MINE, THAT IS YOURS
© 1990 PAWS, INC. All Rights Reserved.
GARFIELD
DO YOU HAVE THAT?
NO
GARFIELD
BUT, THE INSTANT YOU AVERT YOUR ATTENTION, I WILL
JIM DAVIS 8-2
GARFIELD

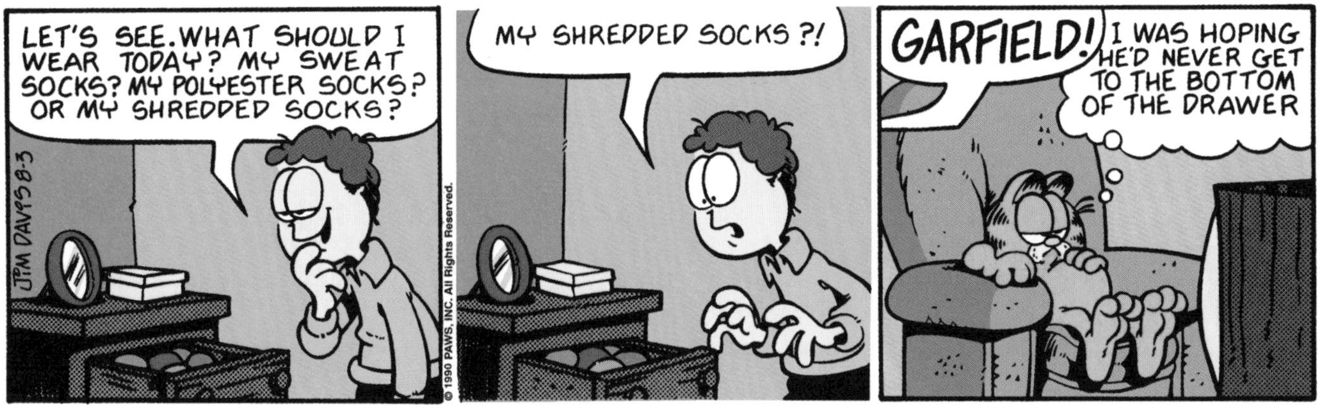
LET'S SEE. WHAT SHOULD I WEAR TODAY? MY SWEAT SOCKS? MY POLYESTER SOCKS? OR MY SHREDDED SOCKS?
JIM DAVIS 8-3
© 1990 PAWS, INC. All Rights Reserved.
MY SHREDDED SOCKS?!
GARFIELD!
I WAS HOPING HE'D NEVER GET TO THE BOTTOM OF THE DRAWER

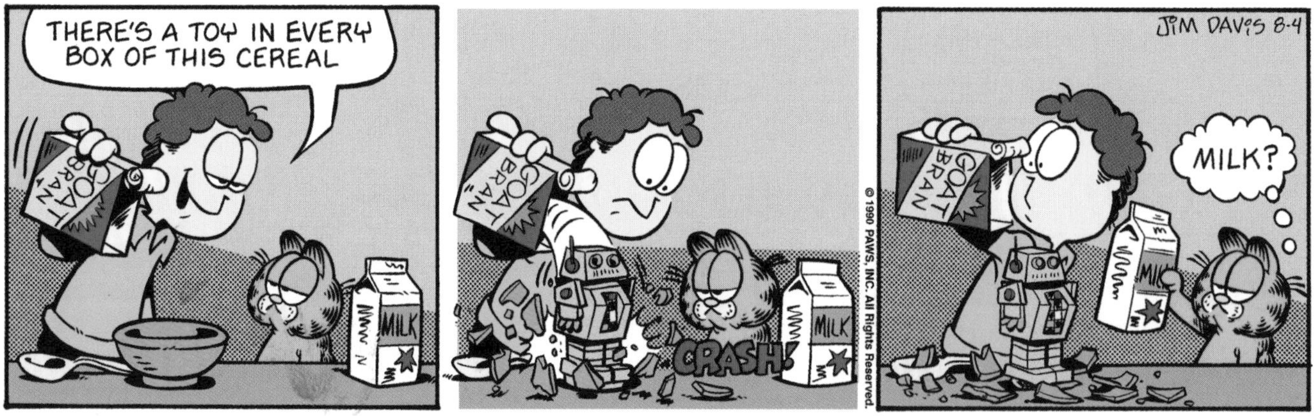
THERE'S A TOY IN EVERY BOX OF THIS CEREAL
GOAT BRAN
MILK
GOAT BRAN
MILK
CRASH!
© 1990 PAWS, INC. All Rights Reserved.
JIM DAVIS 8-4
GOAT BRAN
MILK?
MILK

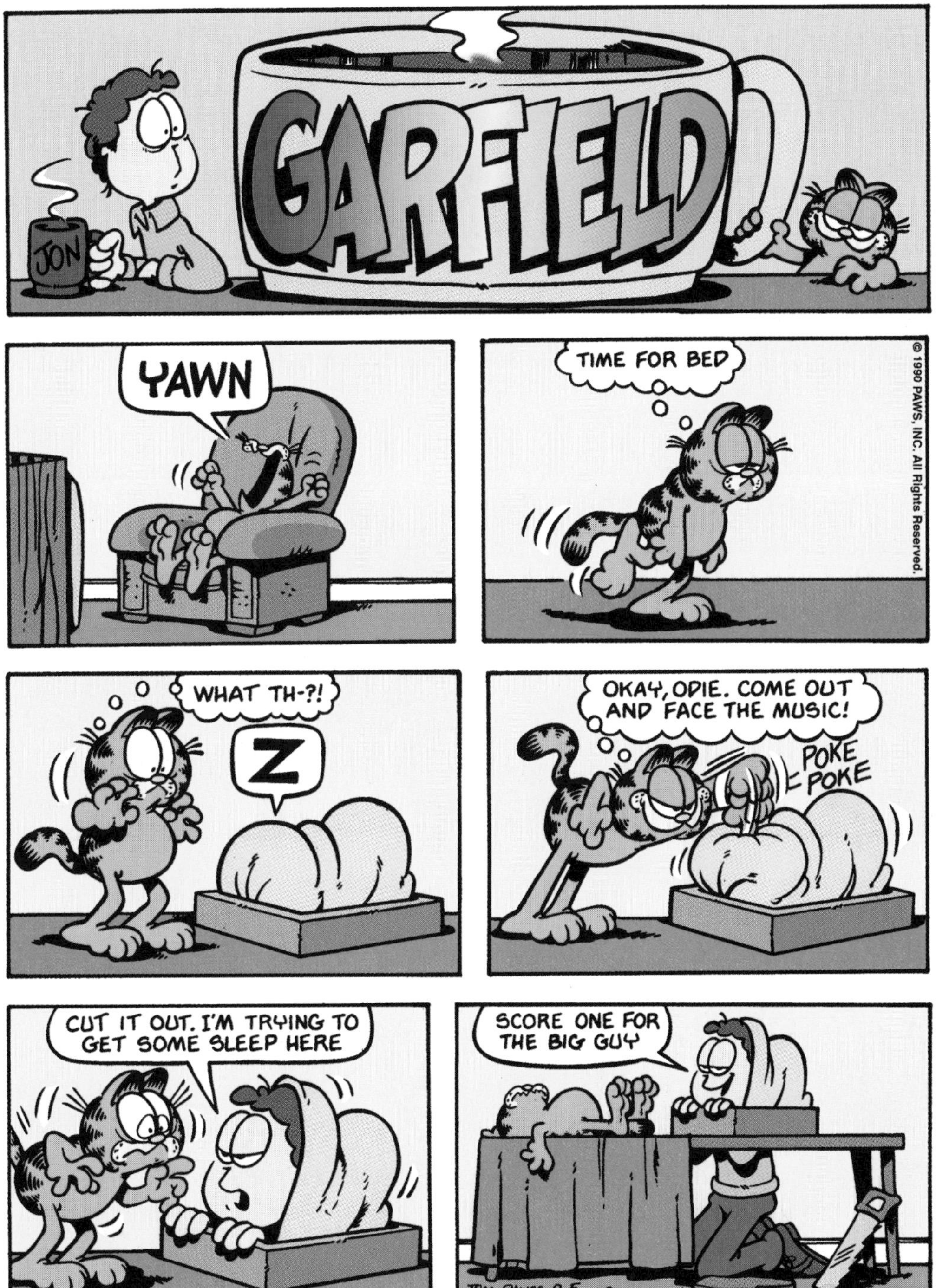
GARFIELD
JON
YAWN
TIME FOR BED
WHAT TH-?!
Z
OKAY, ODIE. COME OUT AND FACE THE MUSIC!
POKE POKE
CUT IT OUT. I'M TRYING TO GET SOME SLEEP HERE
SCORE ONE FOR THE BIG GUY
JIM DAVIS 8-5

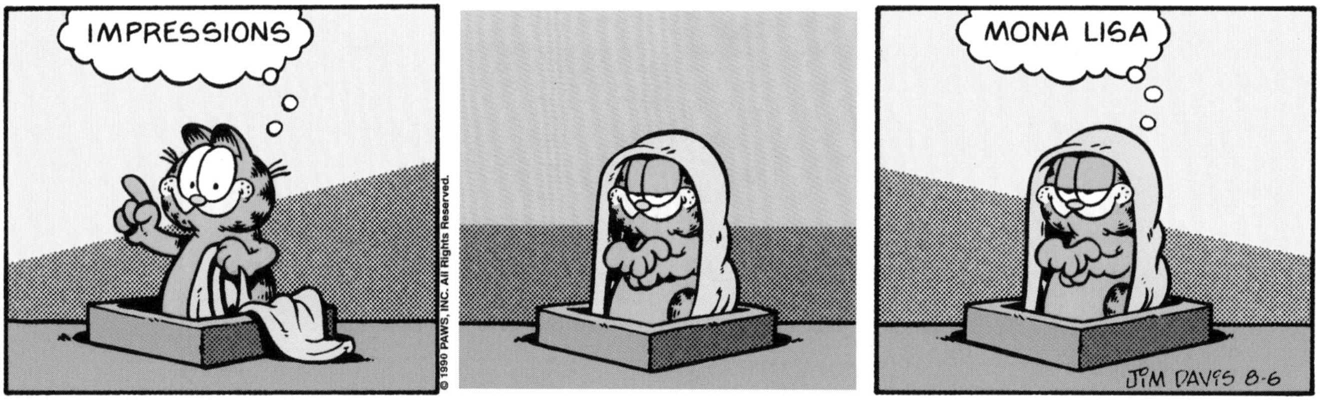
IMPRESSIONS
© 1990 PAWS, INC. All Rights Reserved.
MONA LISA
JIM DAVIS 8-6

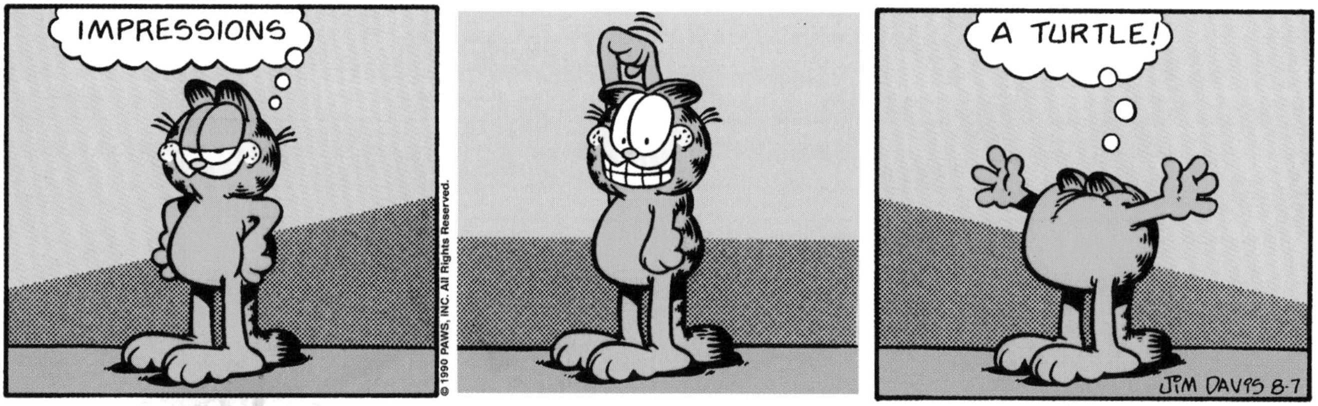
IMPRESSIONS
© 1990 PAWS, INC. All Rights Reserved.
A TURTLE!
JIM DAVIS 8-7

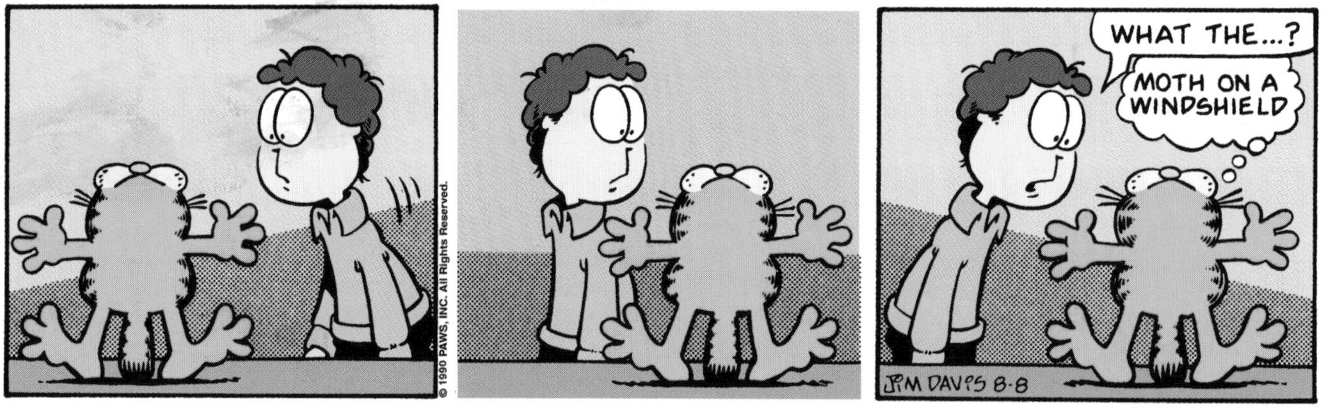
© 1990 PAWS, INC. All Rights Reserved.
WHAT THE...?
MOTH ON A WINDSHIELD
JIM DAVIS 8-8

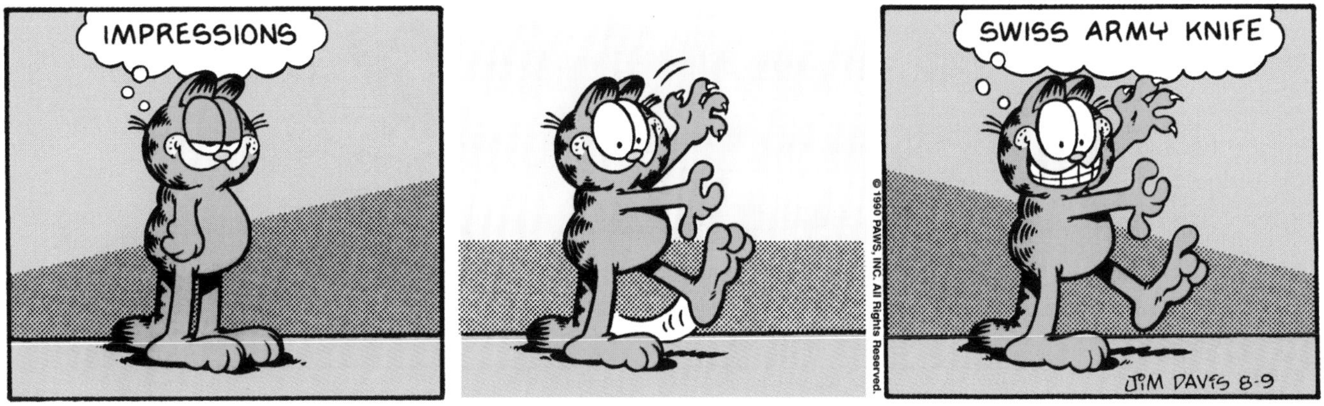
IMPRESSIONS
SWISS ARMY KNIFE
JIM DAVIS 8-9
© 1990 PAWS, INC. All Rights Reserved.

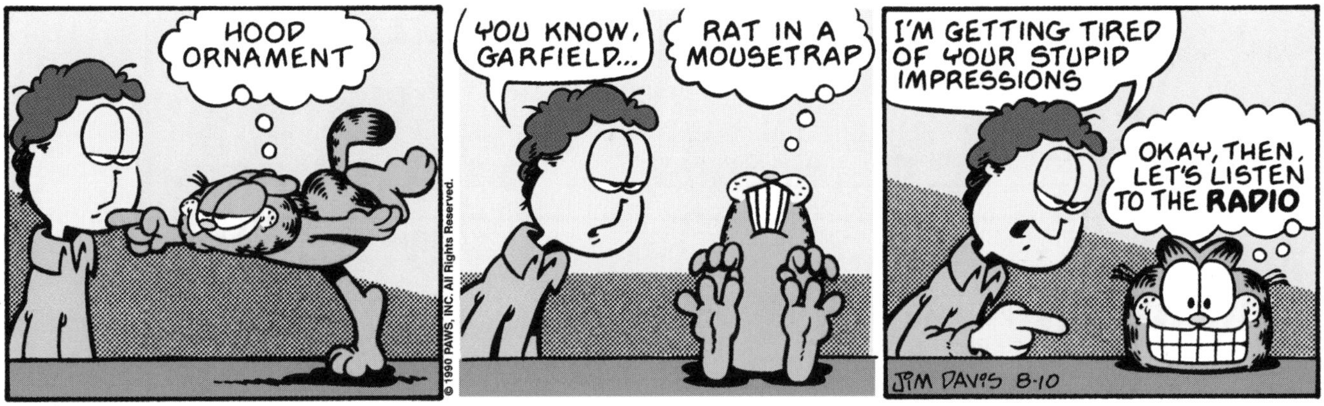
HOOD ORNAMENT
YOU KNOW, GARFIELD...
RAT IN A MOUSETRAP
I'M GETTING TIRED OF YOUR STUPID IMPRESSIONS
OKAY, THEN, LET'S LISTEN TO THE **RADIO**
JIM DAVIS 8-10
© 1990 PAWS, INC. All Rights Reserved.

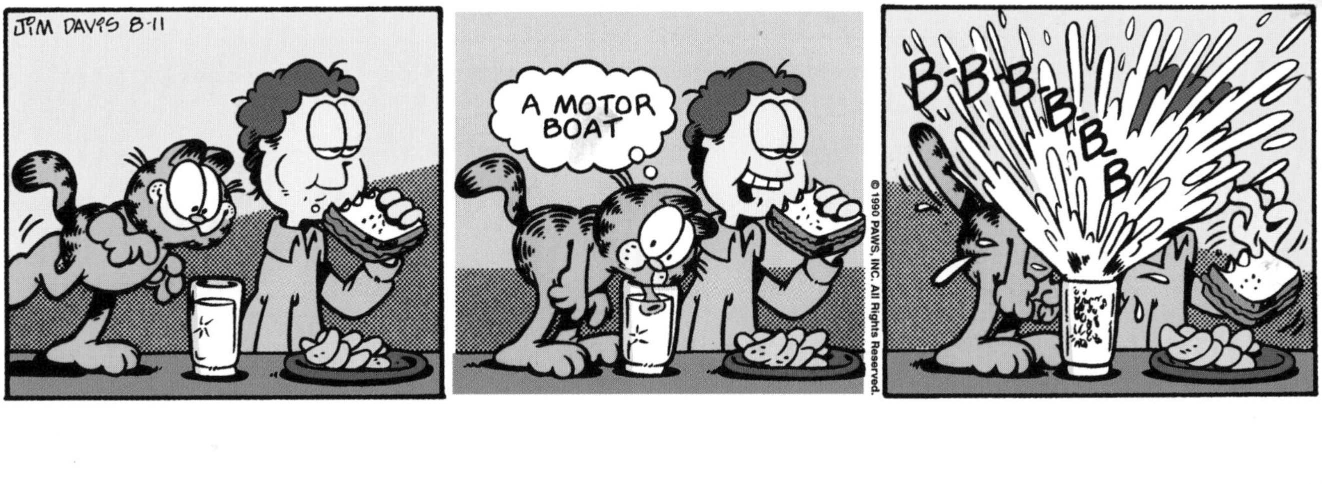
JIM DAVIS 8-11
A MOTOR BOAT
B-B-B-B-B-B-B
© 1990 PAWS, INC. All Rights Reserved.

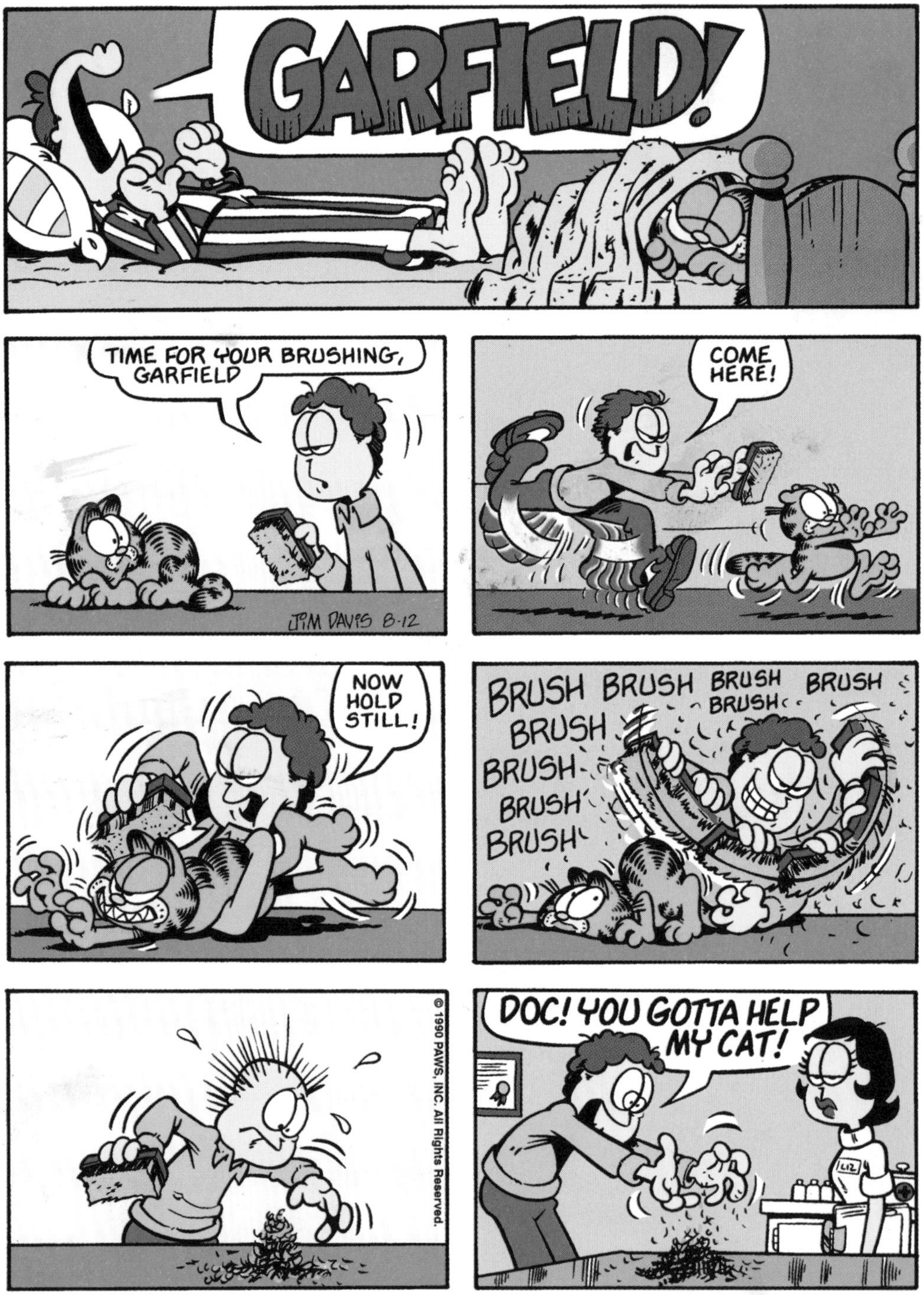
GARFIELD!
TIME FOR YOUR BRUSHING, GARFIELD
JIM DAVIS 8-12
COME HERE!
NOW HOLD STILL!
BRUSH BRUSH BRUSH BRUSH BRUSH
BRUSH
BRUSH
BRUSH
BRUSH
BRUSH
© 1990 PAWS, INC. All Rights Reserved.
DOC! YOU GOTTA HELP MY CAT!
LIZ

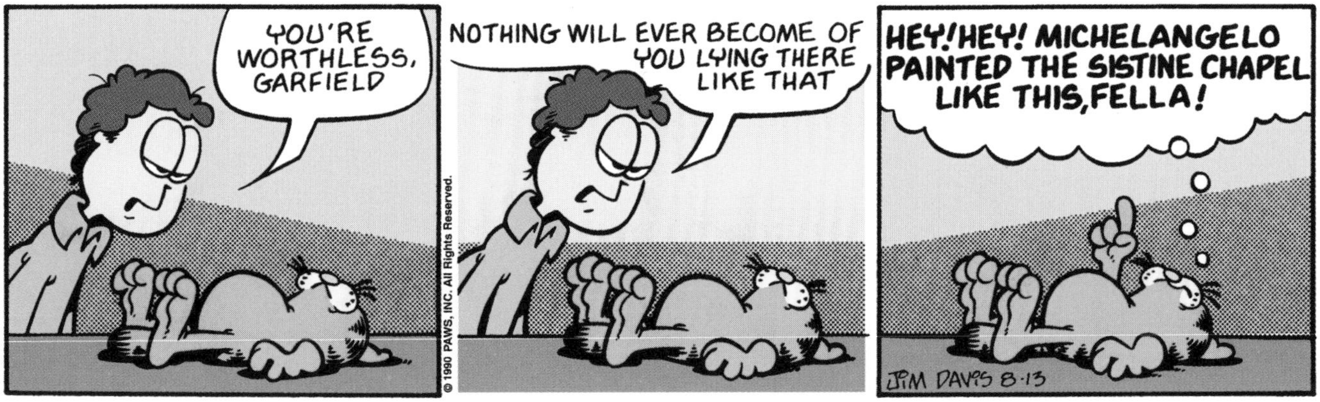
YOU'RE WORTHLESS, GARFIELD
© 1990 PAWS, INC. All Rights Reserved.
NOTHING WILL EVER BECOME OF YOU LYING THERE LIKE THAT
HEY! HEY! MICHELANGELO PAINTED THE SISTINE CHAPEL LIKE THIS, FELLA!
JIM DAVIS 8-13

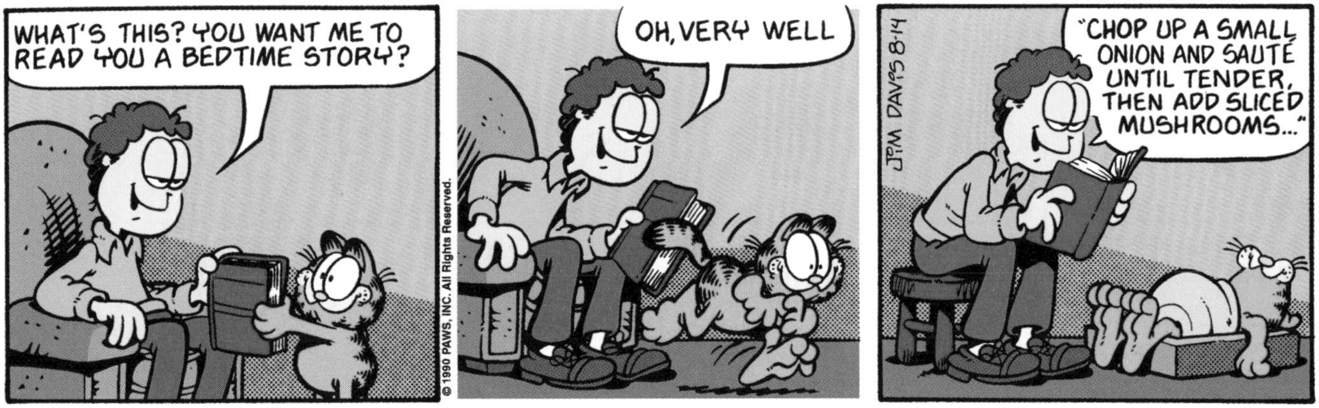
WHAT'S THIS? YOU WANT ME TO READ YOU A BEDTIME STORY?
© 1990 PAWS, INC. All Rights Reserved.
OH, VERY WELL
JIM DAVIS 8-14
"CHOP UP A SMALL ONION AND SAUTÉ UNTIL TENDER, THEN ADD SLICED MUSHROOMS..."

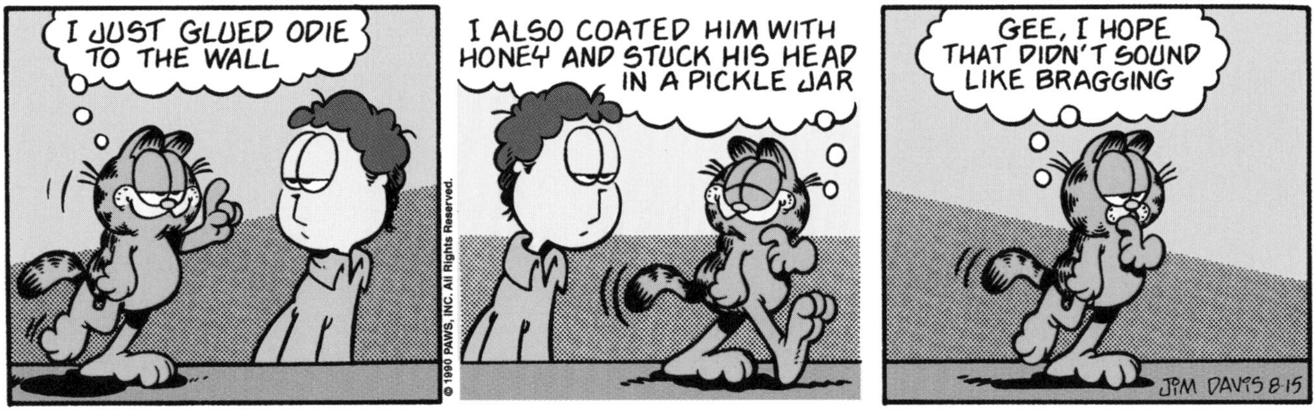
I JUST GLUED ODIE TO THE WALL
© 1990 PAWS, INC. All Rights Reserved.
I ALSO COATED HIM WITH HONEY AND STUCK HIS HEAD IN A PICKLE JAR
GEE, I HOPE THAT DIDN'T SOUND LIKE BRAGGING
JIM DAVIS 8-15

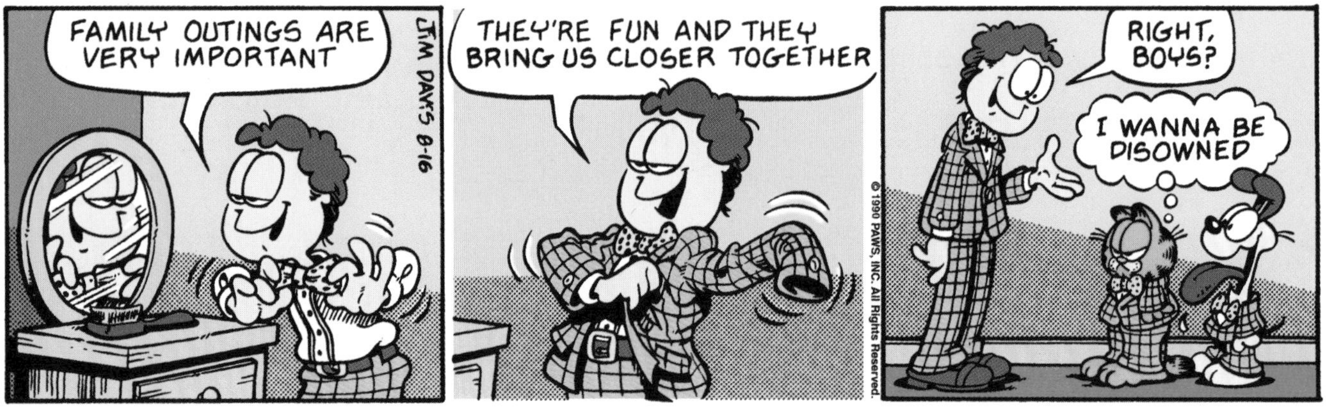
JIM DAVIS 8-16
FAMILY OUTINGS ARE VERY IMPORTANT
THEY'RE FUN AND THEY BRING US CLOSER TOGETHER
RIGHT, BOYS?
I WANNA BE DISOWNED
© 1990 PAWS, INC. All Rights Reserved.

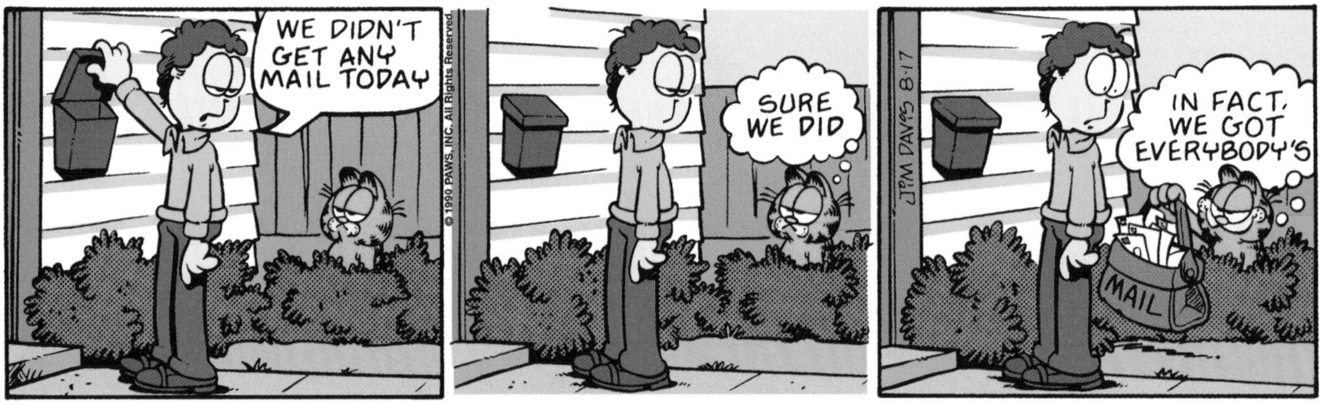
WE DIDN'T GET ANY MAIL TODAY
© 1990 PAWS, INC. All Rights Reserved.
SURE WE DID
JIM DAVIS 8-17
IN FACT, WE GOT EVERYBODY'S
MAIL

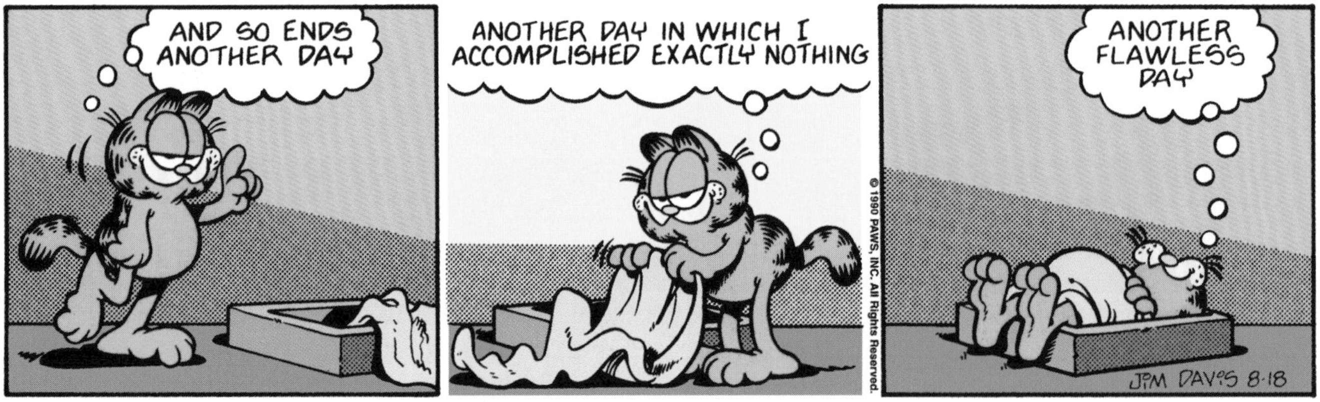
AND SO ENDS ANOTHER DAY
ANOTHER DAY IN WHICH I ACCOMPLISHED EXACTLY NOTHING
© 1990 PAWS, INC. All Rights Reserved.
ANOTHER FLAWLESS DAY
JIM DAVIS 8-18

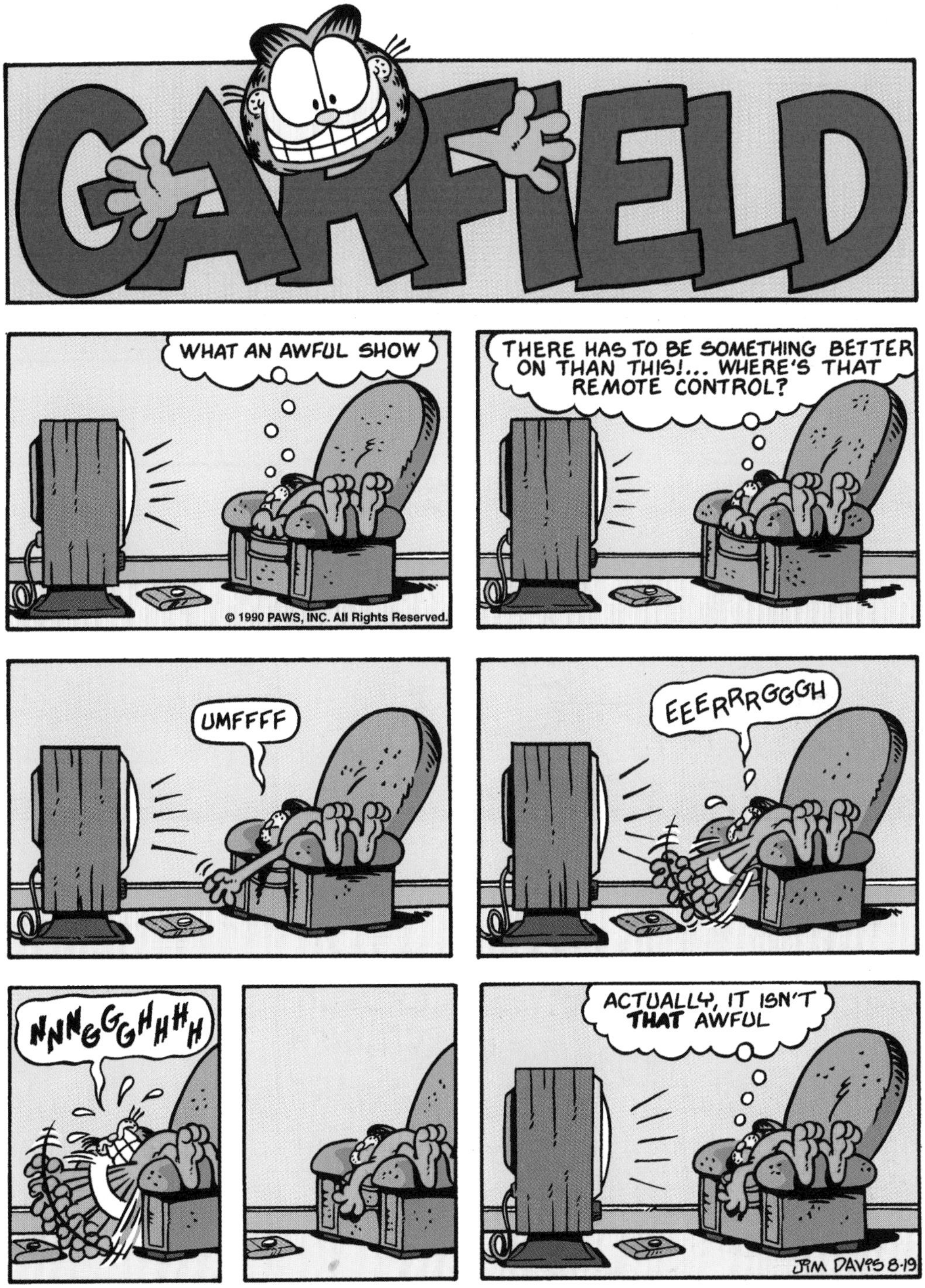
GARFIELD
WHAT AN AWFUL SHOW
© 1990 PAWS, INC. All Rights Reserved.
THERE HAS TO BE SOMETHING BETTER ON THAN THIS!... WHERE'S THAT REMOTE CONTROL?
UMFFFF
EEERRRRGGGH
NNNGGGHHHH
ACTUALLY, IT ISN'T **THAT** AWFUL
JIM DAVIS 8-19

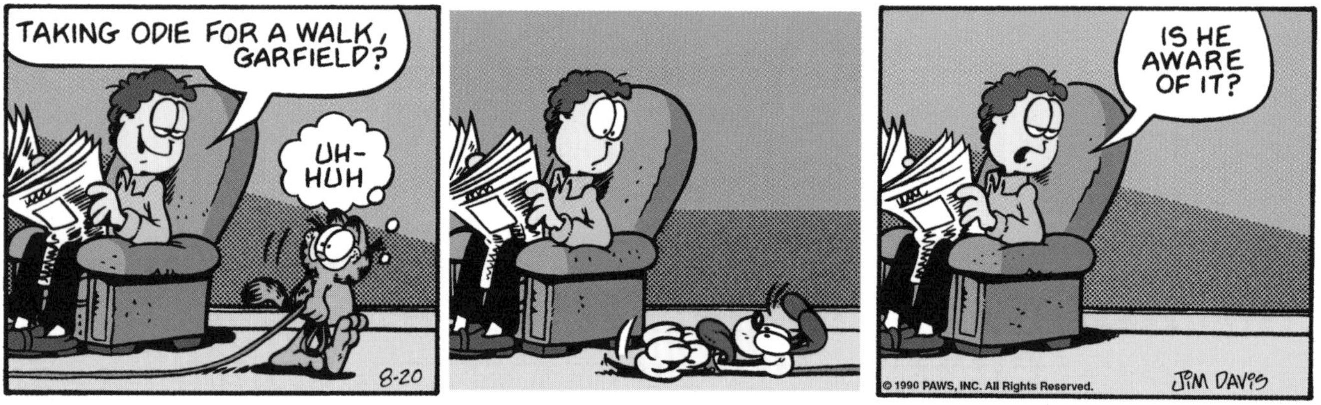
TAKING ODIE FOR A WALK, GARFIELD?
UH-HUH
8-20
IS HE AWARE OF IT?
© 1990 PAWS, INC. All Rights Reserved.
JIM DAVIS

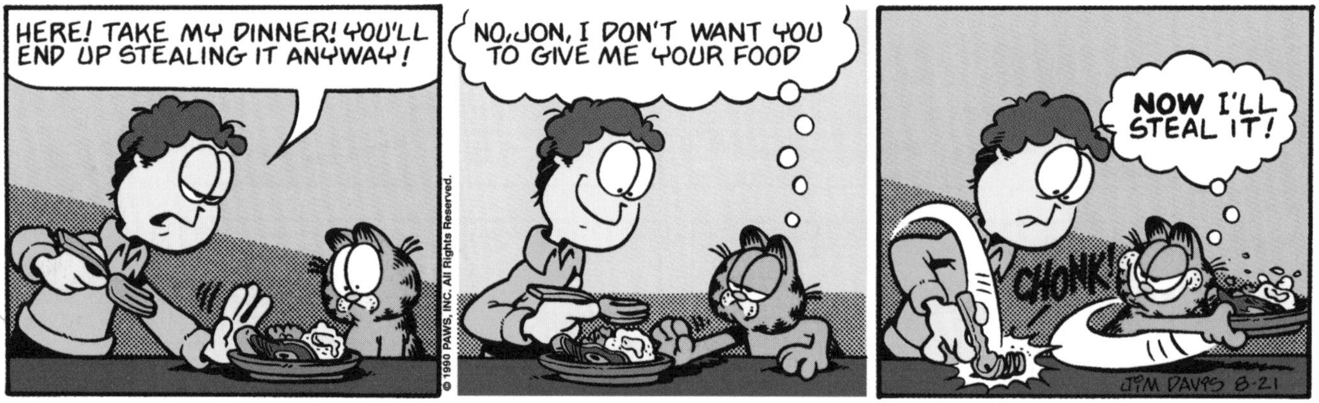
HERE! TAKE MY DINNER! YOU'LL END UP STEALING IT ANYWAY!
© 1990 PAWS, INC. All Rights Reserved.
NO, JON, I DON'T WANT YOU TO GIVE ME YOUR FOOD
NOW I'LL STEAL IT!
CHONK!
JIM DAVIS 8-21

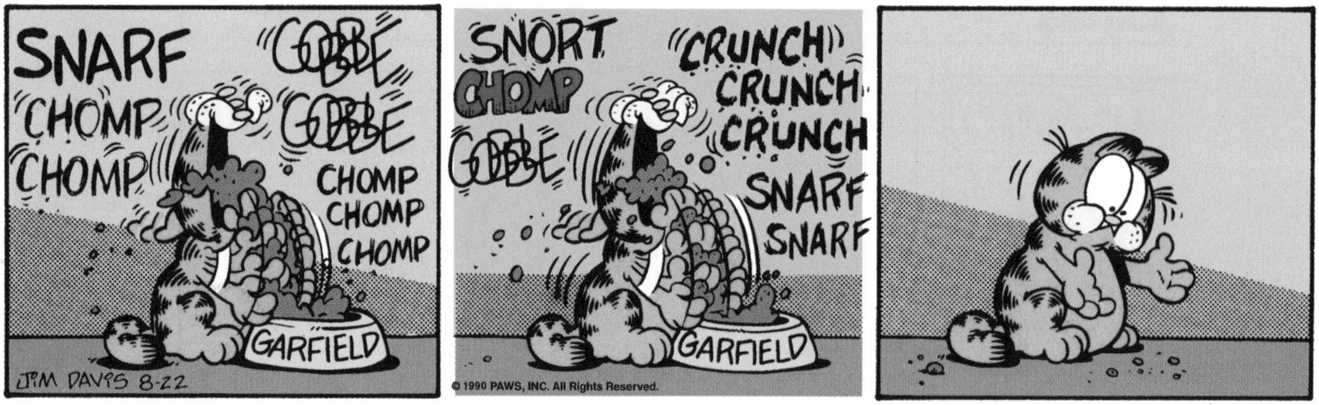
SNARF
CHOMP
CHOMP
CHOMP
CHOMP
CHOMP
GARFIELD
JIM DAVIS 8-22
SNORT
CHOMP
CRUNCH
CRUNCH
CRUNCH
SNARF
SNARF
GARFIELD
© 1990 PAWS, INC. All Rights Reserved.

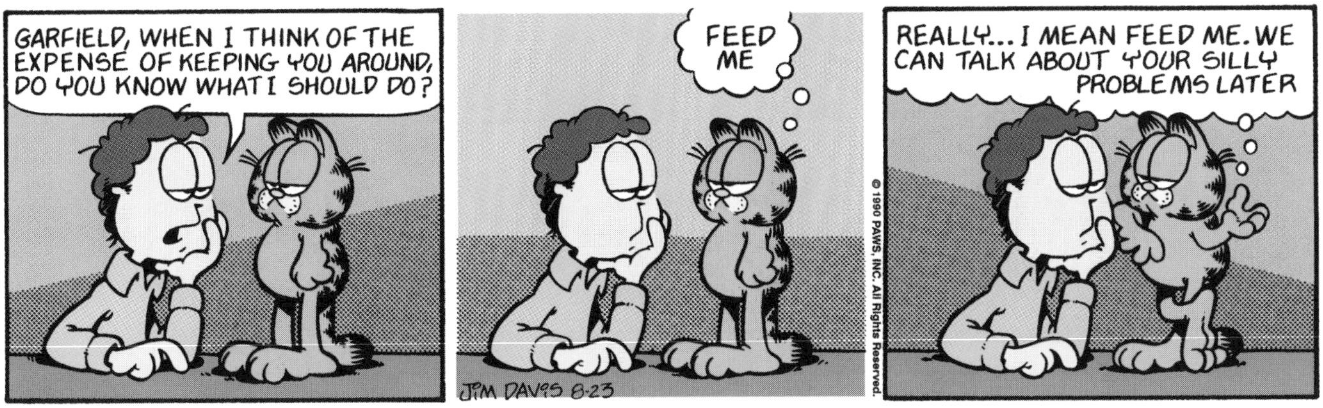
GARFIELD, WHEN I THINK OF THE EXPENSE OF KEEPING YOU AROUND, DO YOU KNOW WHAT I SHOULD DO?
FEED ME
JIM DAVIS 8-23
© 1990 PAWS, INC. All Rights Reserved.
REALLY... I MEAN FEED ME. WE CAN TALK ABOUT YOUR SILLY PROBLEMS LATER

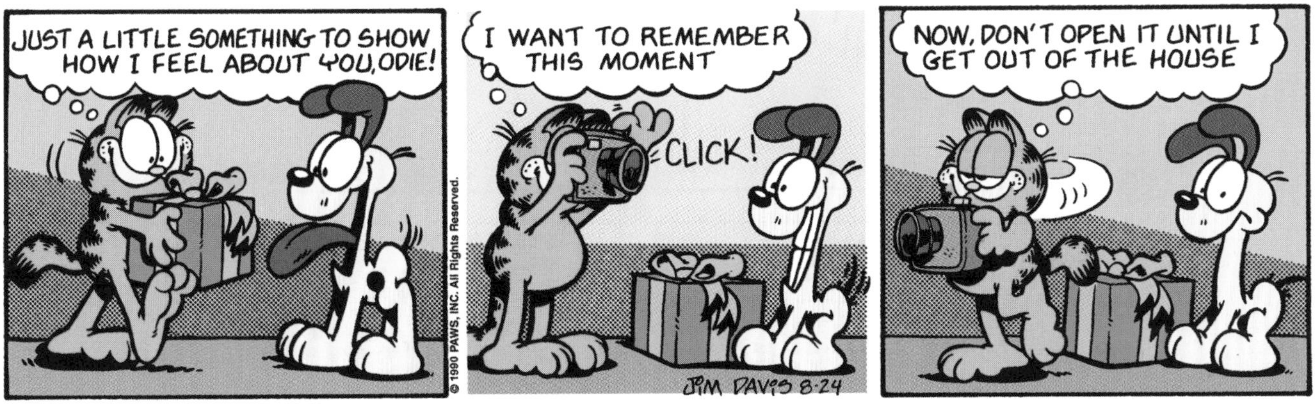
JUST A LITTLE SOMETHING TO SHOW HOW I FEEL ABOUT YOU, ODIE!
© 1990 PAWS, INC. All Rights Reserved.
I WANT TO REMEMBER THIS MOMENT
CLICK!
JIM DAVIS 8-24
NOW, DON'T OPEN IT UNTIL I GET OUT OF THE HOUSE

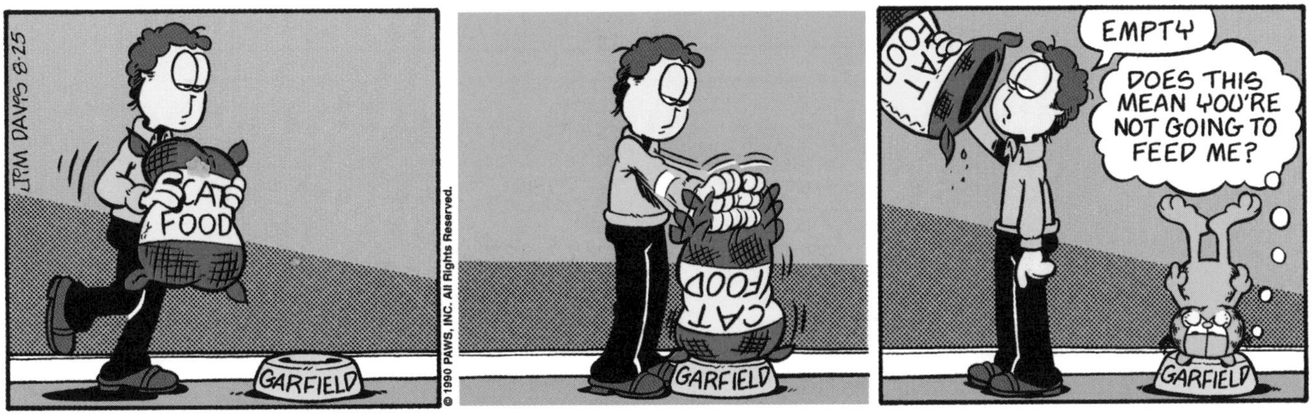
JIM DAVIS 8-25
CAT FOOD
GARFIELD
© 1990 PAWS, INC. All Rights Reserved.
CAT FOOD
GARFIELD
CAT FOOD
EMPTY
DOES THIS MEAN YOU'RE NOT GOING TO FEED ME?
GARFIELD

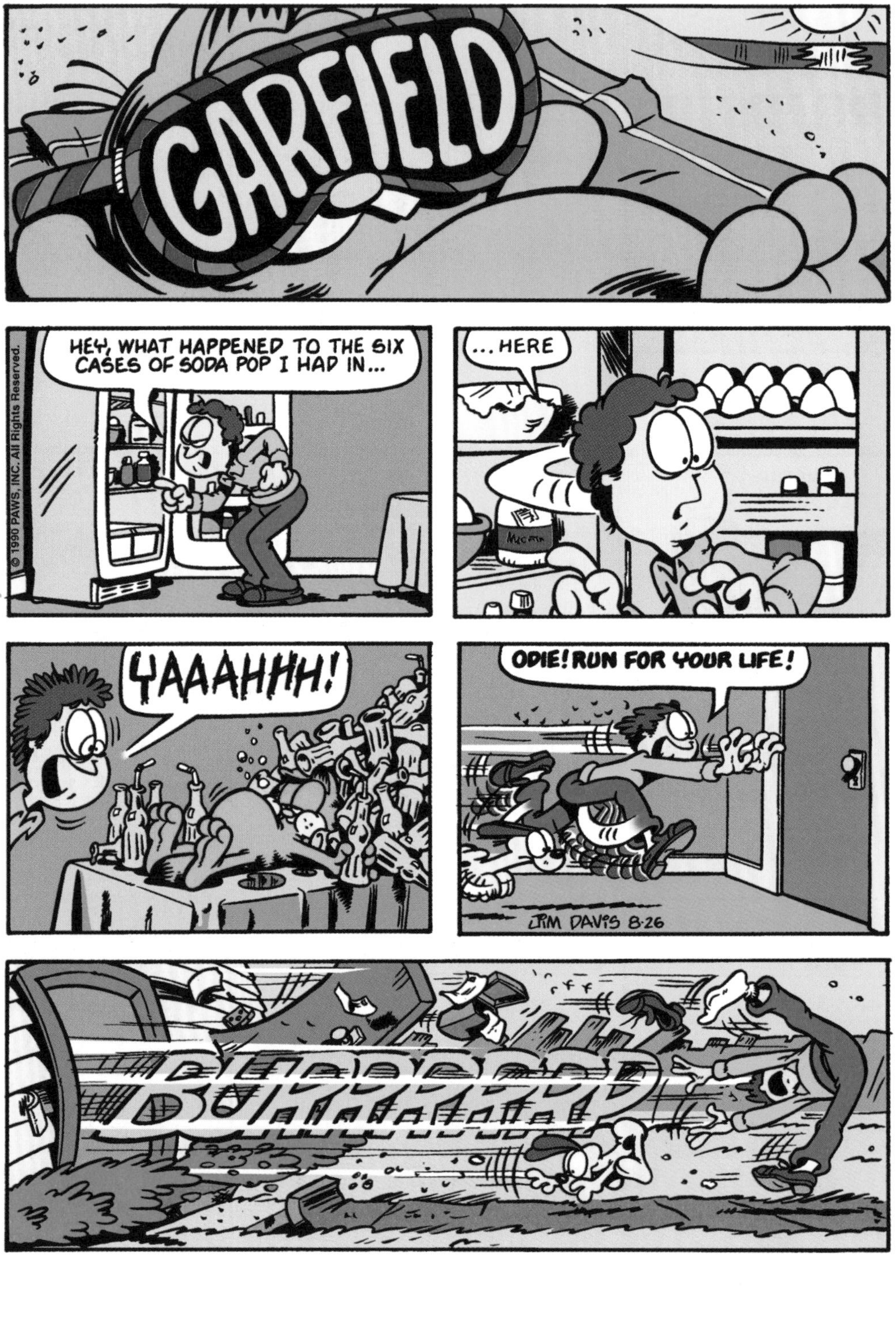
GARFIELD
© 1990 PAWS, INC. All Rights Reserved.
HEY, WHAT HAPPENED TO THE SIX CASES OF SODA POP I HAD IN...
... HERE
YAAAHHH!
ODIE! RUN FOR YOUR LIFE!
JIM DAVIS 8-26
BURRRRRRP

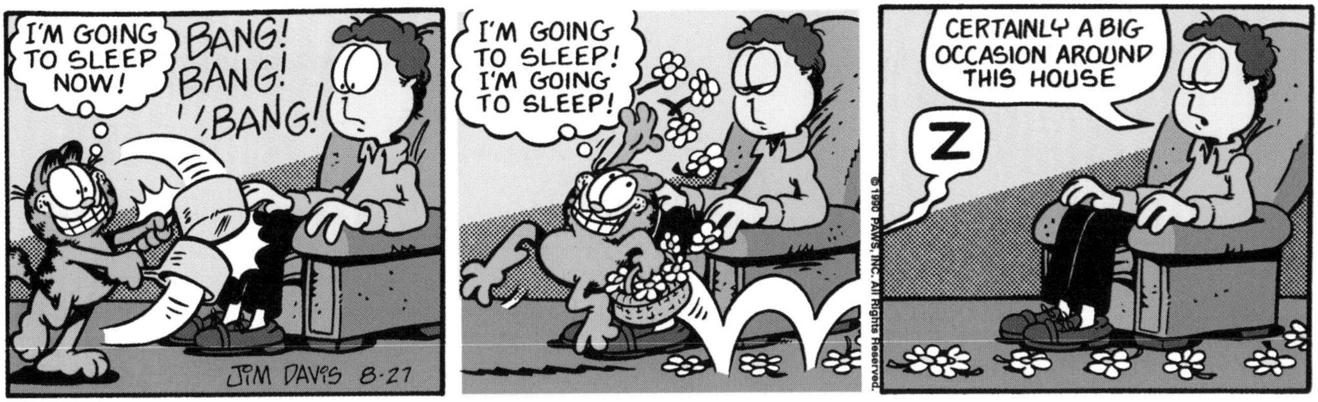
I'M GOING TO SLEEP NOW!
BANG! BANG! BANG!
JIM DAVIS 8-27
I'M GOING TO SLEEP! I'M GOING TO SLEEP!
© 1990 PAWS, INC. All Rights Reserved.
CERTAINLY A BIG OCCASION AROUND THIS HOUSE
Z

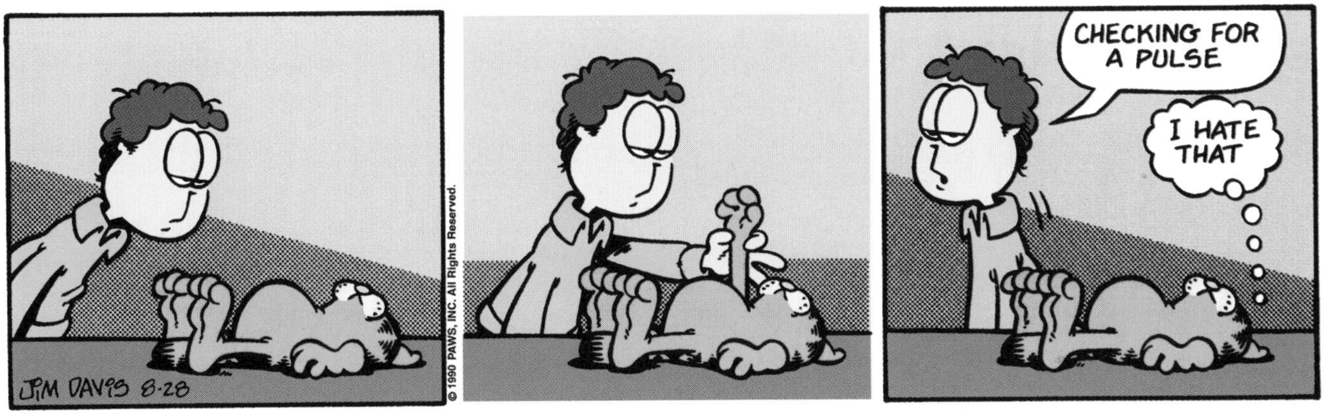
JIM DAVIS 8-28
© 1990 PAWS, INC. All Rights Reserved.
CHECKING FOR A PULSE
I HATE THAT

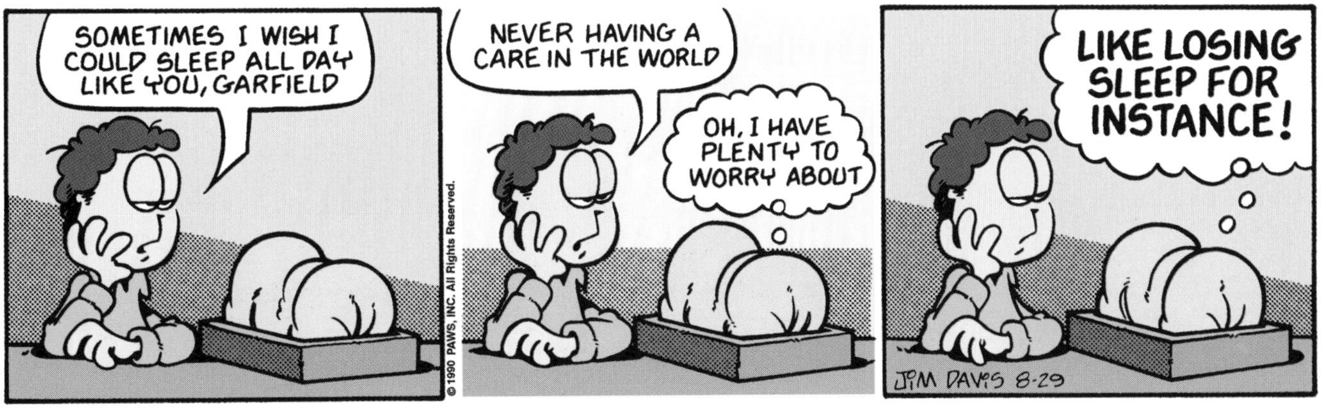
SOMETIMES I WISH I COULD SLEEP ALL DAY LIKE YOU, GARFIELD
© 1990 PAWS, INC. All Rights Reserved.
NEVER HAVING A CARE IN THE WORLD
OH, I HAVE PLENTY TO WORRY ABOUT
LIKE LOSING SLEEP FOR INSTANCE!
JIM DAVIS 8-29

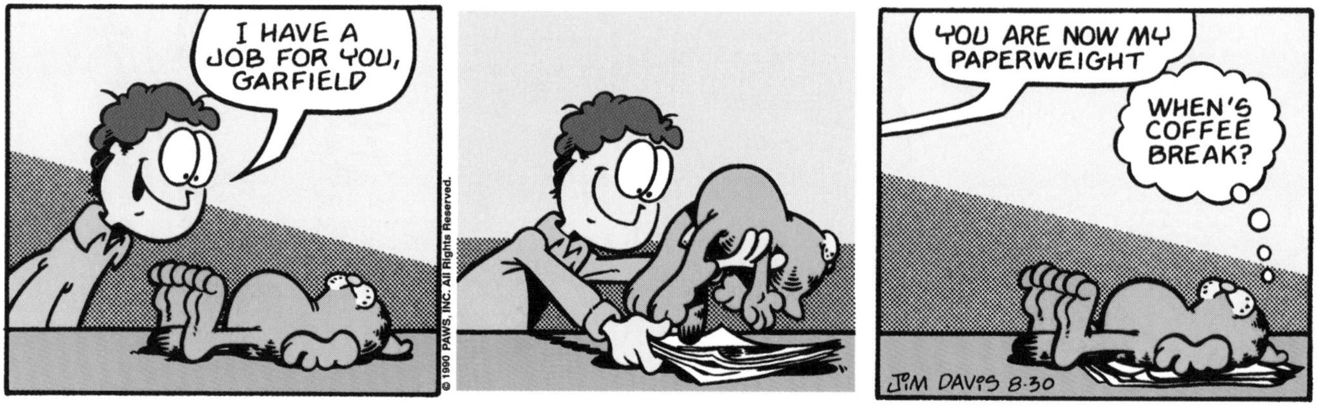
I HAVE A JOB FOR YOU, GARFIELD
© 1990 PAWS, INC. All Rights Reserved.
YOU ARE NOW MY PAPERWEIGHT
WHEN'S COFFEE BREAK?
JIM DAVIS 8-30

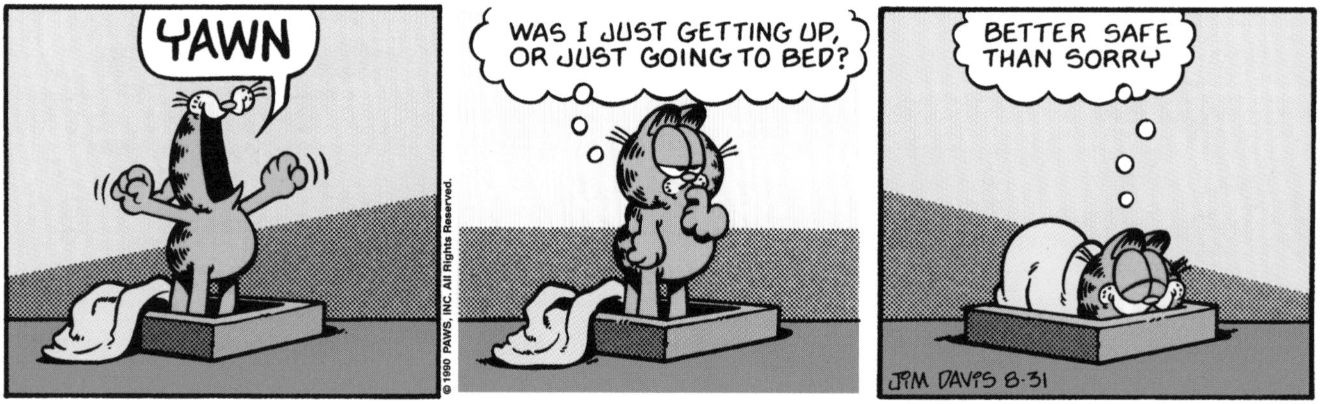
YAWN
© 1990 PAWS, INC. All Rights Reserved.
WAS I JUST GETTING UP, OR JUST GOING TO BED?
BETTER SAFE THAN SORRY
JIM DAVIS 8-31

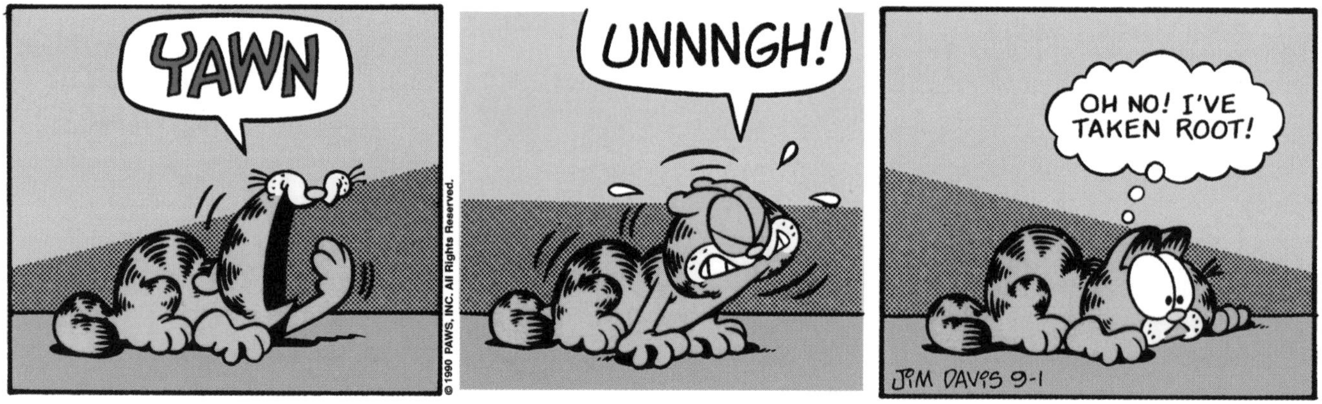
YAWN
© 1990 PAWS, INC. All Rights Reserved.
UNNNGH!
OH NO! I'VE TAKEN ROOT!
JIM DAVIS 9-1

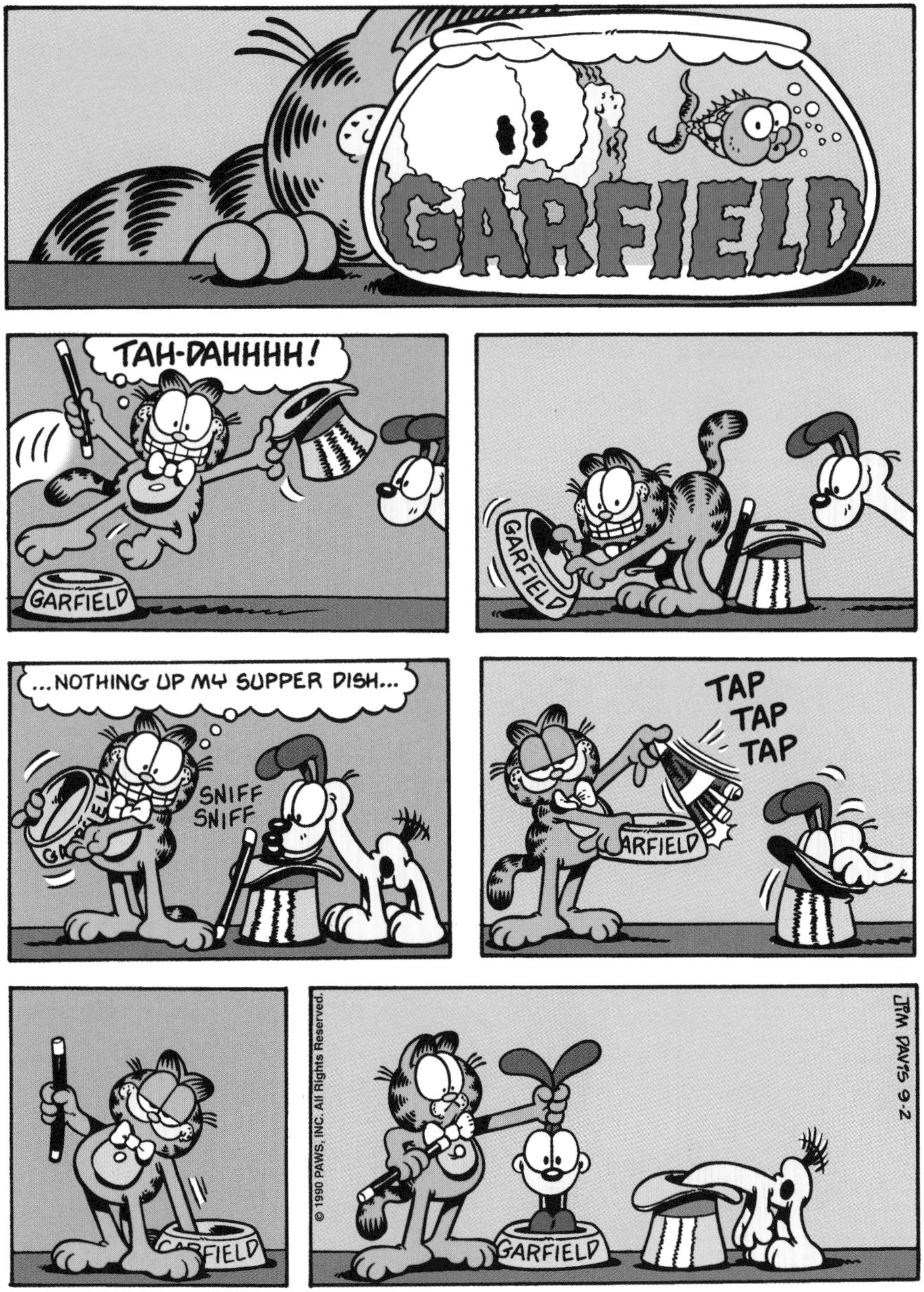
GARFIELD
TAH-DAHHHH!
GARFIELD
GARFIELD
...NOTHING UP MY SUPPER DISH...
GARFIELD
SNIFF SNIFF
TAP TAP TAP
GARFIELD
GARFIELD
GARFIELD
© 1990 PAWS, INC. All Rights Reserved.
JIM DAVIS 9-2

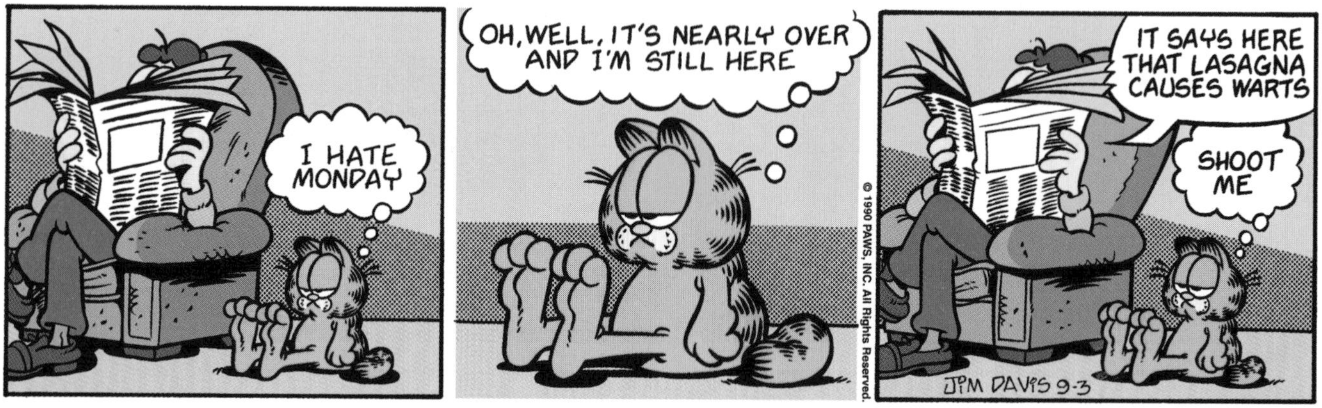
I HATE MONDAY
OH, WELL, IT'S NEARLY OVER AND I'M STILL HERE
© 1990 PAWS, INC. All Rights Reserved.
IT SAYS HERE THAT LASAGNA CAUSES WARTS
SHOOT ME
JIM DAVIS 9-3

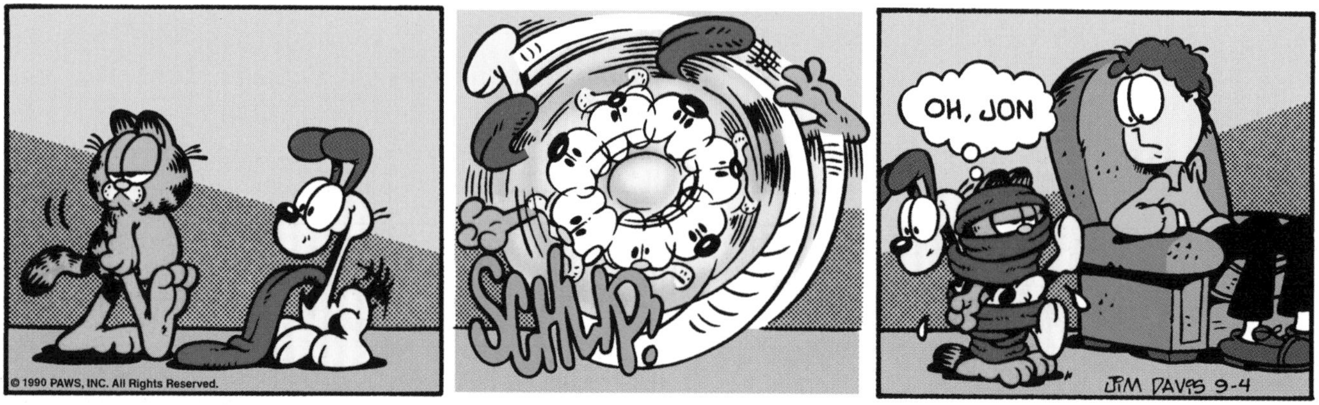
© 1990 PAWS, INC. All Rights Reserved.
SCHLUP!
OH, JON
JIM DAVIS 9-4

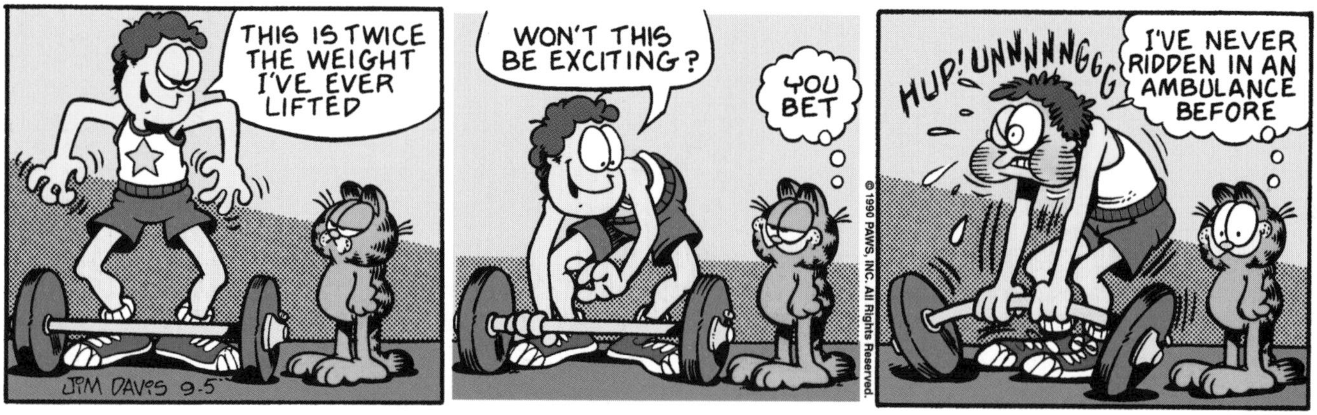
THIS IS TWICE THE WEIGHT I'VE EVER LIFTED
JIM DAVIS 9-5
WON'T THIS BE EXCITING?
YOU BET
© 1990 PAWS, INC. All Rights Reserved.
HUP! UNNNNNGGG
I'VE NEVER RIDDEN IN AN AMBULANCE BEFORE

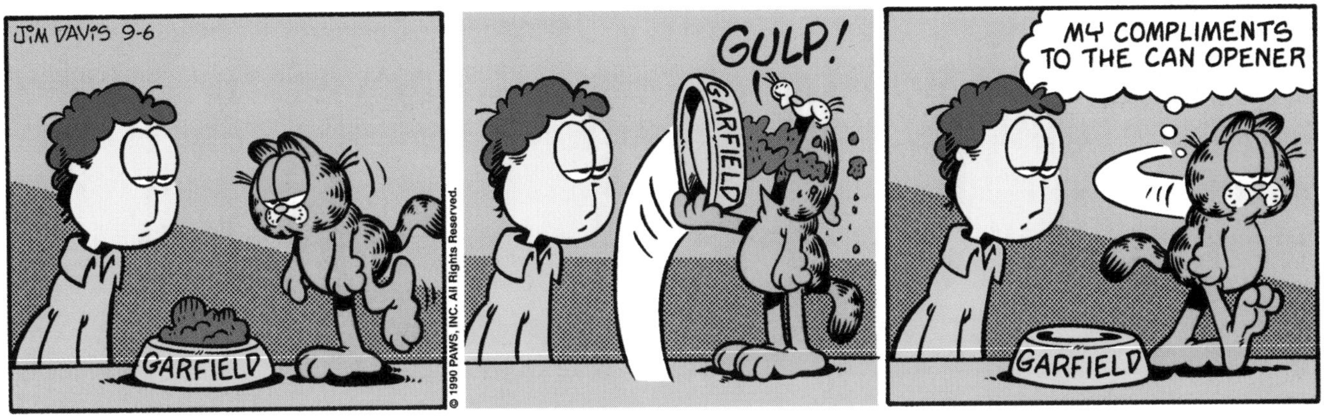
JIM DAVIS 9-6
GULP!
MY COMPLIMENTS TO THE CAN OPENER
© 1990 PAWS, INC. All Rights Reserved.

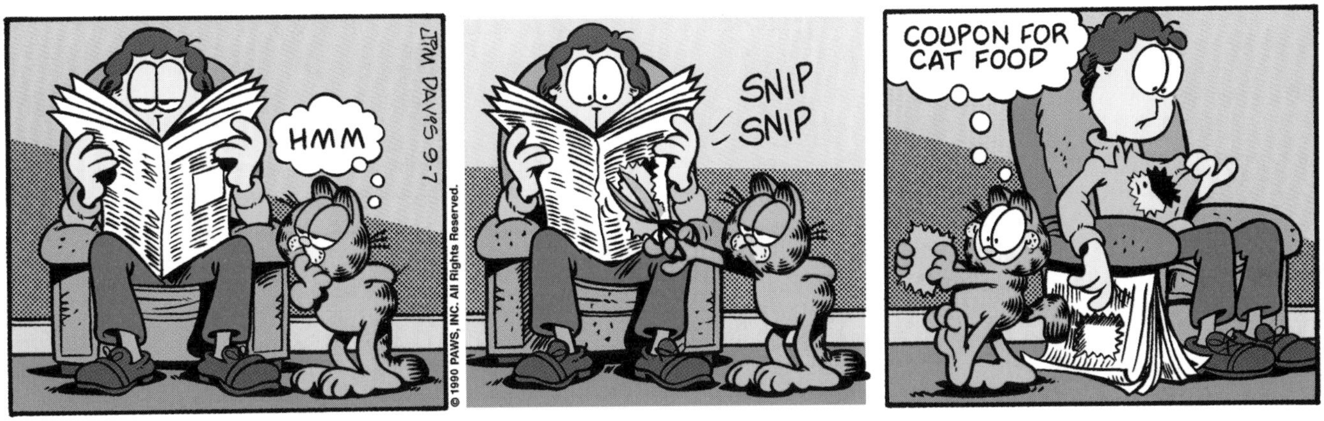
JIM DAVIS 9-7
HMM
SNIP SNIP
COUPON FOR CAT FOOD
© 1990 PAWS, INC. All Rights Reserved.

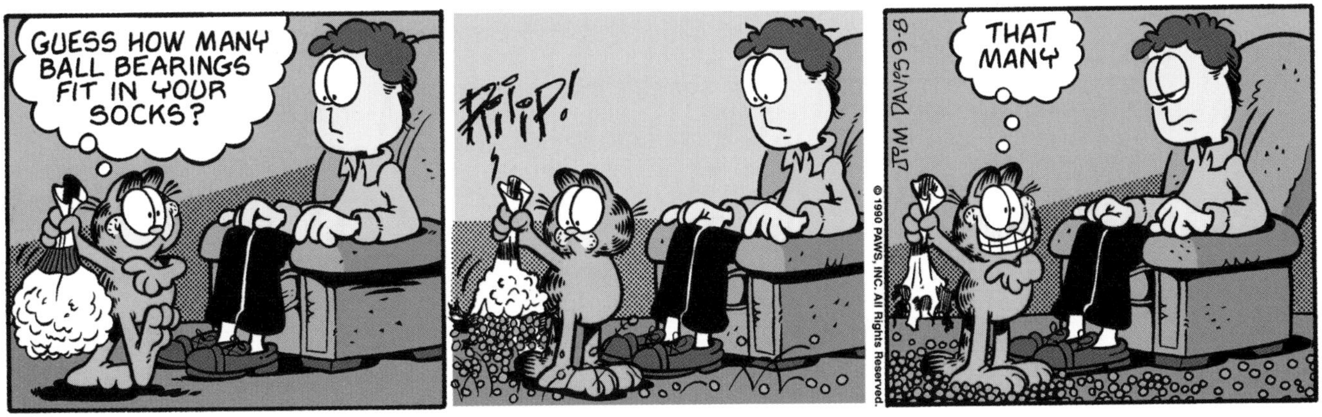
GUESS HOW MANY BALL BEARINGS FIT IN YOUR SOCKS?
RIIIP!
JIM DAVIS 9-8
THAT MANY
© 1990 PAWS, INC. All Rights Reserved.

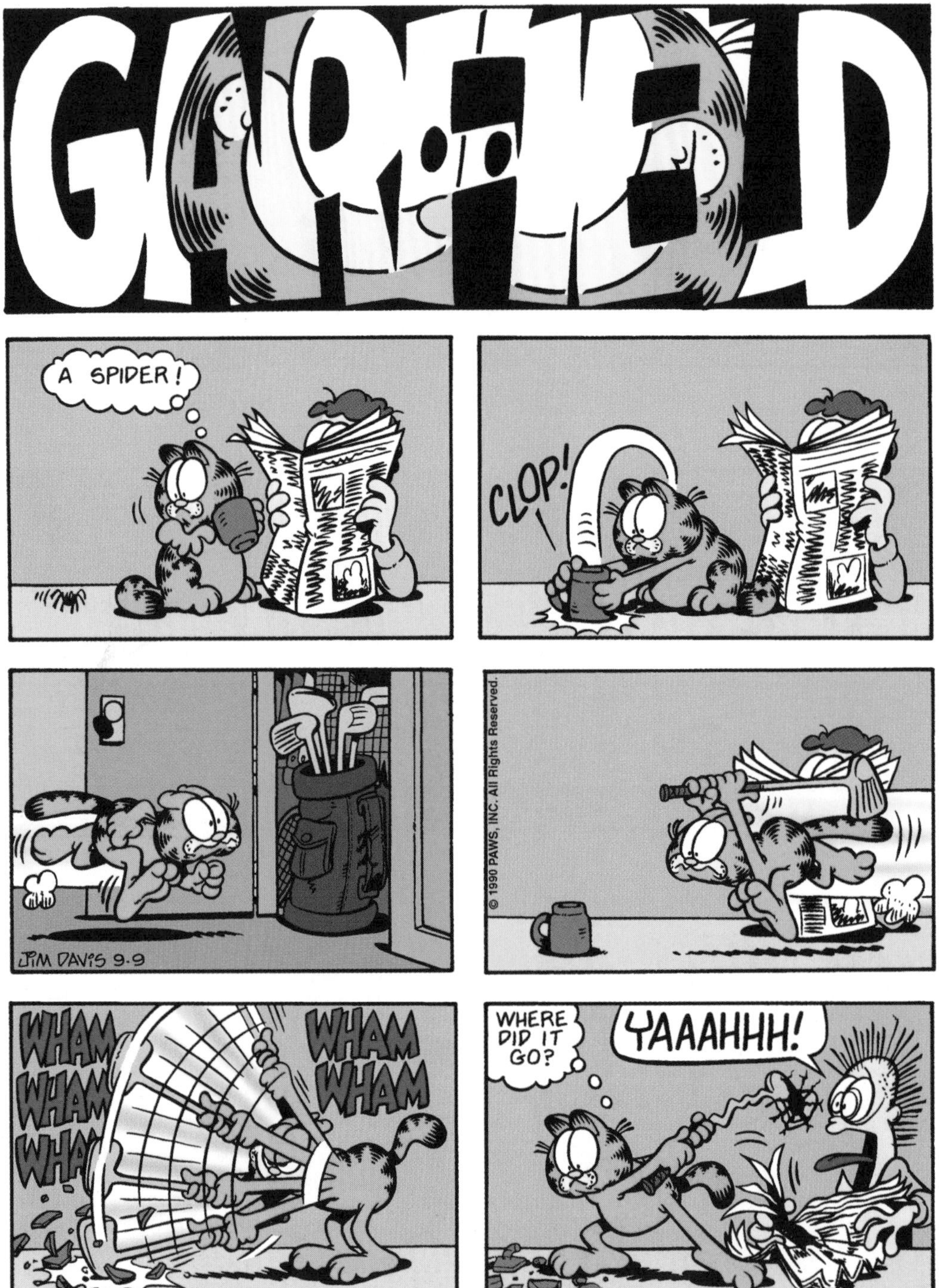
GARFIELD
A SPIDER!
CLOP!
JIM DAVIS 9-9
© 1990 PAWS, INC. All Rights Reserved.
WHAM
WHAM
WHAM
WHAM
WHAM
WHERE DID IT GO?
YAAAHHH!

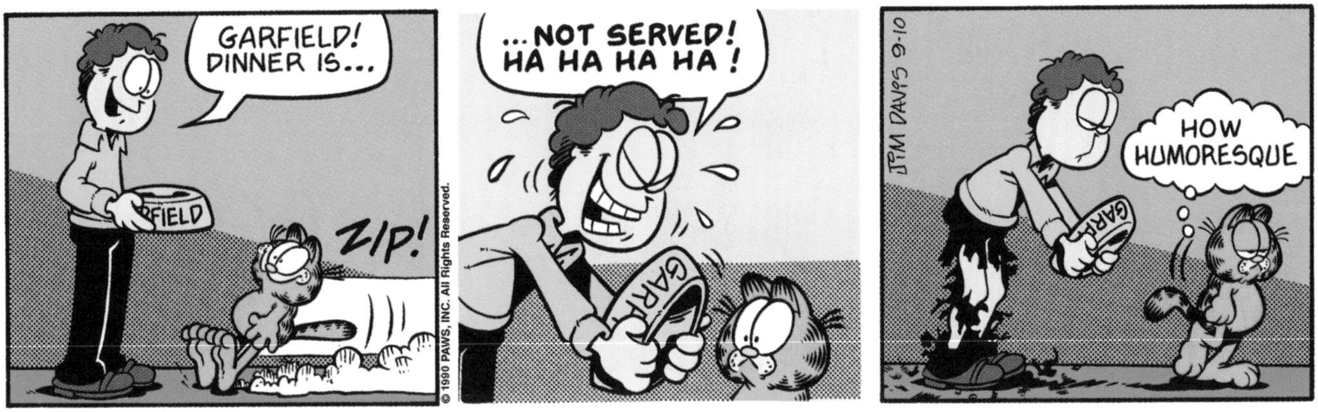
GARFIELD! DINNER IS...
FIELD
ZIP!
© 1990 PAWS, INC. All Rights Reserved.
...NOT SERVED! HA HA HA HA!
GARF
JIM DAVIS 9-10
HOW HUMORESQUE
GARF

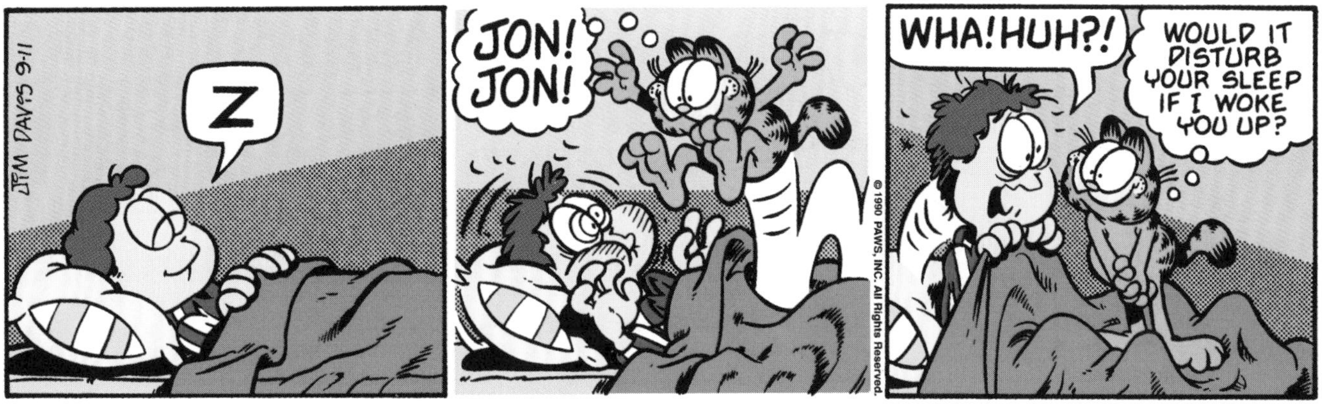
JIM DAVIS 9-11
Z
JON! JON!
© 1990 PAWS, INC. All Rights Reserved.
WHA! HUH?!
WOULD IT DISTURB YOUR SLEEP IF I WOKE YOU UP?

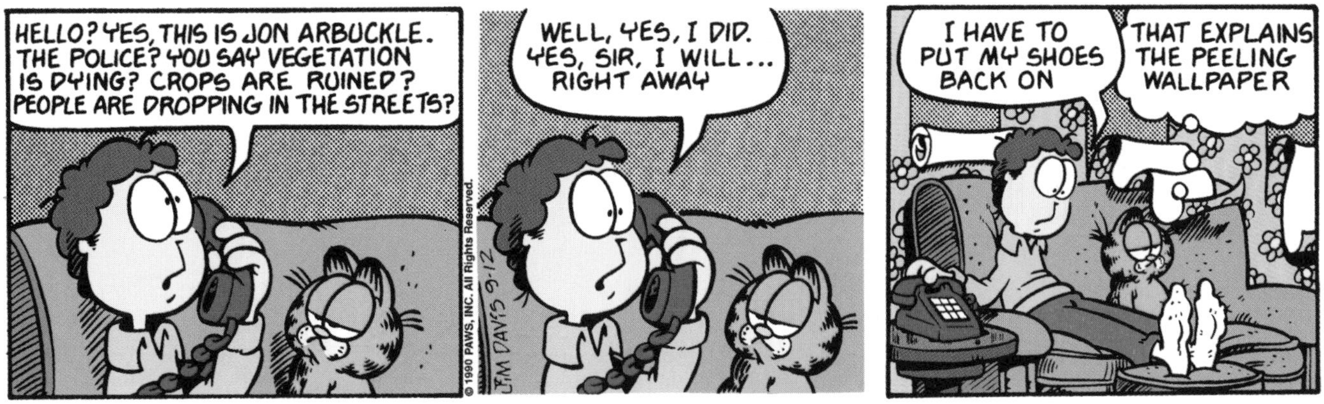
HELLO? YES, THIS IS JON ARBUCKLE. THE POLICE? YOU SAY VEGETATION IS DYING? CROPS ARE RUINED? PEOPLE ARE DROPPING IN THE STREETS?
© 1990 PAWS, INC. All Rights Reserved.
JIM DAVIS 9-12
WELL, YES, I DID. YES, SIR, I WILL... RIGHT AWAY
I HAVE TO PUT MY SHOES BACK ON
THAT EXPLAINS THE PEELING WALLPAPER

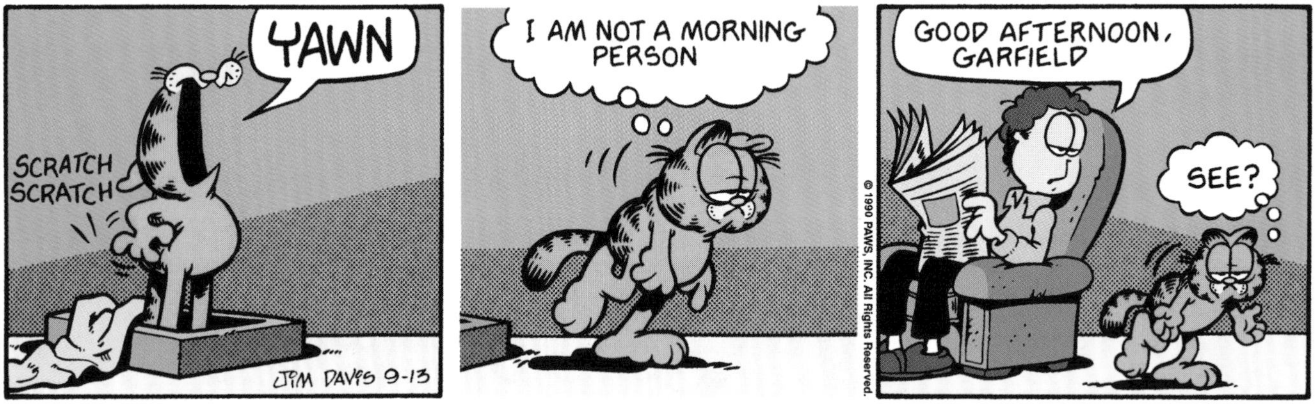
YAWN
SCRATCH SCRATCH
JIM DAVIS 9-13
I AM NOT A MORNING PERSON
GOOD AFTERNOON, GARFIELD
SEE?
© 1990 PAWS, INC. All Rights Reserved.

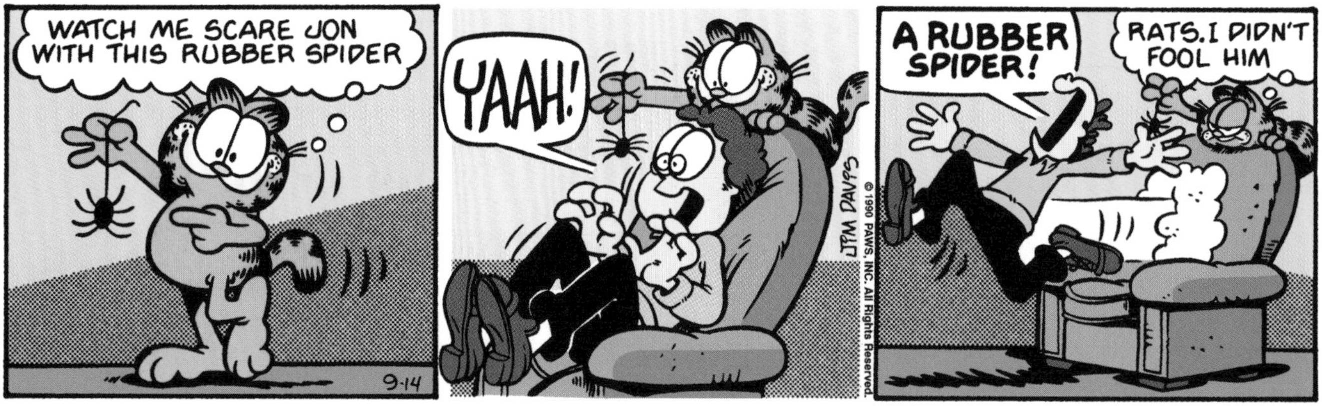
WATCH ME SCARE JON WITH THIS RUBBER SPIDER
9-14
YAAH!
JIM DAVIS
A RUBBER SPIDER!
RATS. I DIDN'T FOOL HIM
© 1990 PAWS, INC. All Rights Reserved.

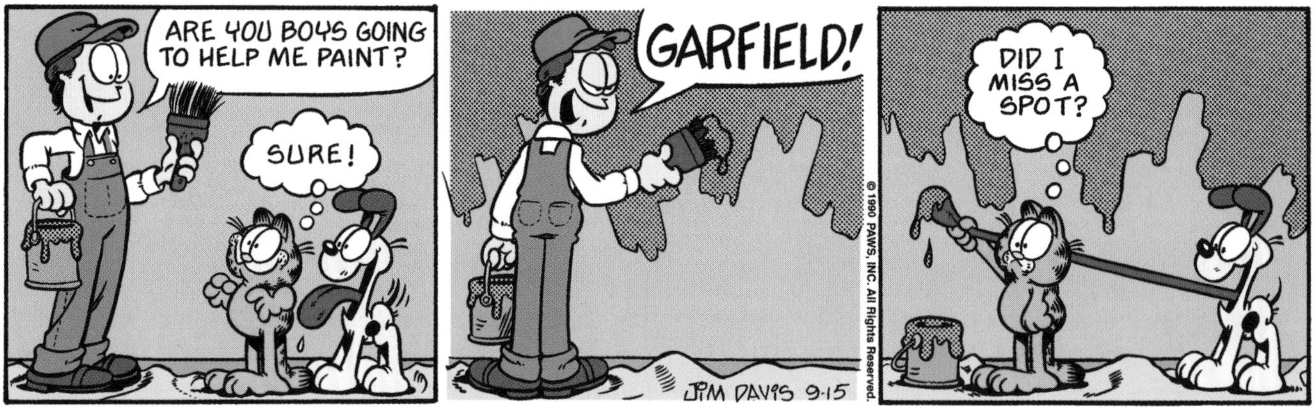
ARE YOU BOYS GOING TO HELP ME PAINT?
SURE!
GARFIELD!
JIM DAVIS 9-15
DID I MISS A SPOT?
© 1990 PAWS, INC. All Rights Reserved.

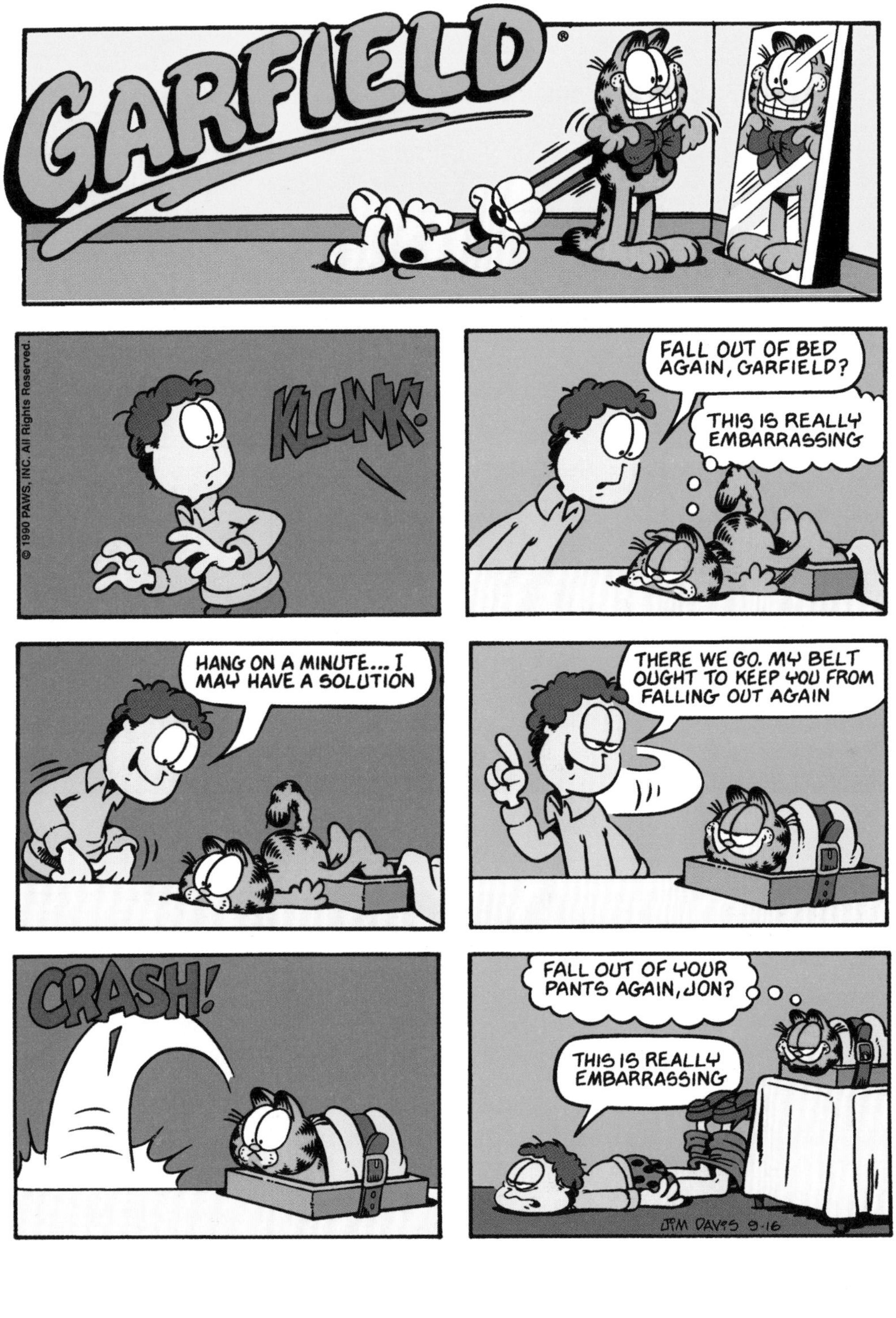
GARFIELD®
KLUNK!
FALL OUT OF BED AGAIN, GARFIELD?
THIS IS REALLY EMBARRASSING
HANG ON A MINUTE... I MAY HAVE A SOLUTION
THERE WE GO. MY BELT OUGHT TO KEEP YOU FROM FALLING OUT AGAIN
CRASH!
FALL OUT OF YOUR PANTS AGAIN, JON?
THIS IS REALLY EMBARRASSING
JIM DAVIS 9-16

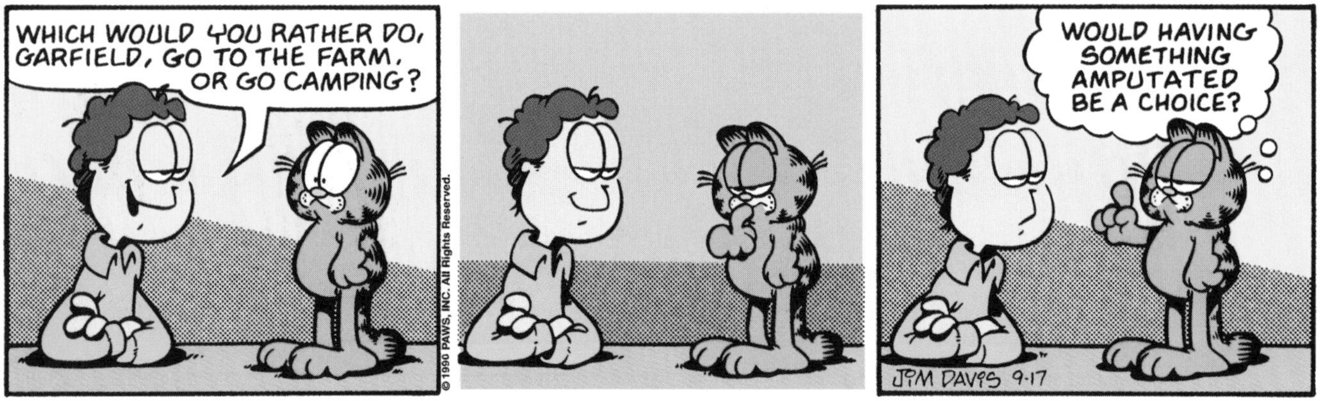
WHICH WOULD YOU RATHER DO, GARFIELD, GO TO THE FARM, OR GO CAMPING?
WOULD HAVING SOMETHING AMPUTATED BE A CHOICE?
© 1990 PAWS, INC. All Rights Reserved.
JIM DAVIS 9-17

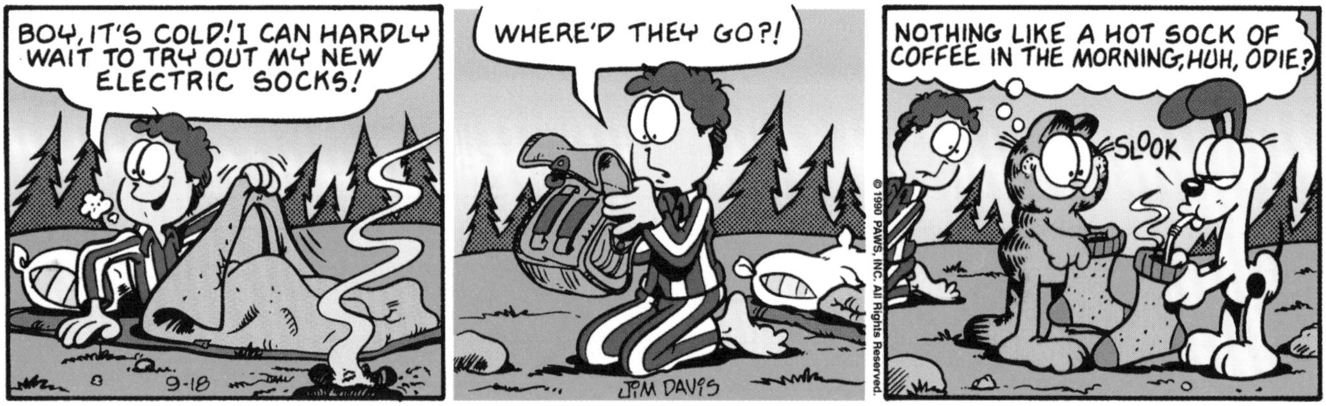
BOY, IT'S COLD! I CAN HARDLY WAIT TO TRY OUT MY NEW ELECTRIC SOCKS!
9-18
WHERE'D THEY GO?!
JIM DAVIS
NOTHING LIKE A HOT SOCK OF COFFEE IN THE MORNING, HUH, ODIE?
SLOOK
© 1990 PAWS, INC. All Rights Reserved.

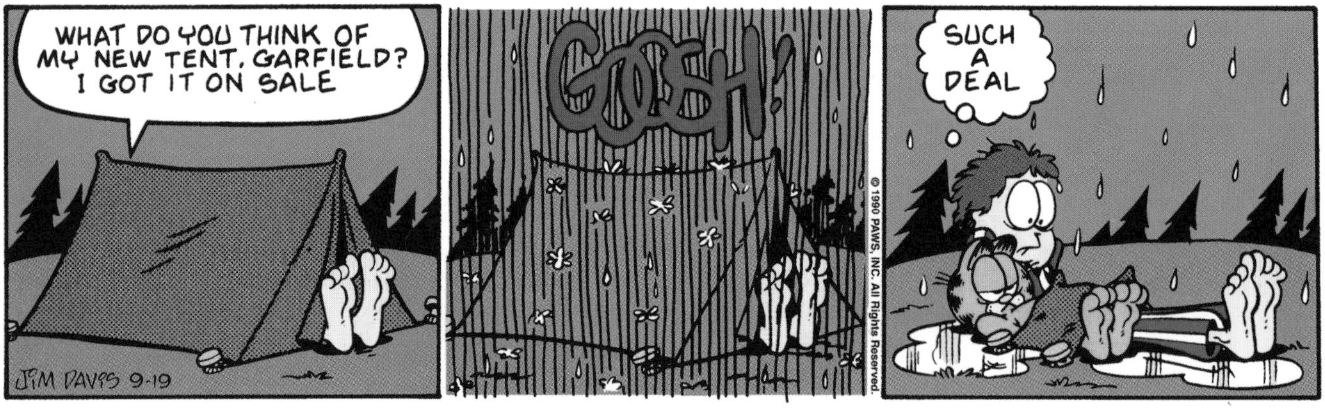
WHAT DO YOU THINK OF MY NEW TENT, GARFIELD? I GOT IT ON SALE
JIM DAVIS 9-19
GOOSH!
SUCH A DEAL
© 1990 PAWS, INC. All Rights Reserved.

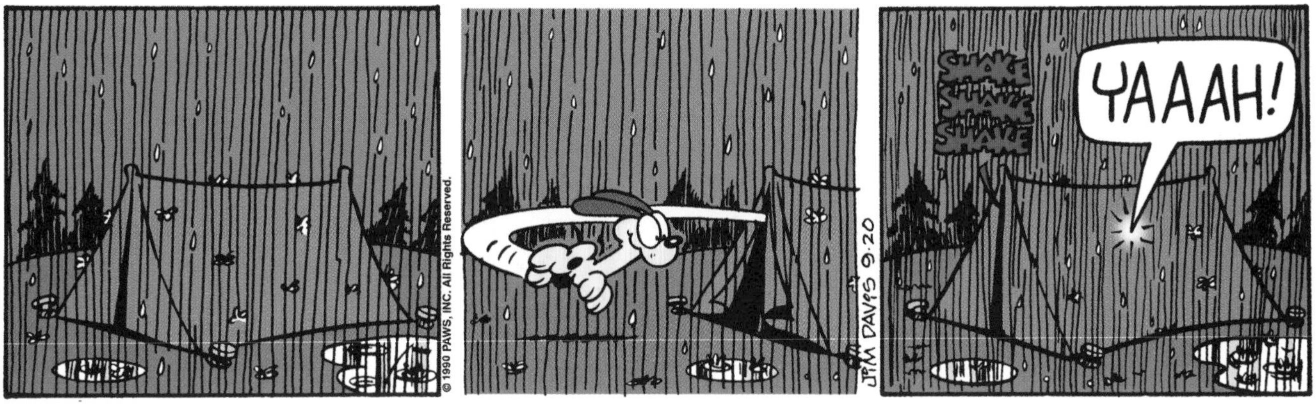
© 1990 PAWS, INC. All Rights Reserved.
JIM DAVIS 9-20
SHAKE SHAKE SHAKE
YAAAH!

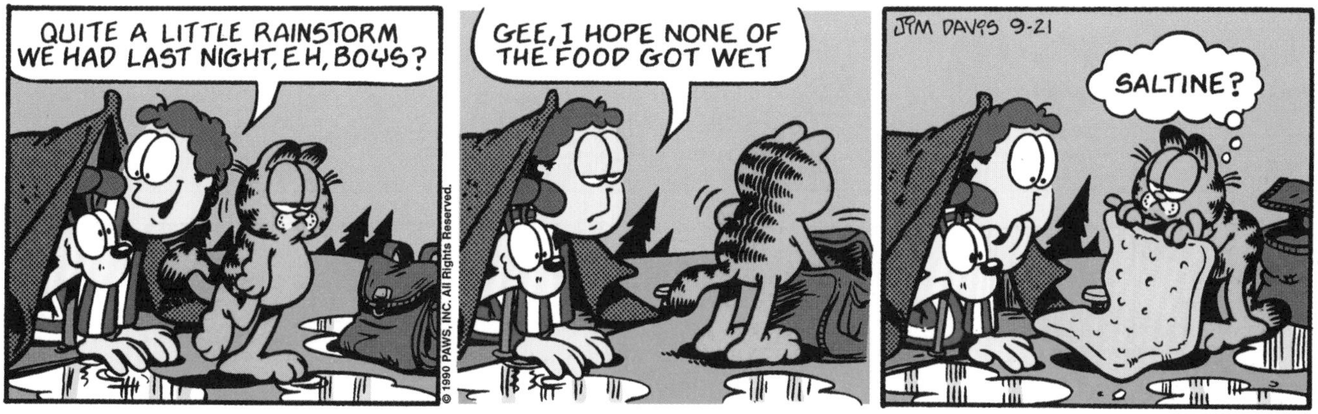
QUITE A LITTLE RAINSTORM WE HAD LAST NIGHT, EH, BOYS?
© 1990 PAWS, INC. All Rights Reserved.
GEE, I HOPE NONE OF THE FOOD GOT WET
JIM DAVIS 9-21
SALTINE?

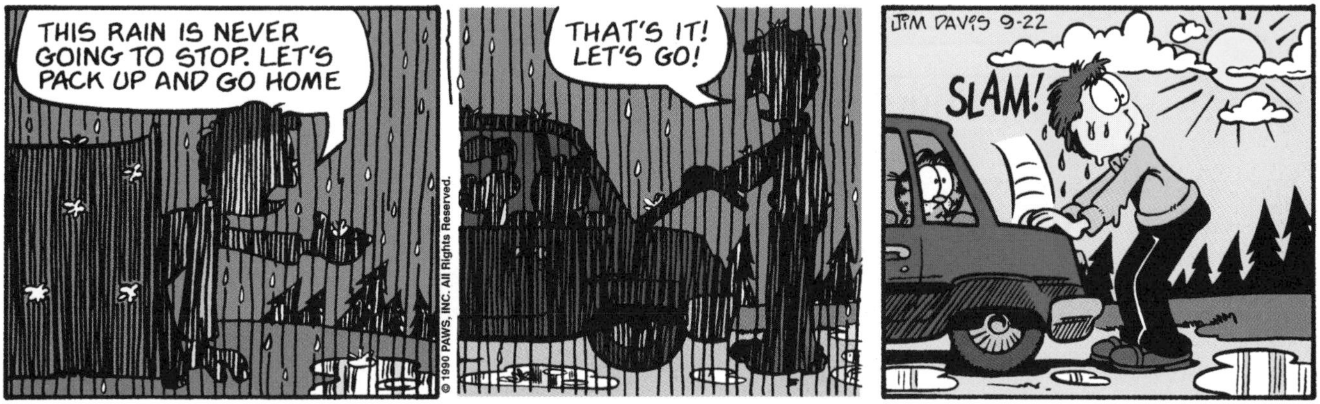
THIS RAIN IS NEVER GOING TO STOP. LET'S PACK UP AND GO HOME
© 1990 PAWS, INC. All Rights Reserved.
THAT'S IT! LET'S GO!
JIM DAVIS 9-22
SLAM!

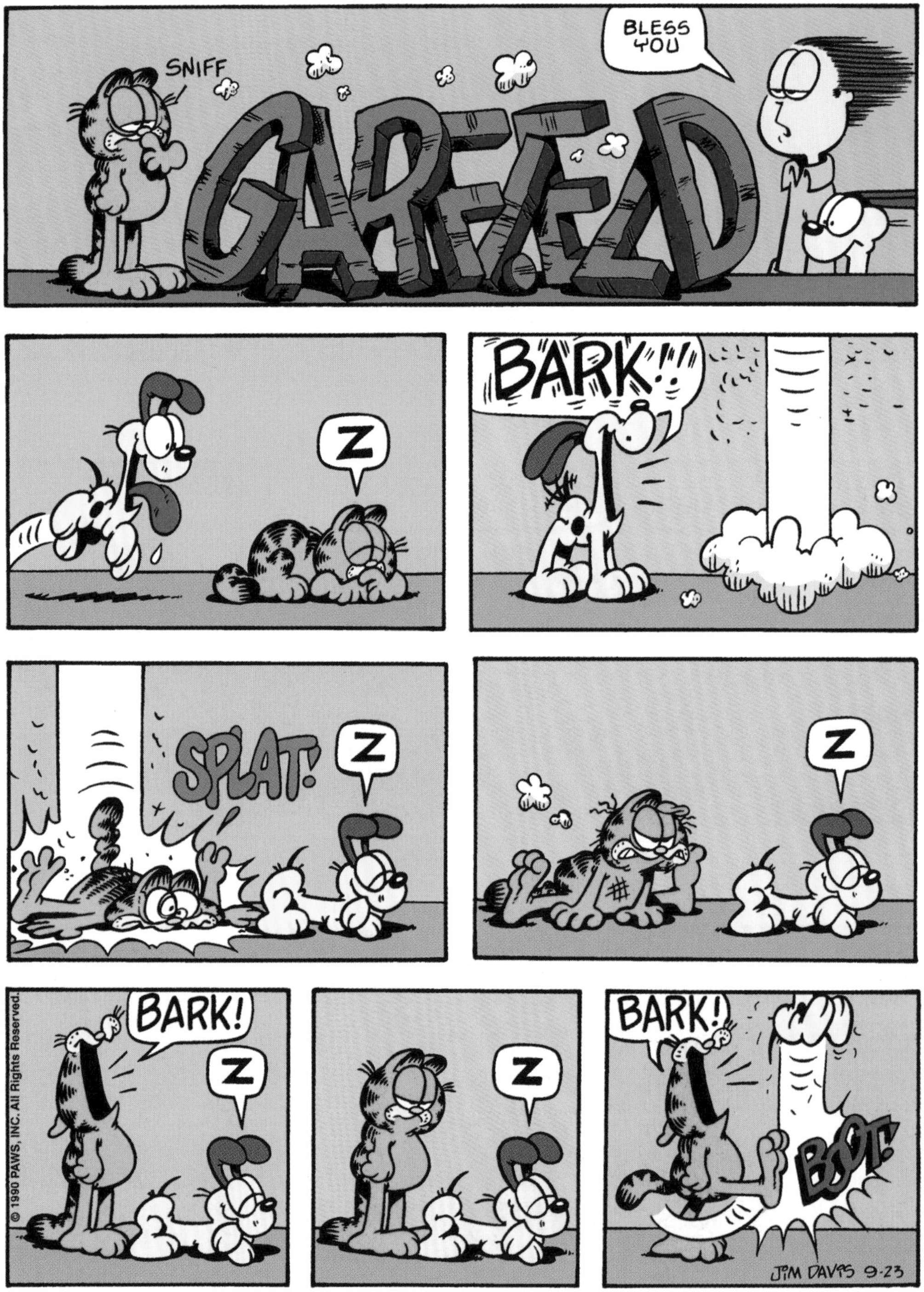
SNIFF
BLESS YOU
GARFIELD
BARK!!
Z
SPLAT!
Z
Z
BARK!
Z
Z
BARK!
BOOT!
JIM DAVIS 9-23
© 1990 PAWS, INC. All Rights Reserved.

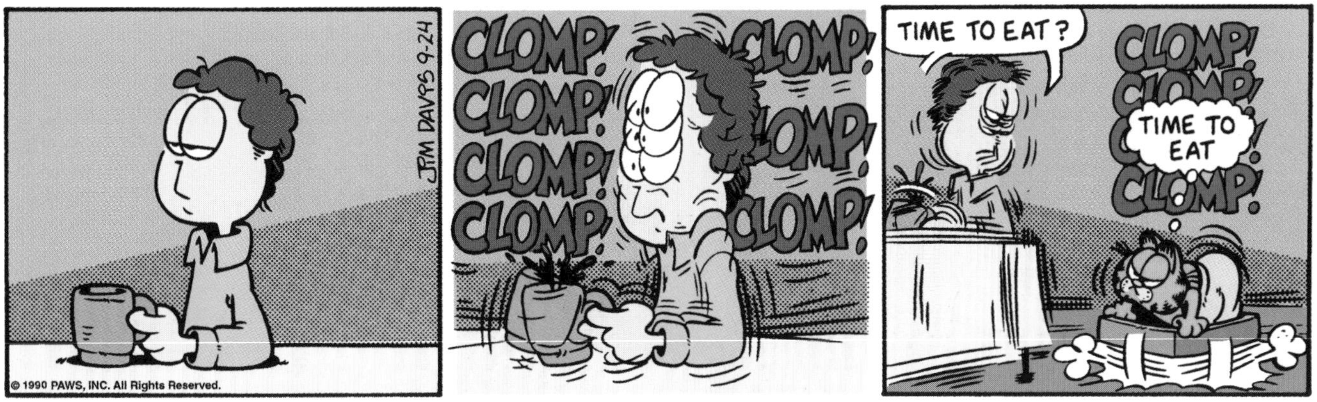
JPM DAVPS 9-24
© 1990 PAWS, INC. All Rights Reserved.
CLOMP! CLOMP! CLOMP! CLOMP!
CLOMP! CLOMP! CLOMP!
TIME TO EAT?
CLOMP! CLOMP! CLOMP!
TIME TO EAT

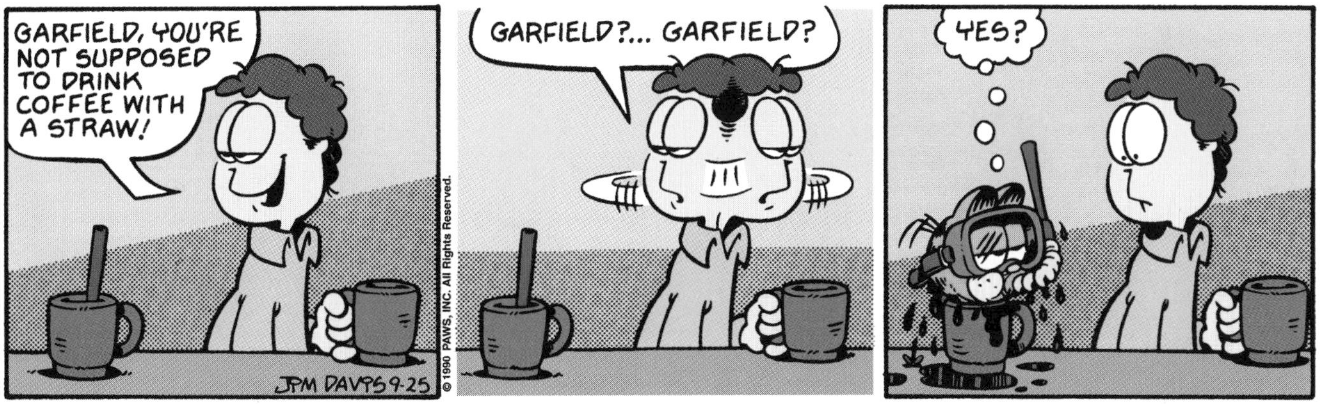
GARFIELD, YOU'RE NOT SUPPOSED TO DRINK COFFEE WITH A STRAW!
JPM DAVPS 9-25
© 1990 PAWS, INC. All Rights Reserved.
GARFIELD?... GARFIELD?
YES?

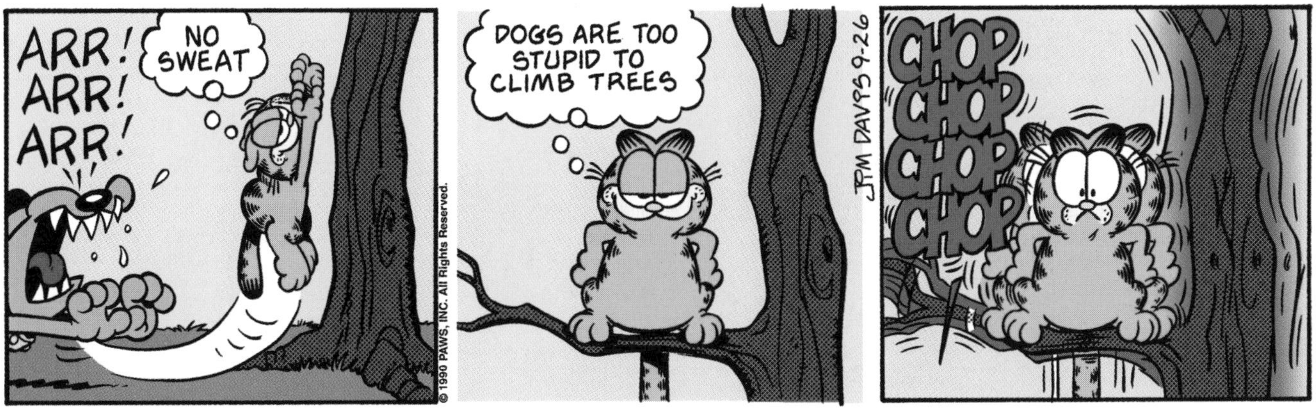
ARR! ARR! ARR!
NO SWEAT
© 1990 PAWS, INC. All Rights Reserved.
DOGS ARE TOO STUPID TO CLIMB TREES
JPM DAVPS 9-26
CHOP CHOP CHOP CHOP

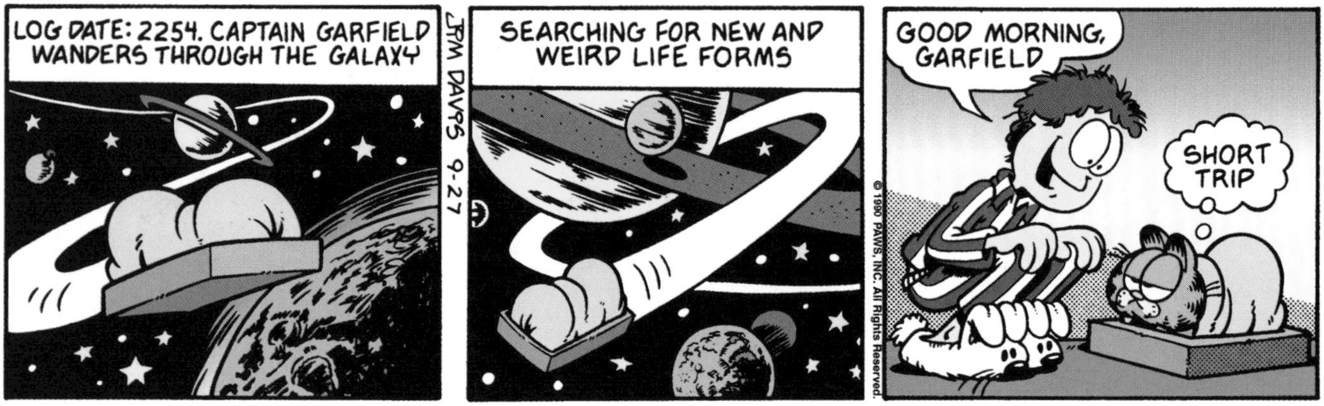
LOG DATE: 2254. CAPTAIN GARFIELD WANDERS THROUGH THE GALAXY
JPM DAVPS 9-27
SEARCHING FOR NEW AND WEIRD LIFE FORMS
GOOD MORNING, GARFIELD
SHORT TRIP
© 1990 PAWS, INC. All Rights Reserved.

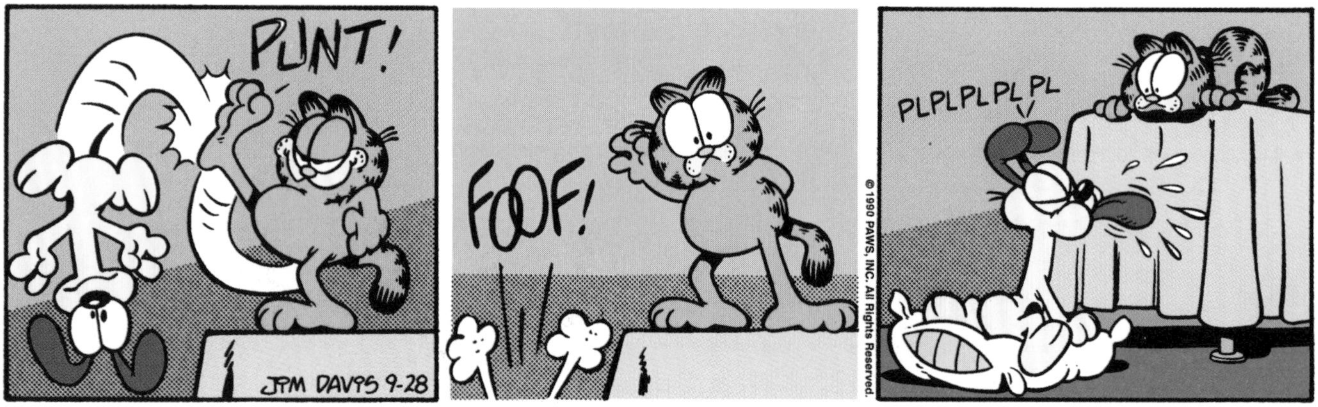
PUNT!
JPM DAVPS 9-28
FOOF!
PLPLPLPLPL
© 1990 PAWS, INC. All Rights Reserved.

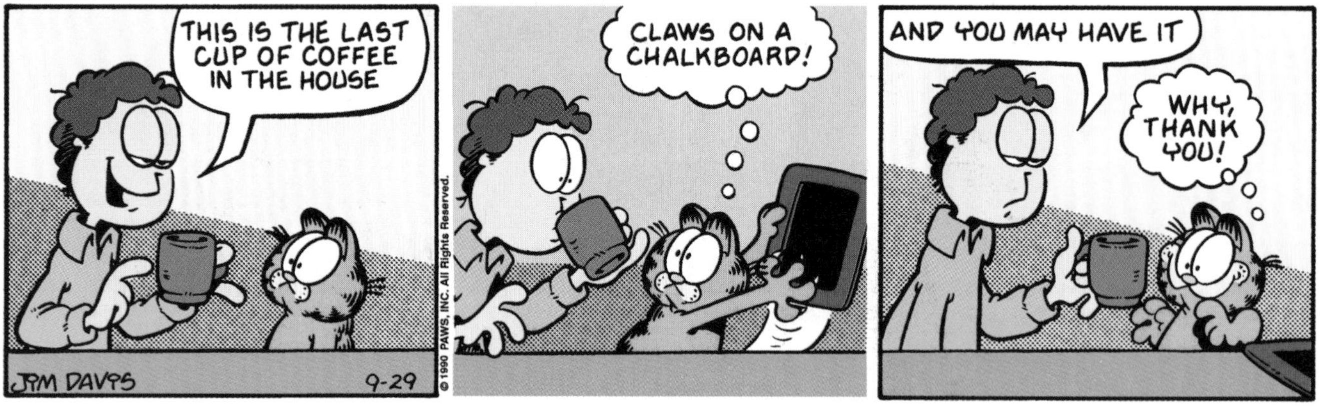
THIS IS THE LAST CUP OF COFFEE IN THE HOUSE
JPM DAVPS 9-29
© 1990 PAWS, INC. All Rights Reserved.
CLAWS ON A CHALKBOARD!
AND YOU MAY HAVE IT
WHY, THANK YOU!

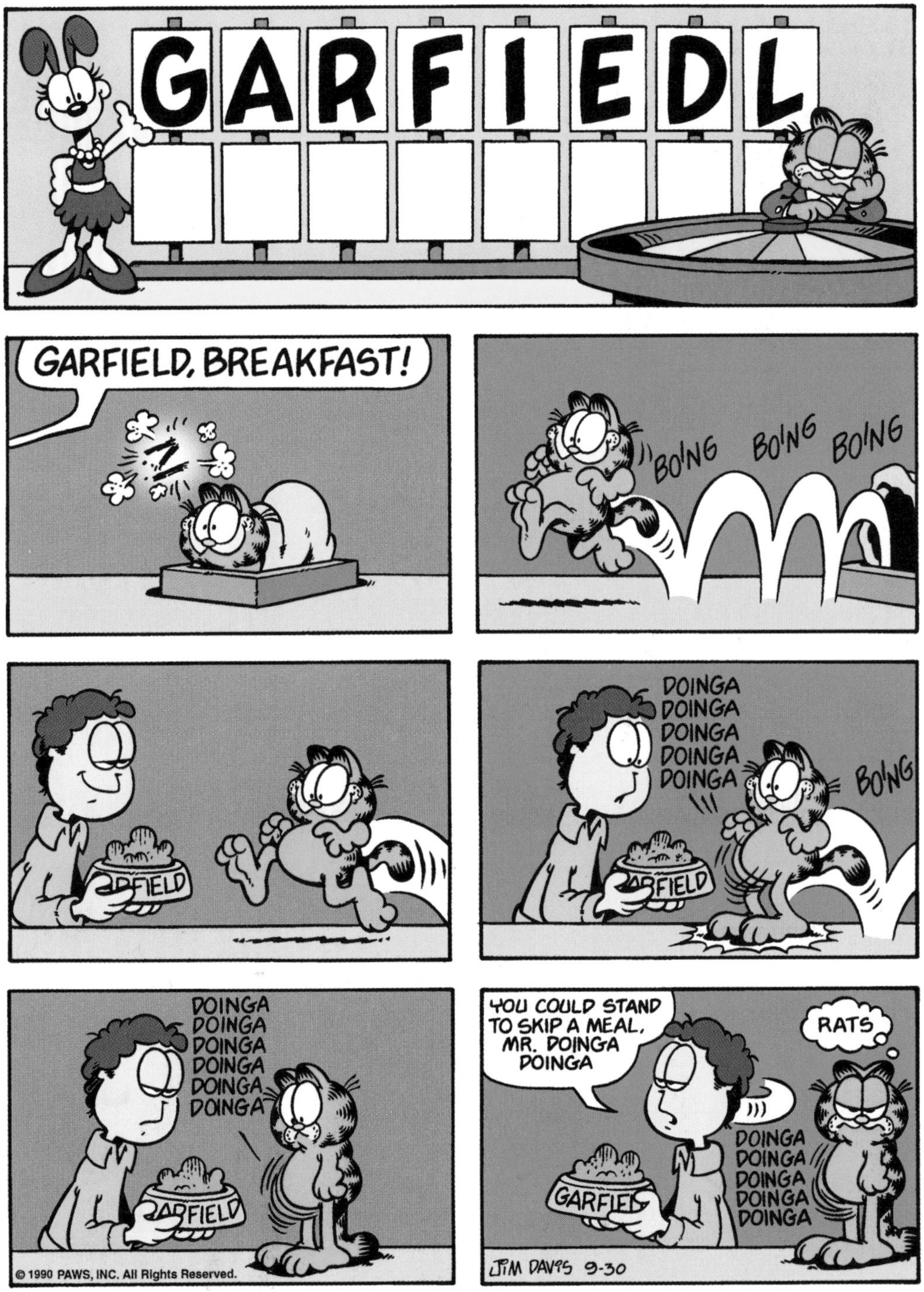
GARFIEDL
GARFIELD, BREAKFAST!
Z
BOING BOING BOING
GARFIELD
DOINGA DOINGA DOINGA DOINGA DOINGA
BOING
GARFIELD
DOINGA DOINGA DOINGA DOINGA DOINGA DOINGA
GARFIELD
YOU COULD STAND TO SKIP A MEAL, MR. DOINGA DOINGA
RATS
DOINGA DOINGA DOINGA DOINGA DOINGA
GARFIEL
JIM DAVIS 9-30

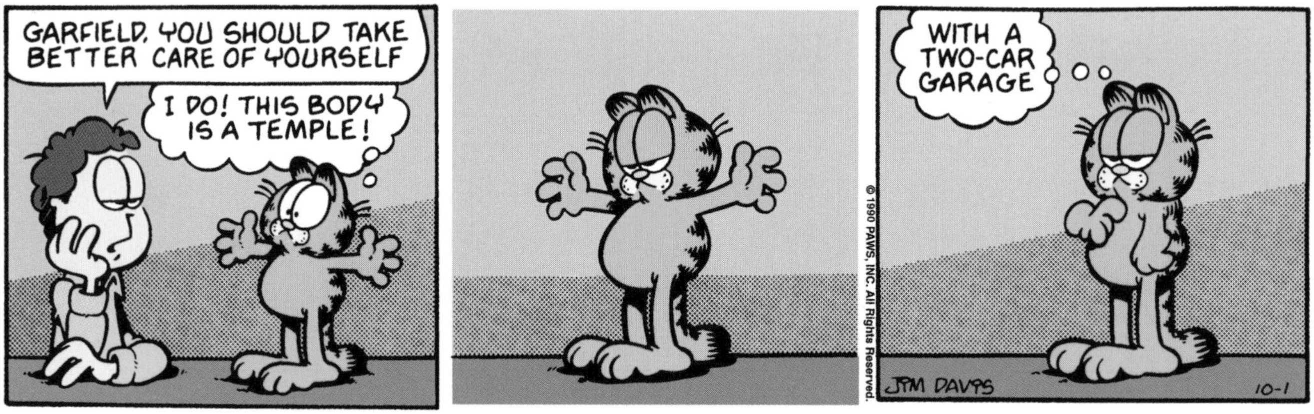
GARFIELD, YOU SHOULD TAKE BETTER CARE OF YOURSELF
I DO! THIS BODY IS A TEMPLE!
WITH A TWO-CAR GARAGE
© 1990 PAWS, INC. All Rights Reserved.
JIM DAVIS
10-1

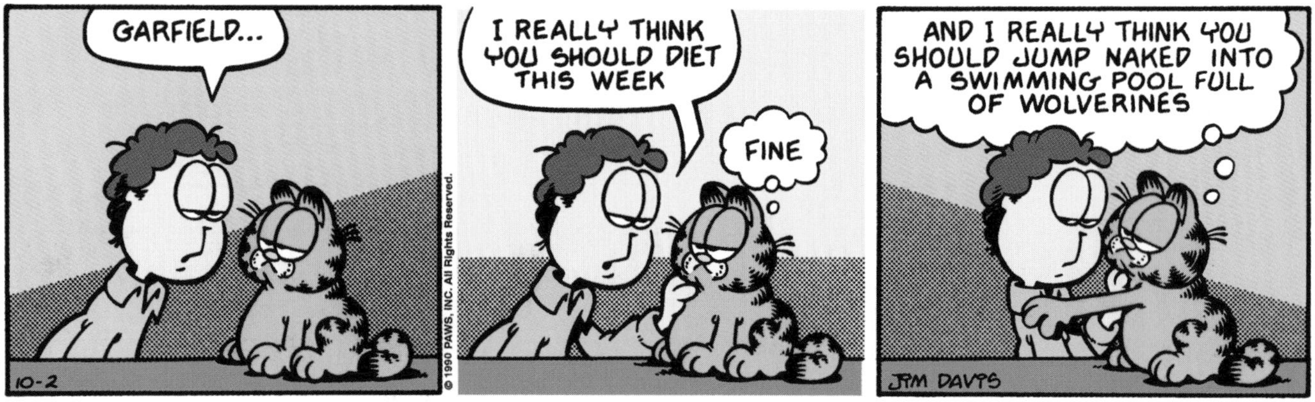
GARFIELD...
10-2
© 1990 PAWS, INC. All Rights Reserved.
I REALLY THINK YOU SHOULD DIET THIS WEEK
FINE
AND I REALLY THINK YOU SHOULD JUMP NAKED INTO A SWIMMING POOL FULL OF WOLVERINES
JIM DAVIS

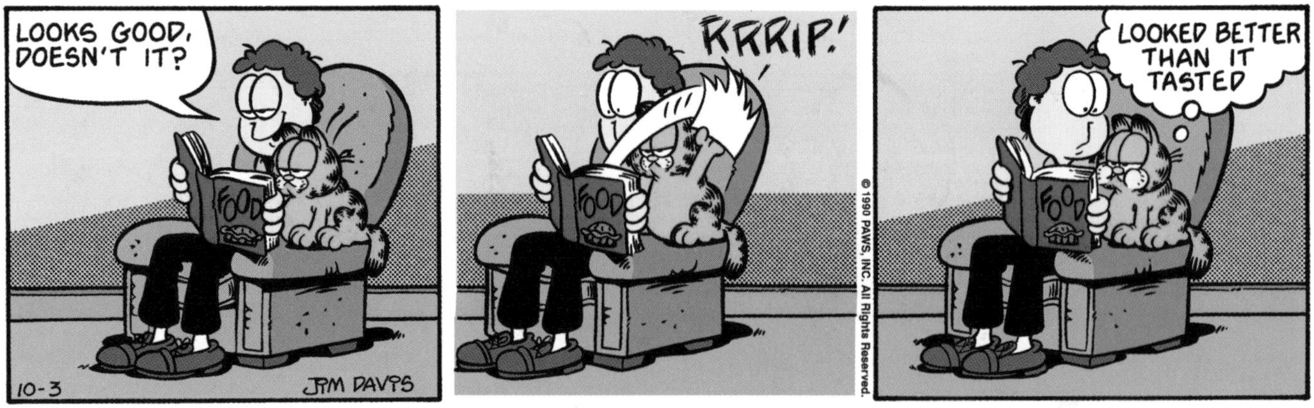
LOOKS GOOD, DOESN'T IT?
FOOD
10-3
JIM DAVIS
KRRRIP!
© 1990 PAWS, INC. All Rights Reserved.
LOOKED BETTER THAN IT TASTED

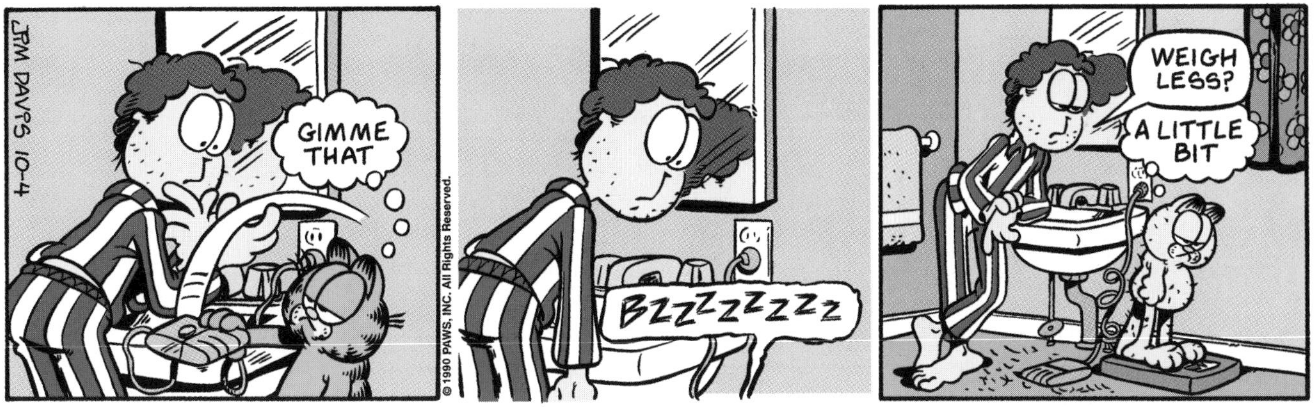
JIM DAVIS 10-4
GIMME THAT
© 1990 PAWS, INC. All Rights Reserved.
BZZZZZZZZZ
WEIGH LESS?
A LITTLE BIT

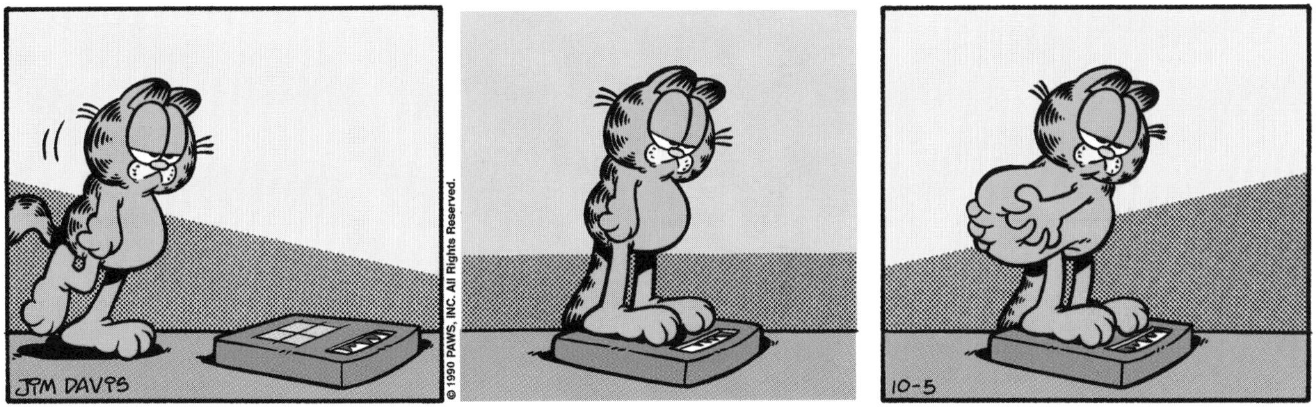
JIM DAVIS
© 1990 PAWS, INC. All Rights Reserved.
10-5

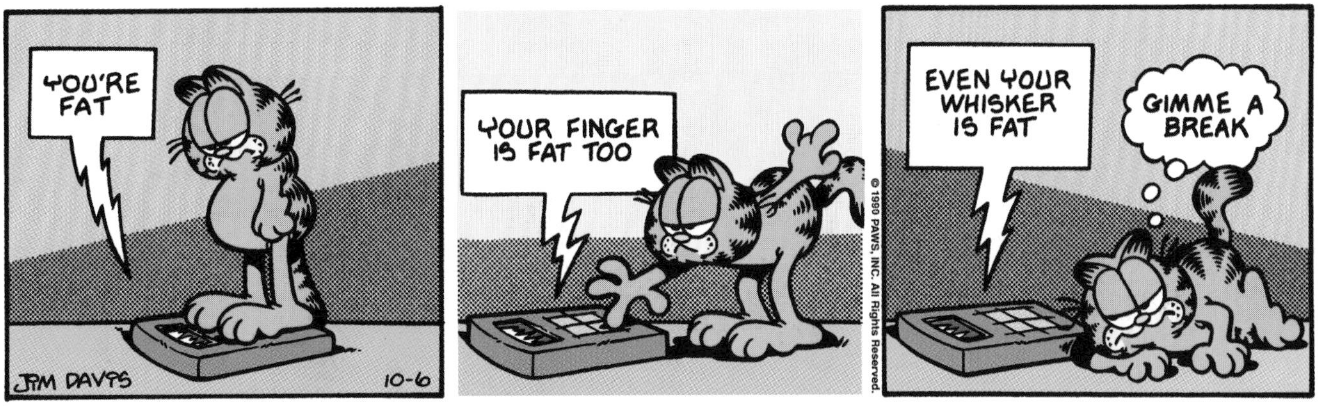
YOU'RE FAT
JIM DAVIS
10-6
YOUR FINGER IS FAT TOO
© 1990 PAWS, INC. All Rights Reserved.
EVEN YOUR WHISKER IS FAT
GIMME A BREAK

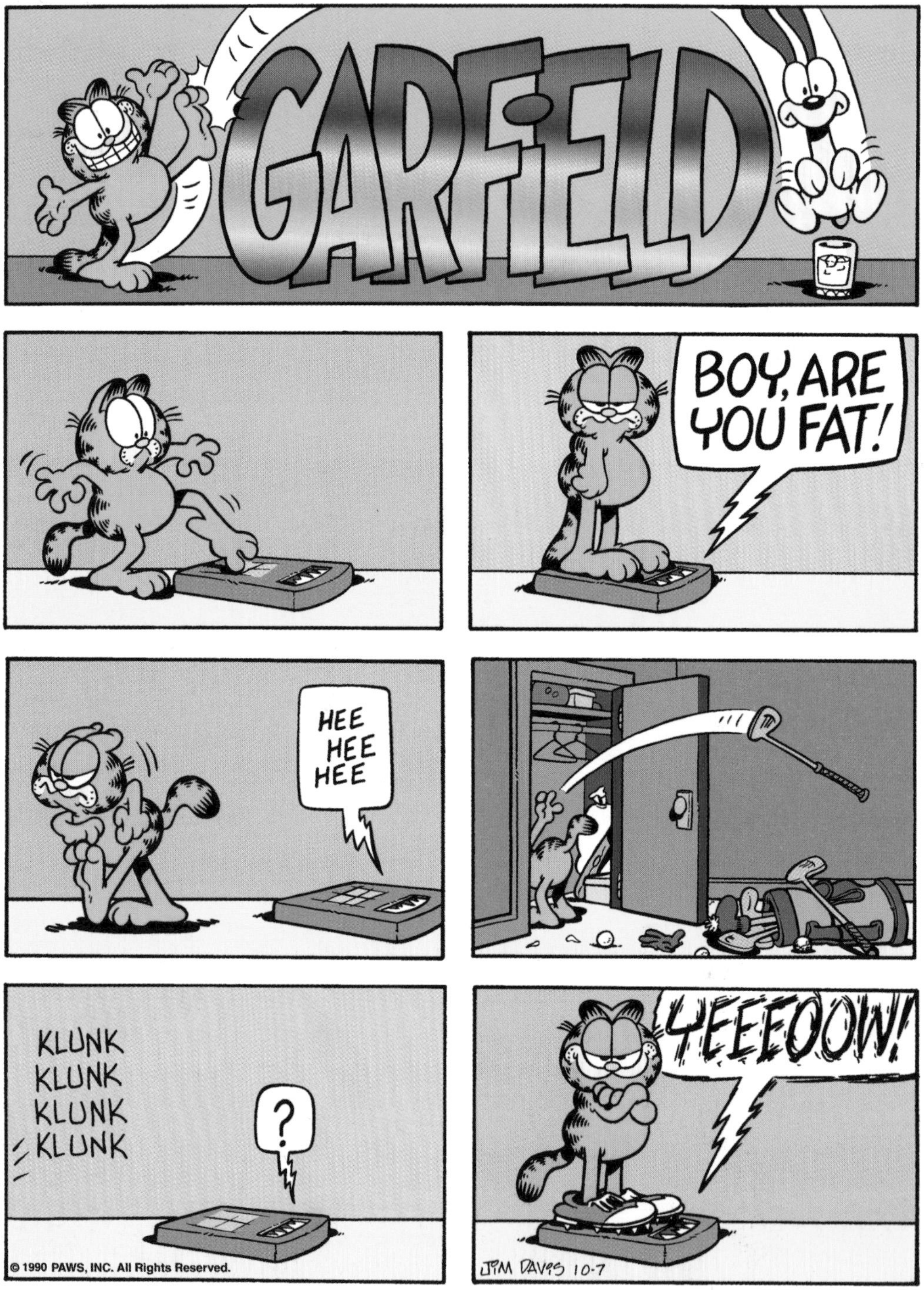
GARFIELD
BOY, ARE YOU FAT!
HEE HEE HEE
KLUNK KLUNK KLUNK KLUNK
?
YEEEOOW!
© 1990 PAWS, INC. All Rights Reserved.
JIM DAVIS 10-7

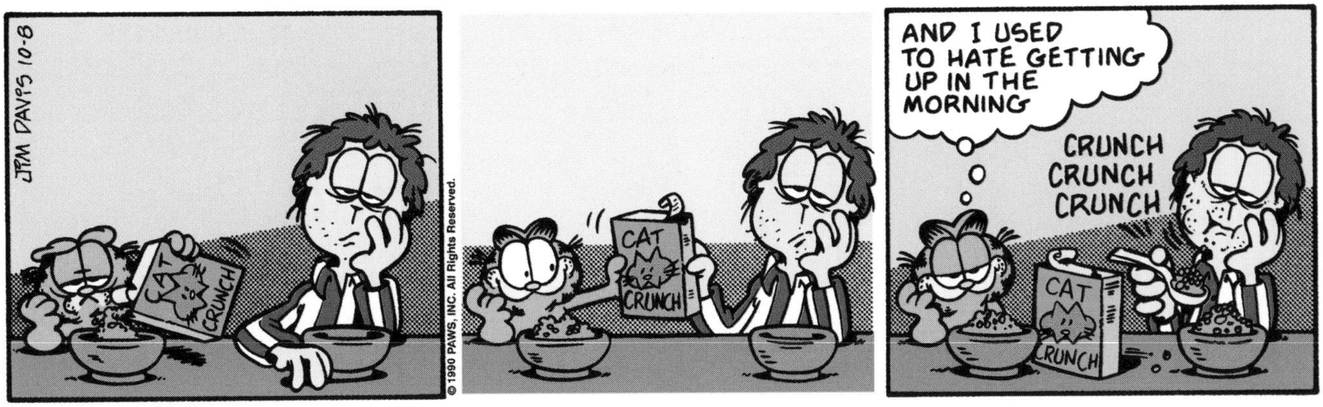
JIM DAVIS 10-8
CAT CRUNCH
© 1990 PAWS, INC. All Rights Reserved.
CAT CRUNCH
AND I USED TO HATE GETTING UP IN THE MORNING
CRUNCH CRUNCH CRUNCH
CAT CRUNCH

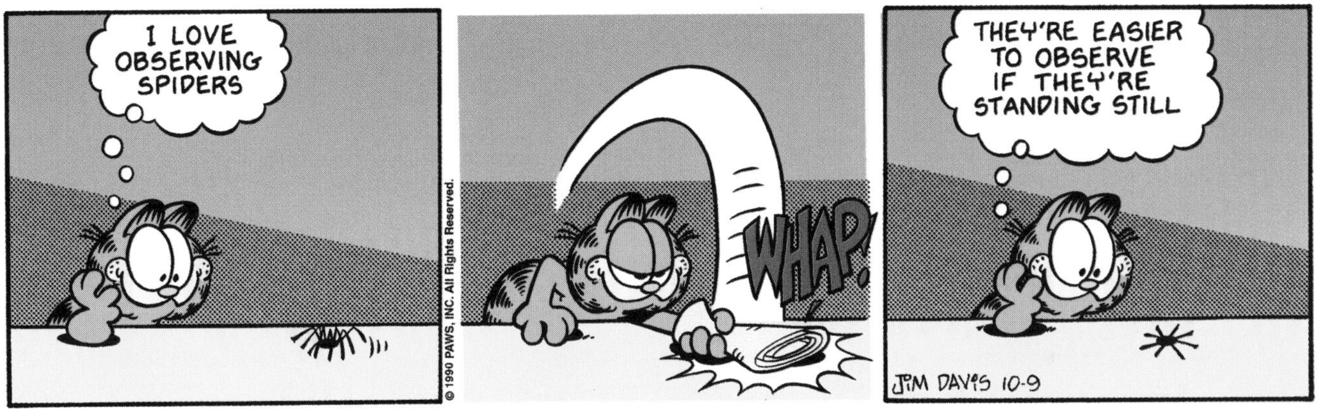
I LOVE OBSERVING SPIDERS
© 1990 PAWS, INC. All Rights Reserved.
WHAP!
THEY'RE EASIER TO OBSERVE IF THEY'RE STANDING STILL
JIM DAVIS 10-9

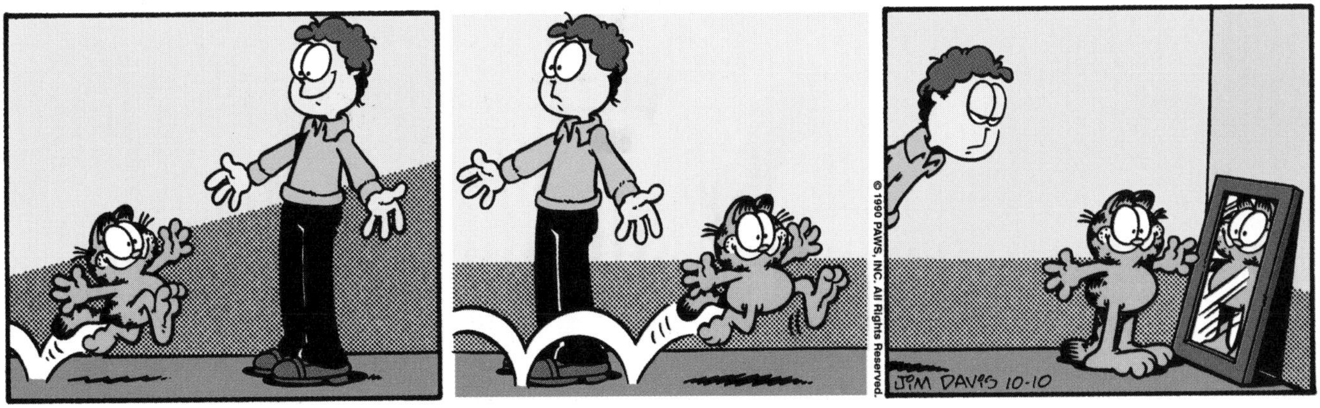
© 1990 PAWS, INC. All Rights Reserved.
JIM DAVIS 10-10

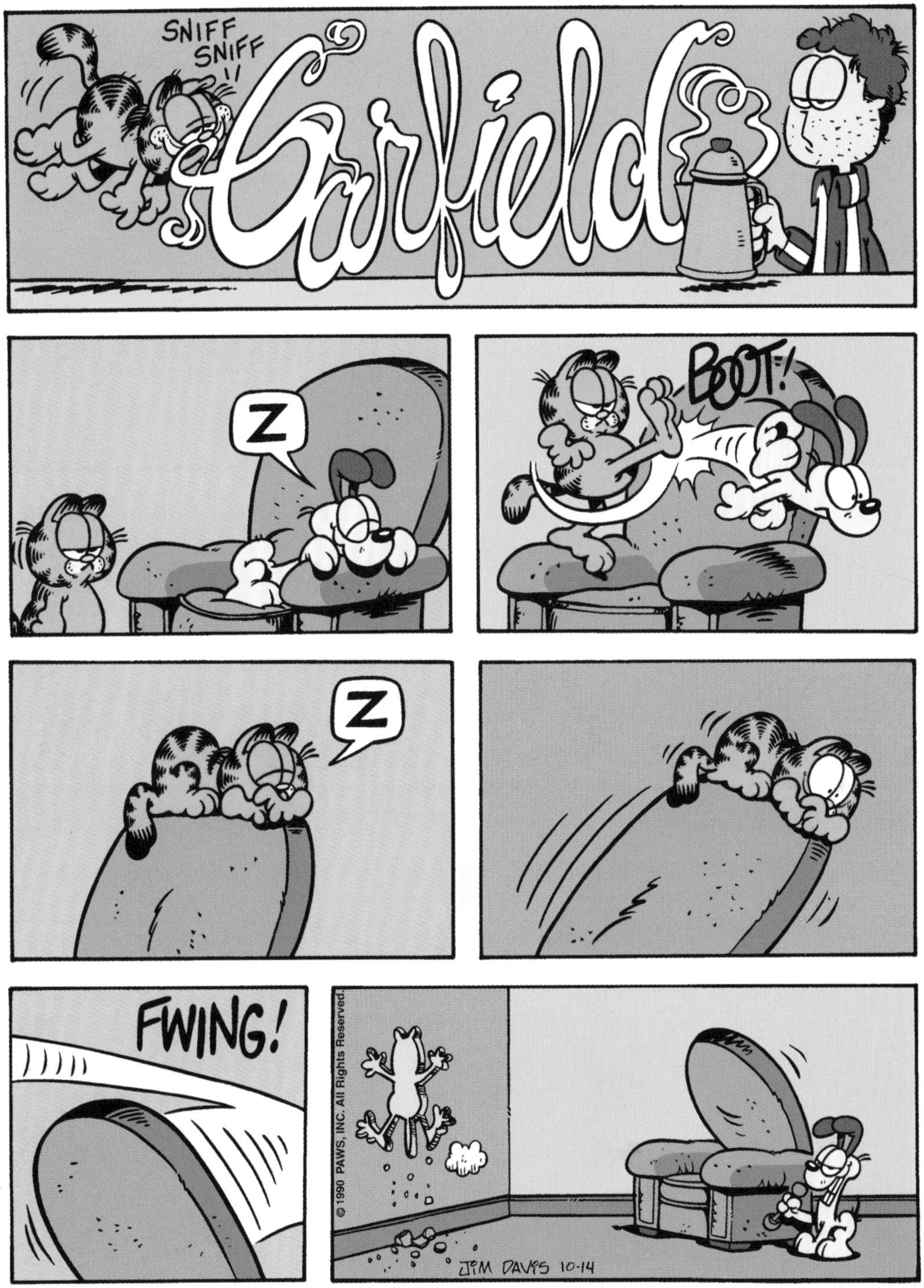
SNIFF SNIFF
Garfield
Z
BOOT!
Z
FWING!
© 1990 PAWS, INC. All Rights Reserved.
JIM DAVIS 10-14

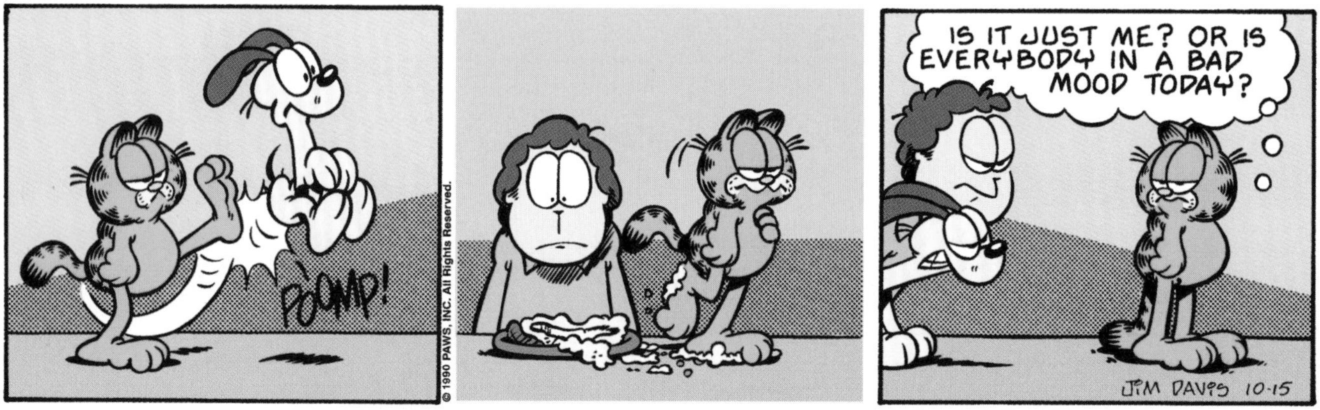
POOMP!
© 1990 PAWS, INC. All Rights Reserved.
IS IT JUST ME? OR IS EVERYBODY IN A BAD MOOD TODAY?
JIM DAVIS 10-15

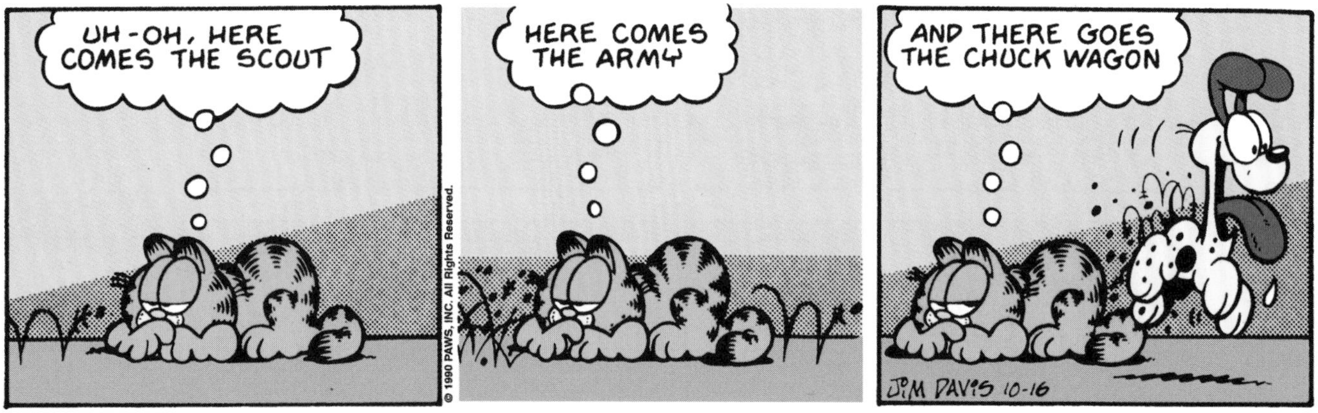
UH-OH, HERE COMES THE SCOUT
© 1990 PAWS, INC. All Rights Reserved.
HERE COMES THE ARMY
AND THERE GOES THE CHUCK WAGON
JIM DAVIS 10-16

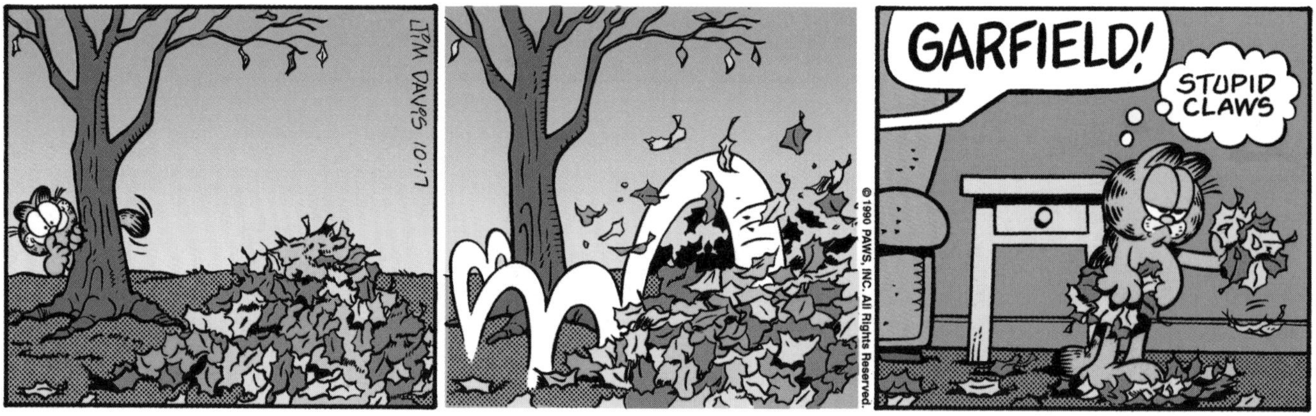
JIM DAVIS 10-17
© 1990 PAWS, INC. All Rights Reserved.
GARFIELD!
STUPID CLAWS

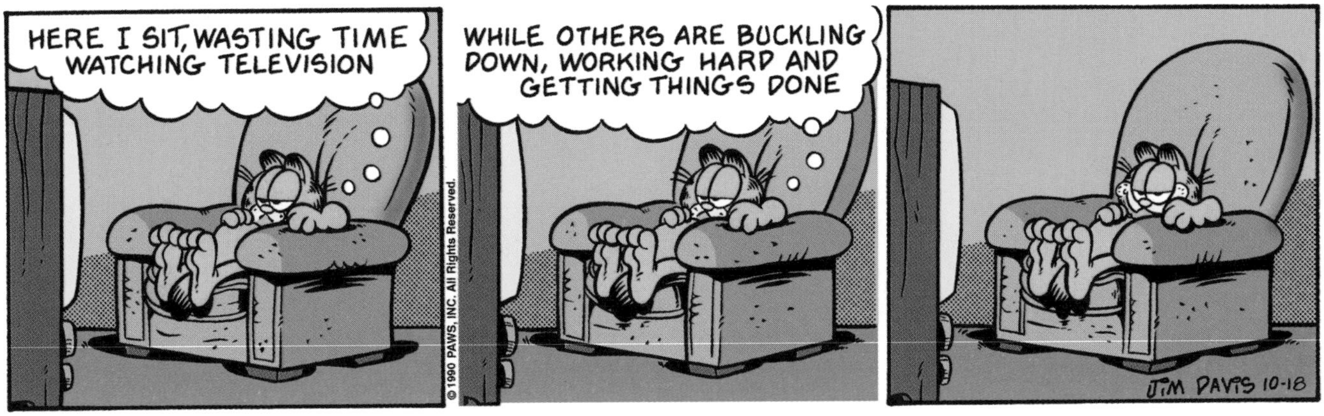
HERE I SIT, WASTING TIME WATCHING TELEVISION
WHILE OTHERS ARE BUCKLING DOWN, WORKING HARD AND GETTING THINGS DONE
© 1990 PAWS, INC. All Rights Reserved.
JIM DAVIS 10-18

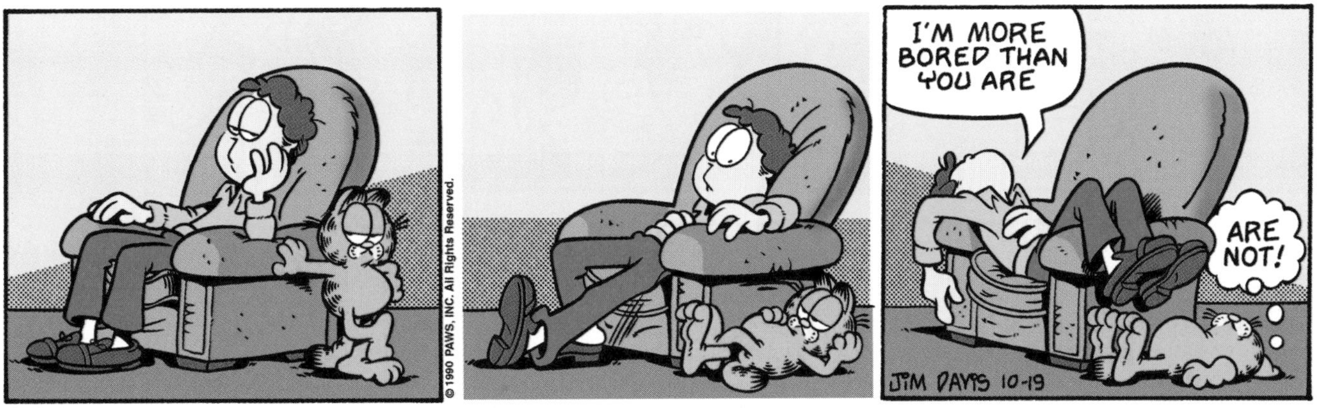
© 1990 PAWS, INC. All Rights Reserved.
I'M MORE BORED THAN YOU ARE
ARE NOT!
JIM DAVIS 10-19

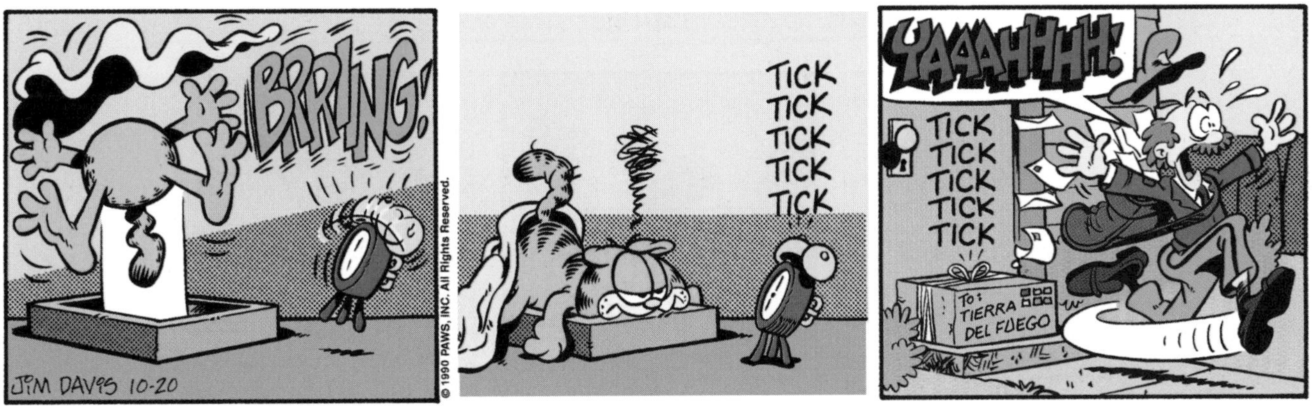
BRRING!
JIM DAVIS 10-20
© 1990 PAWS, INC. All Rights Reserved.
TICK TICK TICK TICK TICK
YAAAHHHH!
TICK TICK TICK TICK TICK
TO: TIERRA DEL FUEGO

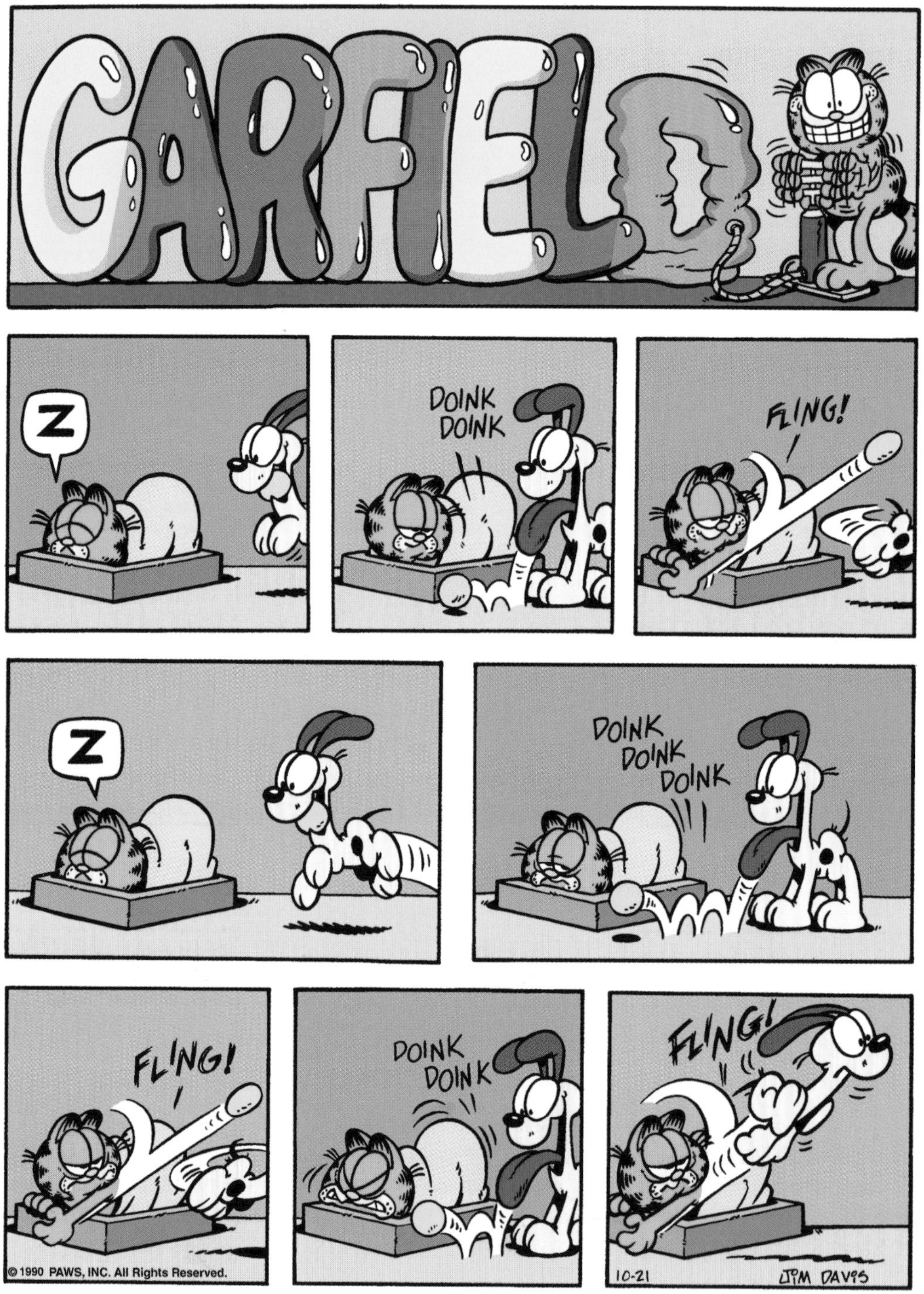
GARFIELD
Z
DOINK DOINK
FLING!
Z
DOINK DOINK DOINK
FLING!
DOINK DOINK
FLING!
10-21
JIM DAVIS

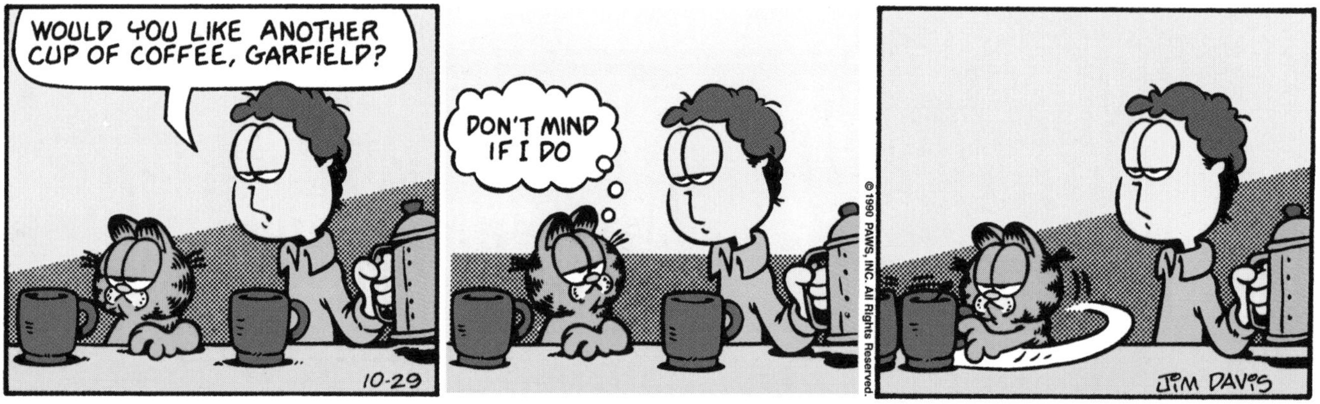
WOULD YOU LIKE ANOTHER CUP OF COFFEE, GARFIELD?
10-29
DON'T MIND IF I DO
© 1990 PAWS, INC. All Rights Reserved.
JIM DAVIS

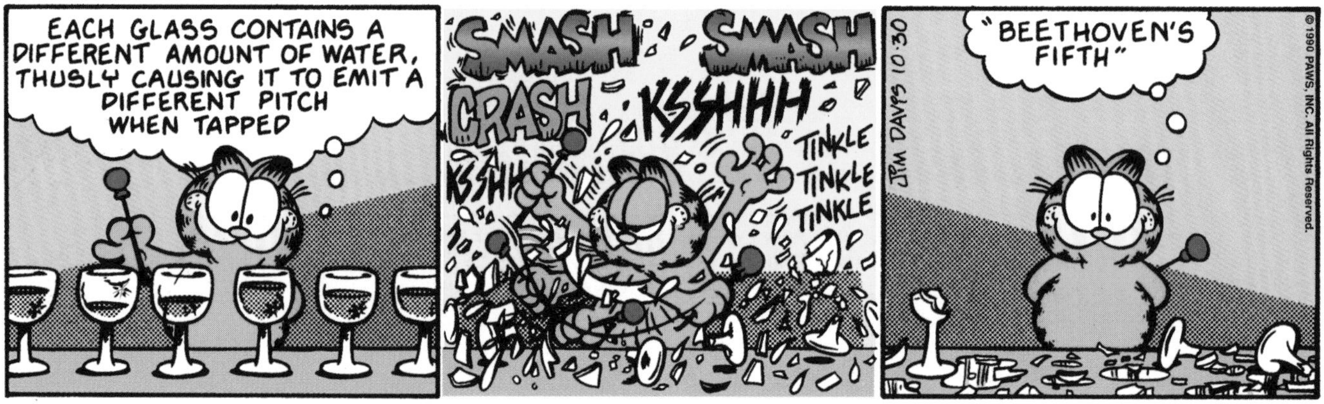
EACH GLASS CONTAINS A DIFFERENT AMOUNT OF WATER, THUSLY CAUSING IT TO EMIT A DIFFERENT PITCH WHEN TAPPED
SMASH SMASH
CRASH
KSSHHH
KSSHH
TINKLE
TINKLE
TINKLE
JIM DAVIS 10-30
"BEETHOVEN'S FIFTH"
© 1990 PAWS, INC. All Rights Reserved.

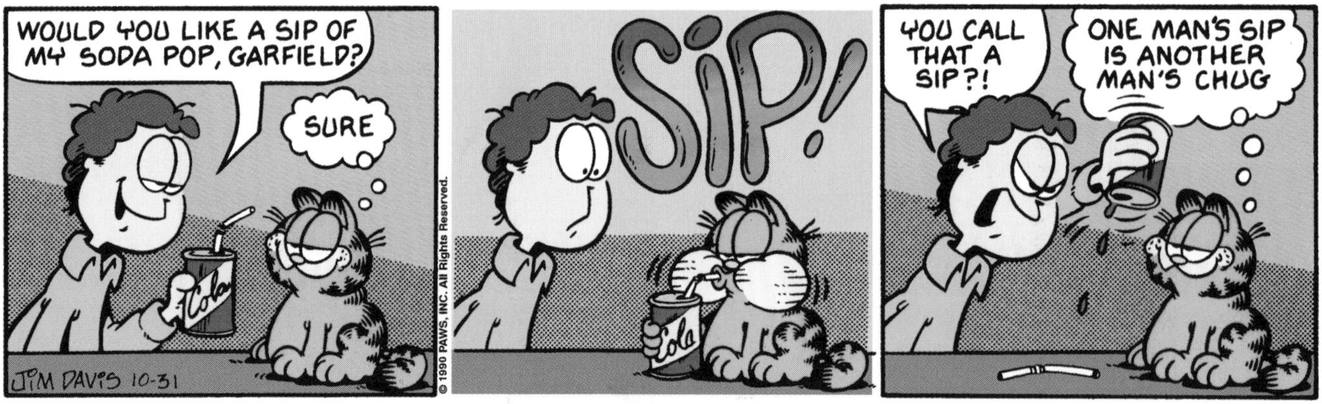
WOULD YOU LIKE A SIP OF MY SODA POP, GARFIELD?
SURE
Cola
JIM DAVIS 10-31
© 1990 PAWS, INC. All Rights Reserved.
SIP!
Cola
YOU CALL THAT A SIP?!
ONE MAN'S SIP IS ANOTHER MAN'S CHUG

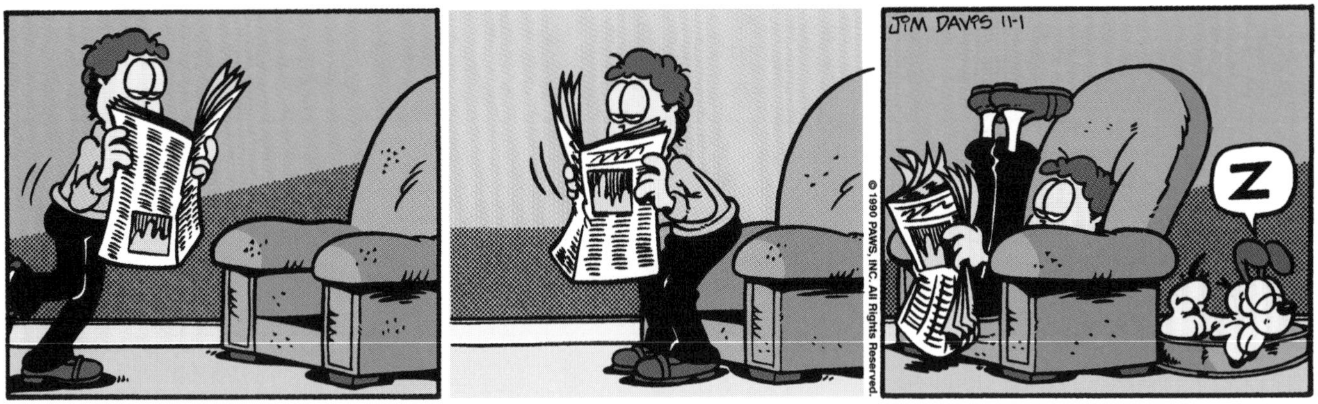
JIM DAVIS 11-1
© 1990 PAWS, INC. All Rights Reserved.
Z

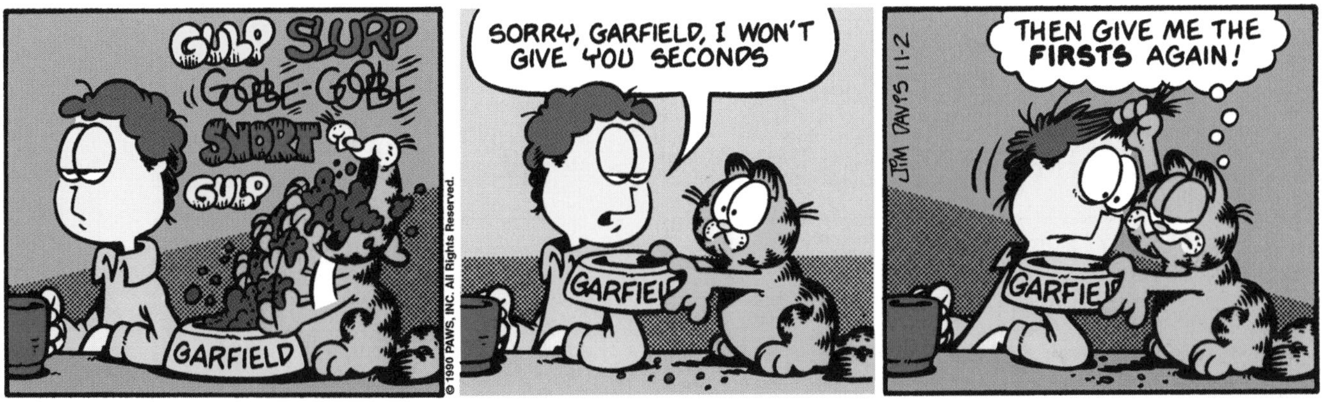
GULP SLURP
GOBBLE-GOBBLE
SNORT
GULP
GARFIELD
© 1990 PAWS, INC. All Rights Reserved.
SORRY, GARFIELD, I WON'T GIVE YOU SECONDS
GARFIELD
JIM DAVIS 11-2
THEN GIVE ME THE **FIRSTS** AGAIN!
GARFIELD

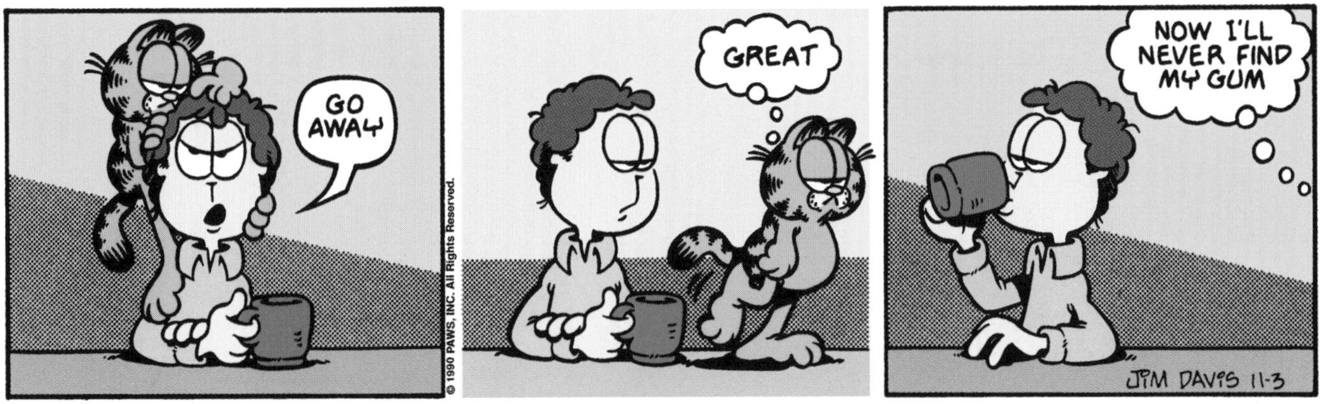
GO AWAY
© 1990 PAWS, INC. All Rights Reserved.
GREAT
NOW I'LL NEVER FIND MY GUM
JIM DAVIS 11-3

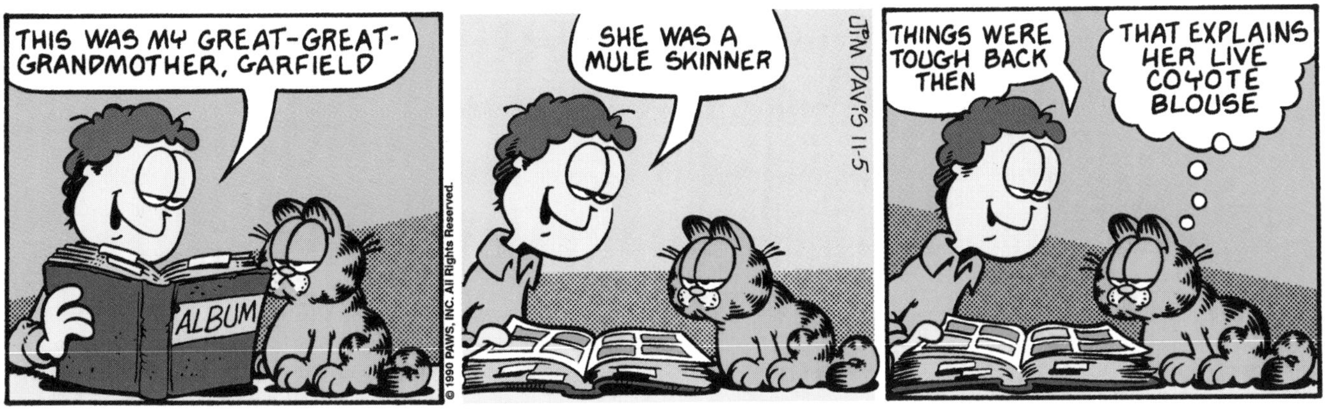
THIS WAS MY GREAT-GREAT-GRANDMOTHER, GARFIELD
ALBUM
© 1990 PAWS, INC. All Rights Reserved.
SHE WAS A MULE SKINNER
JIM DAVIS 11-5
THINGS WERE TOUGH BACK THEN
THAT EXPLAINS HER LIVE COYOTE BLOUSE

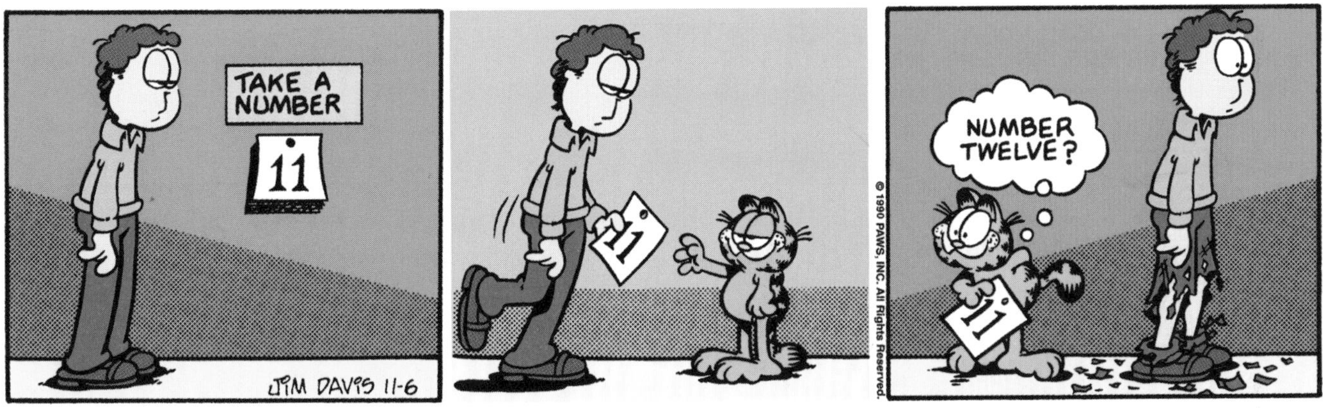
TAKE A NUMBER
11
JIM DAVIS 11-6
11
© 1990 PAWS, INC. All Rights Reserved.
NUMBER TWELVE?
11

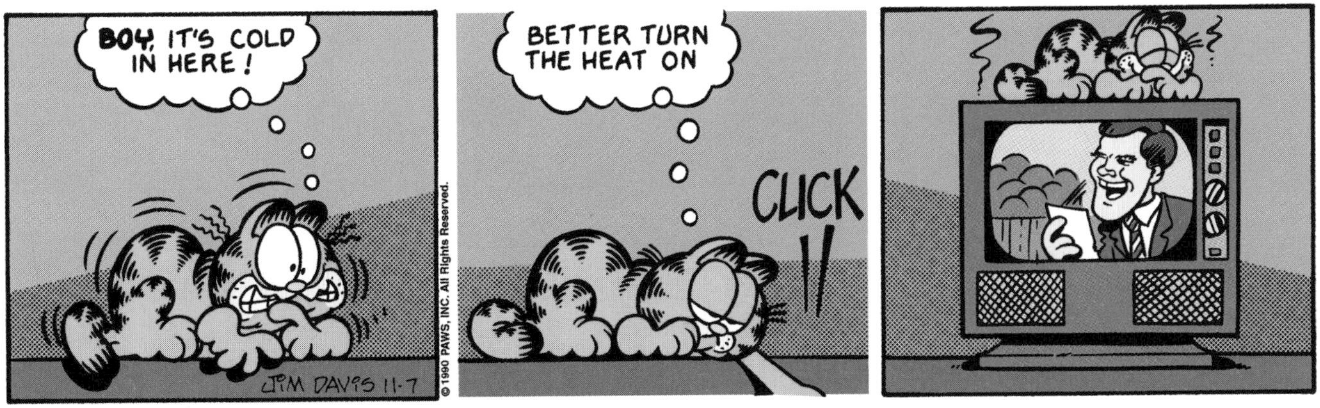
BOY, IT'S COLD IN HERE!
JIM DAVIS 11-7
© 1990 PAWS, INC. All Rights Reserved.
BETTER TURN THE HEAT ON
CLICK

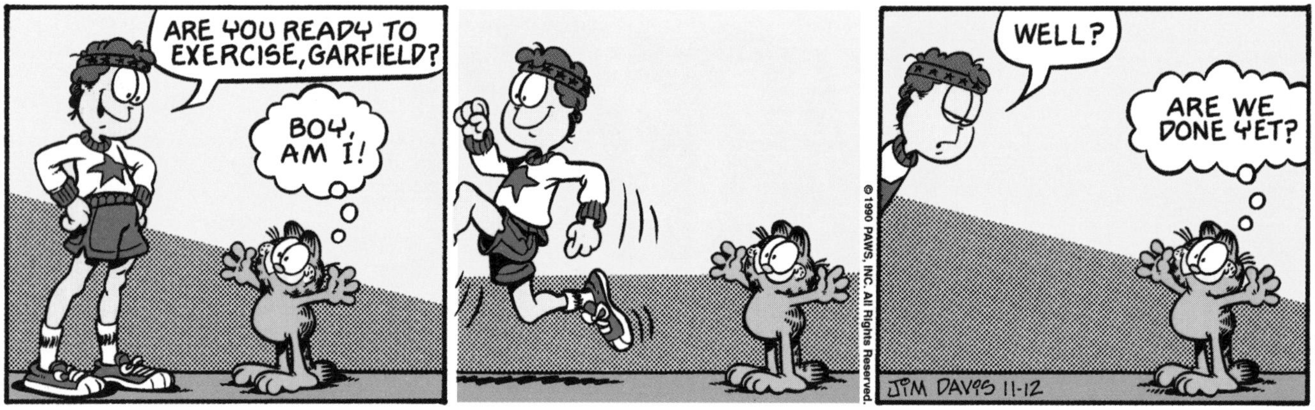
ARE YOU READY TO EXERCISE, GARFIELD?
BOY, AM I!
© 1990 PAWS, INC. All Rights Reserved.
WELL?
ARE WE DONE YET?
JIM DAVIS 11-12

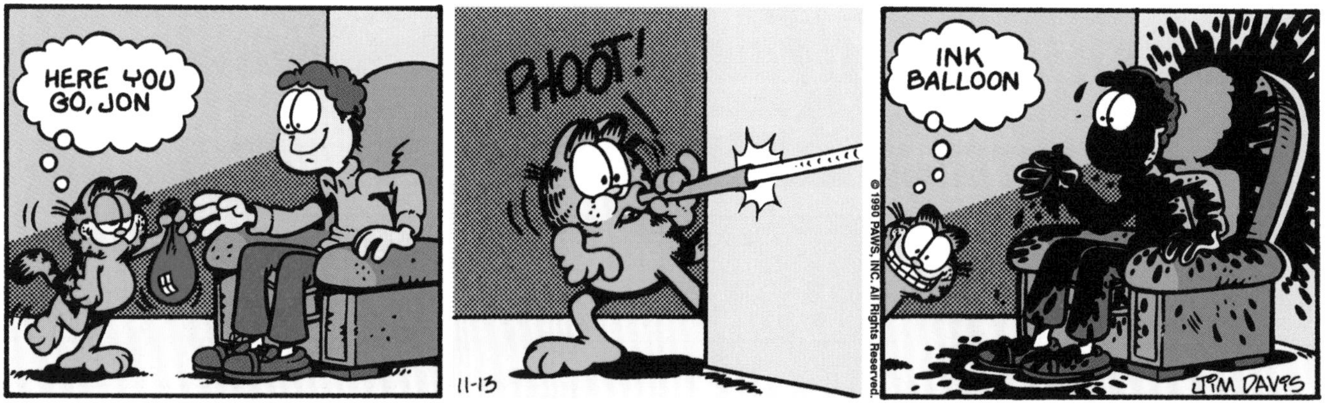
HERE YOU GO, JON
PHOOT!
11-13
© 1990 PAWS, INC. All Rights Reserved.
INK BALLOON
JIM DAVIS

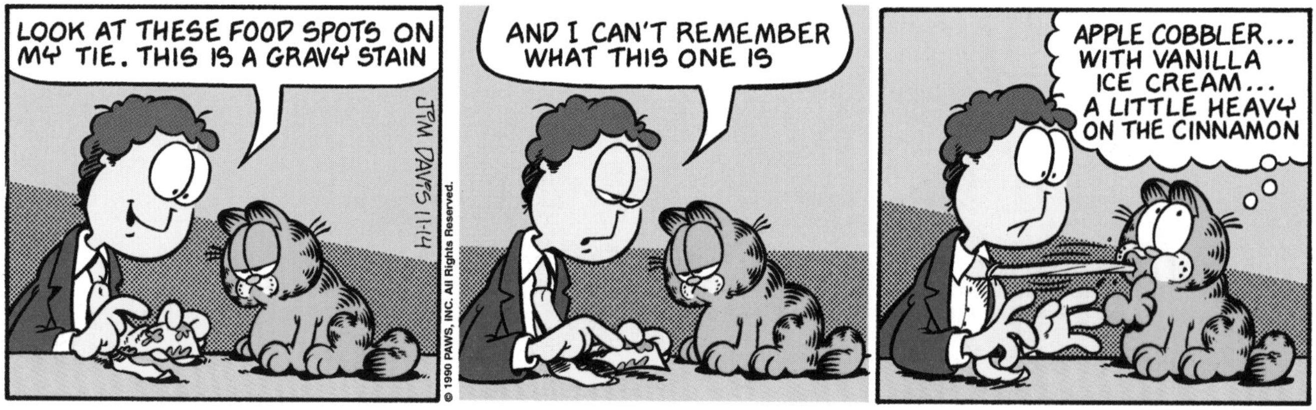
LOOK AT THESE FOOD SPOTS ON MY TIE. THIS IS A GRAVY STAIN
JIM DAVIS 11-14
© 1990 PAWS, INC. All Rights Reserved.
AND I CAN'T REMEMBER WHAT THIS ONE IS
APPLE COBBLER... WITH VANILLA ICE CREAM... A LITTLE HEAVY ON THE CINNAMON

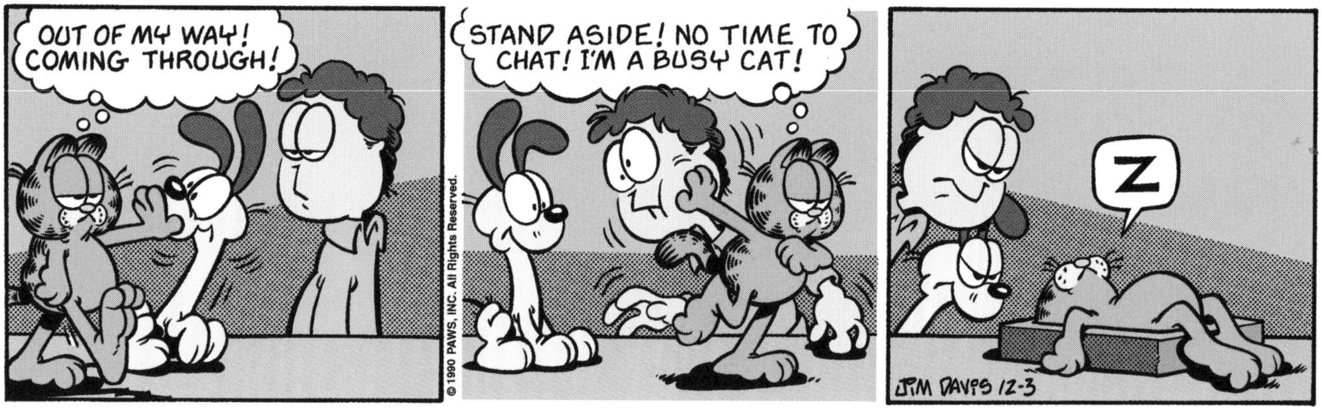
OUT OF MY WAY! COMING THROUGH!
STAND ASIDE! NO TIME TO CHAT! I'M A BUSY CAT!
Z
© 1990 PAWS, INC. All Rights Reserved.
JIM DAVIS 12-3

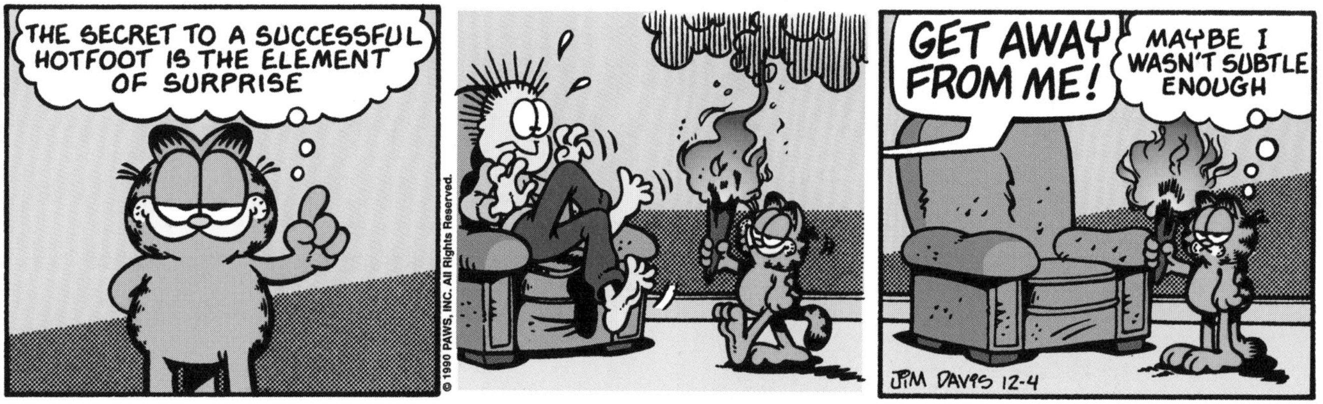
THE SECRET TO A SUCCESSFUL HOTFOOT IS THE ELEMENT OF SURPRISE
GET AWAY FROM ME!
MAYBE I WASN'T SUBTLE ENOUGH
© 1990 PAWS, INC. All Rights Reserved.
JIM DAVIS 12-4

GARFIELD'S TOP TEN NIGHTMARES

10. **Nermal gets cloned**
9. **Vet prescribes "chain saw therapy"**
8. **Falls into vat of Odie drool**
7. **Fleas vote him "Most Bloodsuckable"**
6. **Inhales next to Jon's dirty socks**
5. **Forced to watch the "All Lassie" channel**
4. **Trapped for a week inside health food store**
3. **Cat fur the latest thing for women's coats**
2. **Meets huge spider with an attitude**
1. **Diet Monday!**